RESET

ALSO BY THE AUTHOR

Black Code: Surveillance, Privacy, and the Dark Side of the Internet

Parchment, Printing, and Hypermedia: Communications in World Order Transformation

Ronald J. Deibert

RESET.

Reclaiming the Internet for Civil Society

1 3 5 7 9 10 8 6 4 2

This paperback published in the UK in 2021 by September Publishing
Ebook published in the UK in 2020 by September Publishing
First published in Canada and the USA in 2020 by
House of Anansi Press Inc.

Text design: Ingrid Paulson

Paperback ISBN 9781912836772
Kindle ISBN 9781912836789
Epub ISBN 9781912836796

September Publishing
www.septemberpublishing.org

For Jane:
my love, my lifeline,
my morning coffee confidante

CONTENTS

"Constant experience shows us that every man invested with power is apt to abuse it, and to carry his authority as far as it will go... To prevent this abuse, it is necessary from the very nature of things that power should be a check to power."

Montesquieu, *The Spirit of Laws*

INTRODUCTION

LOOK AT THAT DEVICE in your hand.

No, really, take a good, long look at it.

You carry it around with you wherever you go. You sleep with it, work with it, run with it, you play games on it. You depend on it, and panic when you can't find it. It links you to your relatives and kids. You take photos and videos with it, and share them with friends and family. It alerts you to public emergencies and reminds you of hair appointments.

Traffic is light. If you leave now you will be on time.

You depend on it for directions, weather forecasts, and the news. You talk to it, and it talks back. You monitor the appliances that in turn monitor your house (and you) with it. You book your flights on it and purchase your movie tickets through it. You order groceries and takeout and check recipes on it. It counts your steps and monitors your heartbeat. It reminds you to be mindful. You use it for yoga and meditation.

But if you're like most everyone I know, you also probably feel a bit anxious about it. You realize it (and what it connects you to) is doing things to your lifestyle that you'd probably be better off without. It's encouraging bad habits. Your kids and even some of your friends barely talk to you in person any longer. Sometimes it feels like they don't even look you in the face, their eyeballs glued to it, their thumbs tapping away constantly. Your teen freaks out when their device rings. *You mean I have to actually speak to someone?* How could something so "social" be also so curiously anti-social at the same time?

You check your social media account, and it feels like a toxic mess, but you can't help but swipe for more. Tens of thousands, perhaps millions, of people actually believe the earth is flat because they watched videos extolling conspiracies about it on YouTube. Right-wing, neo-fascist populism flourishes online and off, igniting hatred, murder, and even genocide. A daily assault on the free press rains down unfiltered from the Twitter account of the president of the United States, whose brazen lies since taking office number in the tens of thousands. His tweets are symptomatic of the general malaise: like a car accident, they are grotesque, but somehow you are drawn in and can't look away.

No doubt you have also noticed that social media have taken a drubbing in recent years. The "gee whiz" factor has given way to a kind of dreadful ennui. Your daily news feeds fill with stories about data breaches, privacy infringements, disinformation, spying, and manipulation of political events. Social media executives have been dragged before congressional and parliamentary hearings to face the glare of the cameras and the scrutiny of lawmakers.

The 2016 Brexit referendum and the 2016 U.S. election of president Donald Trump were both major precipitating factors behind the re-examination of social media's impact on society and politics. In both cases, malicious actors, domestic and foreign, used social media to spread malfeasance and ignite real-life protests with the intent to foster chaos and further strain already acute social divisions. Thanks to investigations undertaken in their aftermath, shady data analytics companies like Cambridge Analytica have been flushed out from the shadows to show a glimpse of social media's seamy underworld.

Then there's the *real* dark side to it all. You've read about high-tech mercenary companies selling powerful "cyberwarfare" services to dictators who use them to hack into their adversaries' devices and social networks, often with lethal consequences. First it was Jamal Khashoggi's inner circle, then (allegedly) Jeff Bezos's device. *Maybe I've been hacked too?* you wonder to yourself, suddenly suspicious of that unsolicited text or email with an attachment. The world you're connecting to with that device increasingly feels like a major source of personal risk.

But it's also become your lifeline, now more than ever. When the novel coronavirus (2019-nCoV or COVID-19) swept across the globe after its discovery in

Wuhan, China, in December 2019, business as usual ground to a halt: entire industries shuttered, employees laid off in the millions, and nearly everyone forced into self-isolation and work-from-home. While all other sectors of the global economy were on a rapid downward spiral, the large technology platforms saw use of their services skyrocket. Video conferencing tools, like Zoom, went from obscure office contrivances to something so commonplace your grandparents or children used it, often for hours on end. Netflix, Amazon Prime, and other streaming media services were booming, a welcome distraction from the grim news outside. Bandwidth consumption catapulted to such enormous levels that telecommunications carriers were putting caps on streams and downgrading video quality to ensure the internet didn't overload. Miraculously, it all hung together, and for that you were grateful.

But the global pandemic also accentuated all of social media's shortcomings. Cybercrime and data breaches also skyrocketed as bad actors capitalized on millions of people working from home, their kitchen routers and jerry-rigged network setups never designed to handle sensitive communications. In spite of efforts by social media platforms to remove misleading information and point their users to credible health sources, disinformation was everywhere, sometimes consumed with terrible effects. People perished drinking poisonous cocktails shared over social media (and endorsed by Donald Trump himself) in a desperate attempt to stave off the virus.

The entire situation presented a striking contrast both to the ways in which social media advertise themselves and to how they were widely perceived in the past. Once, it was conventional wisdom to assume that digital technologies would enable greater access to information, facilitate collective organizing, and empower civil society. The Arab Spring, the so-called "coloured revolutions," and other digitally fuelled social movements like them seemed to demonstrate the unstoppable people power unleashed by our always-on, interconnected world. Indeed, for much of the 2000s, technology enthusiasts applauded each new innovation as a way to bring people closer together and revitalize democracy.

Now, social media are increasingly perceived as contributing to a kind of social sickness. A growing number of people believe that social media have a disproportionate influence over important social and political decisions. Others are beginning to notice that we are spending an unhealthy amount of our lives staring at our devices, "socializing," while in reality we are living in isolation and detached from nature. As a consequence of this growing unease, there are calls to regulate social media and to encourage company executives to be better stewards of their platforms, respect privacy, and acknowledge the role of human rights. But where to begin? And what exactly should be done? Answers to these questions are far less clear.

THE TITLE OF THIS BOOK, *Reset*, is intended to prompt a general stocktaking about the unusual and quite disturbing period of time in which we find ourselves. "The arc of the moral universe is long, but it bends toward justice," Martin Luther King Jr. once famously observed. Looking around at the climate crisis, deadly diseases, species extinction, virulent nationalism, systemic racism, audacious kleptocracy, and extreme inequality, it's really hard to share his optimism. These days it feels more like everything's all imploding instead. If there has ever been a time when we needed to rethink what we're collectively doing, this is certainly it.

More specifically, the title is also intended to signal a deeper re-examination of our communications ecosystem that I believe is urgently required, now more than ever. In the language of computers and networking, the term "reset" is used widely to refer to a measure that halts a system and returns it to an initial state. (The term "reboot" is often used interchangeably.) A reset is a way to terminate a runaway process that is causing problems and start over anew. Users of Apple products will be familiar with the "spinning beach ball" that signifies a process that is stuck in a loop, while Microsoft customers will no doubt recall the "blue screen of death." We've all been there at one time or another.

The term "reset" is also used more broadly to refer to a fresh start. As when parents tell their children to take a "time out," a reset is usually suggested when something we are doing has become counterproductive and deserves some reconsideration. It's also common to think about a reset when we do something entirely novel, like begin a new job or move to a new house. Resets allow time to regroup, clean house, take stock and look at the big picture, and launch a new plan. In broader parlance, a reset implies beginning again from well-thought-out first principles. It allows us to discard the errors of the old ways of going about things and start over with a solid foundation.

During the COVID emergency, societies were compelled into an unexpected and enforced reset. Governments around the world, from the municipal to the federal level, mandated quarantines and self-isolation protocols. The global economy effectively went into an indefinite pause as entire sectors were shut down. Emergency measures were introduced. At the time of writing, in spring 2020, we were still at a relatively early stage of the pandemic's spread, and it's unclear how everything will resolve. However it all turns out, the enforced time out has prompted a re-examination of many aspects of our lives and our politics, and social media are certainly not exempt.

I have several objectives in writing *Reset*. One aim is to synthesize what I see as an emerging consensus about the problems related to social media and — by extension — the organization of our entire communications environment. Think of this as a diagnosis of social media: an identification of the illnesses by a close examination of their symptoms. I organize these problems as "painful truths"—"truths" because there is a growing number of scholars and experts who acknowledge these problems, and "painful" because they describe many serious and detrimental effects that are unpleasant to contemplate and difficult to fix. In doing so, I am not so much putting forward a single original argument about social media as combining a lot of disparate research and reporting undertaken by many others who have studied the topic. Of course, not everyone will agree with my synthesis or characterization of these problems. But I have tried as much as possible to capture what I see as the latest evidence-based research and thinking on the topic—to provide a comprehensive picture of the state of the art at the time of writing.

Reset is, therefore, not intended solely for a specialist audience, and it is not sourced in the same manner as a peer-reviewed academic book on the topic would be. I have tried to make *Reset* as accessible as possible, while still being faithful to the recent scholarship on the topic. For those who wish to get into the weeds a little bit more, and to give credit where credit is due, alongside this book I am publishing a detailed bibliography of sources. I feel as though I am part of a large community of scholars who have spent their professional lives dissecting these painful truths about social media—scholars like Rebecca MacKinnon, Tim Wu, Zeynep Tufekci, Siva Vaidhyanathan, danah boyd, Kate Crawford, Bruce Schneier, Ryan Calo, and many others too numerous to list here. In describing the painful truths about social media, I hope to be able to help convey those thinkers' collective concerns as accurately as possible.

Another aim of this work is to move beyond these painful truths and start a conversation about what to do about them. There is a very long and growing list of books, articles, and podcasts that lay bare the problems of social media, but few of them offer a clear alternative or a path forward. Those solutions that are proposed can feel fragmented or incomplete. At best, one might find a few cursory platitudes tacked on in the final paragraphs of an essay or book that hint at, but don't elaborate on, what to do. That is not to say there is a shortage of proposals to reform social media in some fashion; those are plentiful but can also be confusing or seemingly contradictory. Should we break up Facebook and other tech giants, or reform them from within? Should we completely unplug and disconnect, or is there a new app that can help moderate the worst excesses of social media?

My aim is to bring some clarity to this challenge by laying out an underlying framework to help guide us moving forward. However much it may feel like we are in uncharted territory, I don't believe we need to invent some new "cyber" theory to deal with the problems of social media (and we certainly can't pin our hopes on a new app). Humans have faced challenges in other eras similar to our own. We have done this before, albeit at different scales and under different circumstances. There is, in fact, a long tradition of theorizing about security and liberty from which we can draw as we set out to reclaim the internet for civil society. I hope to elaborate on what I see as some of the most promising elements of that tradition.

NOT THAT LONG AGO — and I mean within my adult life — we used information and communications technologies self-consciously and as deliberate one-off acts. We made a telephone call. We watched television. We listened to the radio. We dropped a letter in the postbox. Later, we composed essays or undertook calculations on our desktop computers. These were all relatively self-contained and isolated performances, separate from each other and from other aspects of "normal life." But beginning around the 1980s (at least for those of us living in the industrialized West), things began to change quickly. Those desktop computers were eventually networked together through the internet and internet-based subscription services like CompuServe or America Online. The World Wide Web (1991) brought a kind of Technicolor to the internet while unleashing a dramatically new means of individual self-expression. Thanks to improvements in cellular technologies and miniaturized transistors, telephones went mobile. Before long, Apple gave us the iPod (in 2001), onto which we could download digital music. The iPhone (released in 2007) combined the two and then integrated their various functions via the internet, producing a one-stop, all-purpose, mobile digital networking "smart" device.

Before long, the internet was in everything, from wearables and networked kitchen appliances all the way down to the molecular level with digitally networked implants, like pacemakers and insulin pumps. (Perhaps not surprisingly, security experts have routinely discovered potentially life-threatening software vulnerabilities in many versions of the latter.) Digitally networked neural implants that are presently used for deep-brain and nerve stimulation, as well as to enable mind-controlled prosthetics, are merely at the rudimentary stages of development; engineers are experimenting on systems involving thousands of tiny speck-sized neural implants that would wirelessly communicate with computers outside the brain. Whatever the future brings, we are all now "cyborgs" — a term that once described a hypothetical fusion of "human" and "machine." One can no longer draw a clear separation between our "normal" and our "digital" lives (or, to use older lingo, between "meat" and "virtual spaces"). Our use of information and communications technologies is now less a series of deliberate, self-conscious acts and more like something that just continuously runs in the background. Much of it is rendered invisible through familiarity and habituation. Disparate systems have converged into an always-on, always-connected mega-machine. This profound shift in how we communicate and seek and receive information has occurred largely within the span of a single generation.

To be sure, there is still vast digital inequality (nearly half of the world's population has yet to come online), but those gaps are closing quickly. The fastest growth in mobile internet connectivity is in the global South, as entire populations leapfrog over older legacy systems and "fixed line" connections to plug directly into social media using mobile devices. But the uses towards which those populations (and all next-generation users, for that matter) are putting digital technologies are sometimes quite surprising, and different than what the original designers intended. Human ingenuity can reveal itself in many unexpected ways. The internet gave us access to libraries and hobby boards, but also gave criminal enterprises low-risk opportunities for new types of global malfeasance, like spam, phishing schemes, and (more recently) ransomware and robocalls. Early in the internet's history, many assumed the technology would hamstring dictators and despots, and, to be sure, it has created some control issues for them. But it's also created opportunities for older practices to flourish, such as the way "*kompromat*" (Russian for "compromising material used for blackmail and extortion") has taken on new life in post-Soviet social media. The entire ecosystem was not developed with a single well-thought-out design plan, and security has largely been an afterthought. New applications have been slapped on top of legacy systems and then patched backwards haphazardly, leaving persistent and sometimes gaping vulnerabilities up and down the entire environment for a multitude of bad actors to exploit. It's all an "accidental megastructure," as media theorist Benjamin Bratton aptly put it.

The global communications ecosystem is not a fixed "thing." It's not anywhere near stasis either. It's a continuously evolving mixture of elements, some slow-moving and persistent and others quickly mutating. There are deeper layers, like those legacy standards and protocols, that remain largely fixed. But caked on top of them is a bewildering array of new applications, features, and devices. Weaving through it all are rivers of data, some neatly contained in proper channels, others pouring through the cracks and crevices and spilling out in the form of data breaches. The phrase "data is the new oil" refers to the value to be gained from all the data that is routinely harvested by machines from both humans and other machines — the entire complex bristling with millions of pulsating data-sorting algorithms and sensors. The gradual rollout of fifth-generation cellular technology, known as 5G, will dramatically increase the speed and broadband capacity of cellular networks, fuelling an even greater volume of data circulating among a larger number of networked devices. The combined effect of each of us turning the most intimate aspects of our digital lives inside out has created a new emergent property on a planetary scale that has taken a life of its own — derived from but separate from us, a datasphere.

"Social media" (strictly understood) refers to the breed of applications that emerged in the past decade and a half, thanks largely to the extraordinary business innovations of Google and Facebook, and gave rise to what the political economist and business management professor Shoshana Zuboff has termed "surveillance capitalism." Merriam-Webster defines social media narrowly as "forms of electronic communication (such as websites for social networking and microblogging) through which users create online communities to share information, ideas, personal messages, and other content (such as videos)." But missing from this definition is the underlying business model, an appreciation of which is essential in order to fully understand the dynamics of social media. At their core, social media are vehicles for the relentless collection and monetization of the personal data of their users. Social media are so overwhelming and omnipresent in our lives, it may feel like they have been with us forever. Some of you reading this may have grown up entirely within the universe of Facebook, Google, Snapchat, and TikTok and not know what it's like to live without them. I'm among those living generations that have experienced life before and after social media. I remember standing in a long line with nothing to do but think.

Not everything is social media, but social media influence everything else, so prominent and influential is the business model at their core. The platforms that run social media have huge gravitational force and sweep up most everything else into their orbit (sometimes literally, through acquisitions), absorbing even non-social applications into the galaxy of social media. For example, narrowly understood, drones are not a form of social media. But both developed out of a common family of electronics, robotics, miniaturization, and digitization. Each drone is controlled by software-based, networked applications installed on handheld devices and tablets. The most popular drone is manufactured by a China-based company called DJI, whose apps send data on trips, models, locations, and more to its Shenzhen-based servers as well as numerous advertising firms and other third parties. Much like everything else these days, the influence of social media's business model has infected those applications, and so they too are oriented around personal data surveillance. Overhead remote sensing data are also integral to the functioning of many social media applications, such as Google's maps.

Social media do not stand alone. They are embedded in a vast technological ecosystem. In order to participate in social media, you need some kind of networked device: a smartphone, tablet, laptop, or PC. (The number of networked devices is expanding quickly with 5G networks and the so-called Internet of Things, and now includes internet-enabled fridges, home security systems, dishwashers, and automobiles.) Those devices send electronic signals through radio waves or cables that are transmitted through a physical infrastructure of routers, servers, cell towers, and data farms, in some cases spread throughout multiple countries. Each of these elements is operated by numerous businesses, which can include internet service providers (ISPs), cable companies, cell service providers, satellite services, undersea cable providers, and telecommunications firms as well as the various hardware and software manufacturers supporting them all. Which companies operate the various components of this ecosystem, and according to whose rules, matters enormously for users' security and privacy. For example, policymakers and analysts have raised concerns that China-based communications routing equipment manufacturers Huawei and ZTE may have designed secret "back doors" in their technology that would provide China's security agencies with an intelligence toehold in 5G networks. However valid, these concerns are not unique to China or China-based companies. The history of communications technologies is full of episodes of governments of all sorts cajoling or compelling companies that operate the infrastructure to secretly turn over data they collect. (A decade from now, we'll be worrying about whether the companies that control our brain implants have secretly inserted "back doors.")

The internet, telecommunications, and social media are so foundational to everything else that they have become an object of intense geopolitical competition among states and other actors on the world stage. "Cyber commands," "cyber forces," and "electronic armies" have proliferated. A large, growing, and mostly unaccountable private industry feeds their needs with tools, products, and services. The struggle for information advantage is a by-product of seemingly endless opportunities for data exploitation as a consequence of pervasive insecurity. Defence is expensive and difficult, so everyone goes on the offence instead. The ancient art of intelligence gathering is now a multi-billion-dollar worldwide industry that snakes clandestinely through the catacombs of the planet's electronic infrastructure. To give one illustration of the magnitude of the issue, Google's security team says that on any given day, it tracks around 250 government-backed hacking campaigns operating out of fifty countries. And yet, in spite of it all, the communications ecosystem somehow hangs together. Interdependence runs deep — even closed-off North Korea depends on the internet for illicitly acquired revenues. And so most of the offensive action (even among otherwise sworn adversaries) takes place just below the threshold of armed conflict. Subversion, psychological operations, extortion (through ransomware), and digitally produced propaganda are where the real action is to be found — less violent, to be sure, but no less destructive of the health of the global communications sphere.

The entire ecosystem requires enormous energy to power, and that in turn implicates all of the various components of the global energy grid: power stations, transmission systems, hydroelectric dams, nuclear power plants, coal-fired power plants, and others. The awesome speed with which we can send and retrieve even large amounts of data tends to obscure the vast physical infrastructure through which it all passes. Last year, my family and I did a FaceTime video call between Sydney, Australia, and Toronto, Canada, which at roughly 15,500 kilometres apart are about as distant as two points on Earth can be, and it worked seamlessly... as if it were some kind of magic. But it's not magic at all; it's physics. However immaterial they may seem, our digital experiences rest on a complex and vastly distributed planet-wide infrastructure.

To be sure, it's not all physical. This enormous communications ecosystem could not function without rules, protocols, algorithms, and software that process and order the flows of data. Some of those rules and protocols were developed decades ago and remain foundational still, like the Transmission Control Protocol and Internet Protocol (TCP/IP) underlying pretty much all internet communications, or Signalling System No. 7 (SS7), which was developed in 1975 to route telephone calls but has now unexpectedly become a major source of insecurity used to track the location of smartphones. Other rules and protocols are pasted on top as new applications are developed. Many different terms have been used to describe this entire ecosystem: the internet, cyberspace, the World Wide Web, and more. But because these can quickly date themselves, I prefer to use the more generic "communications ecosystem."

It's important to make this distinction clear, because while we may want to eliminate or temper some of the characteristics of social media, we do not necessarily want to (nor realistically can we) eliminate the vast communications ecosystem of which they are a part. Looking only narrowly at the effects of social media proper may also obscure some of the consequences connected to the broader (and continuously mutating) communications ecosystem. Throughout this book, I'll use "social media" narrowly when referring to those platforms we traditionally associate with the term, but I'll also be spending time examining other technologies connected to them that make up the communications ecosystem as a whole (like that device you hold in your hand).

THERE IS NO SHORTAGE of blame placed on social media for all sorts of social and political pathologies. But assigning causality (in a scientific sense) to social media for any particular outcome, negative or otherwise, is not always simple, given the extensive ecosystem of which it is a part. Sometimes doing so is more manageable, such as through rigorously controlled and peer-reviewed experiments on the effects of digital experiences on human cognition and behaviour. It is from studies such as these that we are beginning to understand some of the addictive qualities of our digital experiences (which may help explain the panic you feel when you lose your device). But higher-level effects — e.g., the impact of social media on political polarization or authoritarianism — are far more difficult to untangle from other "confounding variables" (to use the language of social science). Societies are complex, and monocausal theories about them are almost always incorrect. Some of the effects people may attribute to social media — e.g., decline of trust in public institutions — are almost certainly the result of multiple, overlapping factors, some of which reach back decades. Attributing causality at a massive scale is always tricky for that reason.

One way I like to think about causal relationships at scale is to borrow from theories of biological evolution and describe social media as "environments" within which certain social forces flourish and multiply, or are constrained and wither. Framing causality this way avoids attributing specific effects solely to social media — what scientists sometimes refer to as "reductionism." The relationship between species and the environment of which they are a part is most pronounced when the environment suddenly changes, as with a volcanic eruption or asteroid collision. (Sixty-six million years ago, a ten-to-fifteen-kilometre-wide asteroid slammed into Earth, causing widespread climatic and other changes to the environment, leading to the extinction of roughly three-quarters of Earth's species.) Much as a sudden change in the natural environment can alter conditions in ways that favour some species over others, so too does our changing communications environment favour certain practices, ideas, and institutions over others (both positively and negatively). Seen through this lens, social media do not *generate* practices, ideas, and institutions *de novo*. The spread of disinformation in the public realm is not something Facebook or Twitter alone is responsible for. The practice of deliberately spreading false information is as old as humanity itself. However, social media's algorithms create conditions ripe for its propagation today, and as a consequence, disinformation practices are proliferating, becoming more elaborate, backed up with more resources, and thus potentially have more damaging effects than would be the case in the absence of social media.

Thinking about changing modes of communication as environments has a long pedigree, and a uniquely Canadian connection to boot. Many Canadians may not be aware of our country's important legacy around the study of communications technologies associated with the Toronto School of Communications, and in particular with University of Toronto alumni Harold Innis and Marshall McLuhan. (This family of theorizing is also known as "media ecology," and adherents of it have formed a large professional network called the Media Ecology Association.) Innis and McLuhan both drew attention in their different ways to the material qualities of different modes of communication and how these material qualities affect the nature and quality of communications. McLuhan was fond of speaking in aphorisms, and one of his most famous, "the medium is the message," was intended to encapsulate this thesis: the material properties of any particular communications technology affect the nature and character of the content of communications. Hence societies in which one particular mode of communication is predominant — the oral culture of ancient Greece or the print-based culture of early modern Europe — exhibit characteristics associated with those modes.

Innis, McLuhan, and other media ecologists have drawn attention to how the effects of modes of communication are pronounced in periods of rapid technological change, and in particular when societies transition from one mode of communication to another. The role of chance, or contingency, in human affairs has also been a prominent feature of media ecology, and in particular of the writings of Harold Innis. While human practices congeal and remain stable over long periods of time, making them feel like permanent fixtures (think of sovereign states as an example), they are nonetheless products of history and thus subject to change as nature, technology, and society evolve. In his seminal book *Empire and Communications,* Innis explained how several contingent social, political, technological, and environmental factors all combined to create circumstances advantageous to the rise of the Roman Catholic Church in the early Middle Ages:

> The spread of Mohammedanism cut off exports of papyrus to the east and to the west... Papyrus was produced in a restricted area and met the demands of a centralized administration whereas parchment as the product of an agricultural economy was suited to a decentralized system. The durability of parchment and the convenience of the codex for reference made it particularly suitable for the large books typical of scriptures and legal works. In turn, the difficulties of copying a large book limited the numbers produced. Small libraries

> with a small number of books could be established over large areas. Since the material of a civilization dominated by the papyrus roll had to be recopied into the parchment codex, a thorough system of censorship was involved. Pagan writing was neglected and Christian writing emphasized.

A different set of contingencies later connected to the development of mechanized printing (a wooden block form of which was first invented in eighth-century China and then adapted and improved upon in Europe in the fifteenth century by goldsmith Johannes Gutenberg) led in turn to the demise of the Roman Catholic Church's authority throughout Western Europe (despite that Gutenberg saw the Church as an important early client and sponsor). The invention of mass mechanized printing has also been connected to the rise of individualism (thanks to the silent reading it encouraged) and nationalism (thanks to standardized printed newspapers in vernacular languages), among other social effects.

The purpose of this section is not to simply detour into the history of communications for its own sake, but to remind us of the power of unintended consequences. Technologies designed for one purpose often end up having far-reaching impacts much different than what their designers envisioned. The same holds true not only for social media but for our entire communications ecosystem. Who knew that as social media climbed in popularity and more people acquired always-on mobile devices, these would prove to be a major source of insecurity exploited by autocrats and other bad actors? Who could have foreseen that a tool designed to forge bonds between communities would end up fostering social polarization and discord? Media ecologists remind us that changing technological environments can take human history in unexpected directions.

Media ecology had a major influence on my own intellectual outlook, and in particular on the establishment of the Citizen Lab, the research group I founded at the University of Toronto in 2001 and presently still direct. (My Ph.D. dissertation, which in 1997 became my first published book, titled *Parchment, Printing, and Hypermedia,* was an exploration of the implications for world order of changing modes of communication throughout history.) Innis's attention to material factors prompted me to examine more closely the often overlooked physical infrastructure of the internet — to dig beneath the surface of our communications ecosystem and uncover the exercise of power that goes on in subterranean realms. It is often said that everyone has at most one great idea, and if that's the case, mine was to recognize that there are powerful methods, tools, and techniques in computer and engineering sciences that could help uncover what's going on beneath the surface. Not being formally trained in these domains, I turned to others who were, and as a result the Citizen Lab was born, both interdisciplinary and collaborative from the start.

A colleague of mine once described what we do as a kind of "MRI of the internet," which captures the ways network scanning, reverse engineering, and other computer and engineering science techniques peel back the layers of our communications ecosystem. But I have also been inspired by other, more direct analogies. Since graduate school, I have been fascinated by the way government security agencies have for decades manoeuvred through the communications ecosystem largely outside of public view, thanks to classification and secrecy. Early in my career I became familiar with signals and other electronic intelligence gathering, and was quite shocked to discover how some states had secretly developed sophisticated means and elaborate tools to intercept and monitor telecommunications and other network traffic. The U.S. National Security Agency (NSA) and its partners in the "Five Eyes" alliance (United Kingdom, Canada, New Zealand, and Australia) were doing so on a planetary scale. While marvelling at this capacity (and putting aside legal, ethical, and other reservations), I wondered why a variation of it, based on open-sourced public research, couldn't be developed and used to turn the tables on governments themselves: to "watch the watchers" and reveal the exercise of power going on beneath the surface of our communications environment. A mission was thus established for the Citizen Lab, and our interdisciplinary research came into focus: to serve as "counter-intelligence for global civil society."

There's an old saying that comes to mind, though: *careful what you wish for.* When we first began our work at the Citizen Lab, we had no basis upon which to claim we were undertaking "counter-intelligence" for anyone, let alone global civil society. But gradually the methods, tools, and techniques became more refined; talented personnel were drawn to the mission and the freedom to explore challenging puzzles, the solutions for which had real-world consequences. Important collaborations developed and the case studies accumulated. We found ourselves pulling back the curtain on unaccountable actions that some very powerful actors would rather we did not. Not surprisingly, those powerful actors did not just sit on their hands and do nothing, and we have found ourselves more than once in the crosshairs. *Consider it a mark of success,* we've been told, and I tend to agree. Close to two decades of research, undertaken in collaboration with some enormously talented researchers, has helped inform my perspective on everything reported on in this book. Thanks to the work of the Citizen Lab, I feel as though I've been watching dark clouds forming on the horizon, and I along with my colleagues have been trying to raise the alarm that this is not a good sign.

A MAJOR AIM OF *RESET* is to help get us started thinking about how best to mitigate the harms of social media, and in doing so construct a viable communications ecosystem that supports civil society and contributes to the betterment of the human condition (instead of the opposite). It's clichéd to say that the time in which one lives is a "turning point." But looking around at the massive disruption to humanity's entire operating system, it is no exaggeration to say that we are in the midst of one. Even before the COVID-19 pandemic hit, many existing institutions and assumptions were already under the microscope. So too is the case for social media. In order to move forward positively, we need to have a clear understanding of the nature of the problems in the first place. The first four chapters of *Reset* lay out what I see as the principal "painful truths" about social media and, by extension, the entire technological landscape of which they are a part.

"It's the economy, stupid," political strategist James Carville once remarked, and it's a good reminder of where to begin to understand the pathologies of social media. Chapter 1 explores the economic engine that underlies social media: the personal data surveillance economy, or what Zuboff calls "surveillance capitalism" (a phrase actually first coined in 2014 by the Canada-based sociologist Vincent Mosco). Social media platforms describe themselves in many different, seemingly benign ways: "wiring the world," "connecting friends and family members," "all the world's information at your fingertips," and so on. And on the surface, they often live up to the billing. But regardless of how they present themselves, social media have one fundamental aim: to monitor, archive, analyze, and market as much personal information as they can from those who use their platforms. Constituted on the basis of surveillance capitalism, social media are relentless machines that dig deeper and deeper into our personal lives, attaching more and more sensors to more and more things, in a never-ending quest for unattainable omniscience. Over the course of the past two decades, they have done so spectacularly, accomplishing a degree of intimacy with average people's routines that is unprecedented in human history and flipping the relationship between user and platform. On the surface, it may seem like they're serving us (their customers) something useful and fun, but deeper down we have become their raw material, something akin to unwitting livestock for their massive data farms.

Chapter 2 examines the interplay between social media and social psychology. The job of social media engineers is to design their products in such a way as to capture and retain users' interests. In order to do so, they draw on insights and methods from commercial advertising and behavioural psychology, and they refine their services' features to tap into instincts and cognitive traits related to emotional and other reflexes. This dynamic means that social media's algorithms tend to surface and privilege extreme and sensational content, which in turn degrades the overall quality of discourse on the platforms. (How often have you heard someone remark that Twitter is a "toxic mess"?) It also creates opportunities for malicious actors to deliberately pollute social media and use them as channels to sow division, spread disinformation, and undermine cohesion. This appetite for subversion has even become big business as "dark" PR companies sell disinformation services to a wide range of clients. Although many factors have contributed to the recent descent into tribalism and social polarization, there can be no doubt the environment of social media has created conditions favourable for their flourishing.

Chapter 3 broadens out and scrutinizes the ways in which social media and other related digital technologies have contributed to what I call a "great leap forward in technologies of remote control." In a very short period of time, digital technologies have provided state security agencies with unparalleled capabilities to peer inside our lives, both at a mass scale and down to the atomic level. Part of the reason is the booming surveillance industry, which crosses over relatively seamlessly between private-sector and government clients, and has equipped security agencies with a whole new palette of tools they never previously could have imagined. But part of it is because the social media platforms upon which civil society relies are replete with insecurities. For most people, these insecurities create risks of fraud and other forms of personal data exploitation. For high-risk users, these insecurities can be life-threatening. This great leap forward in the technologies of remote control has taken place mostly in the shadows and in the absence of any compensating measures to prevent abuse. We now have twenty-first-century superpower policing governed by twentieth-century safeguards. As a consequence, already existing authoritarian regimes are tending towards a dystopian system of big-data population control, as exemplified in China's Orwellian "social credit system." Meanwhile, liberal democracies are exhibiting disturbing patterns of unaccountable policing and security practices that challenge existing safeguards against abuse of power. The COVID pandemic heightened these risks as governments declared emergency measures and turned to social media's vast machinery of personal data monitoring for purposes of biomedical surveillance.

Chapter 4 turns to the often overlooked and largely obscured physical and material infrastructure of social media and the communications ecosystem. Although we tend to think of social media and our digital experiences as clean, weightless, and ethereal (an image promoted by the platforms themselves), they are in fact far from it. Every component of our communications ecosystem is implicated in a vast, planet-wide physical and material infrastructure, the raw material for which can be traced back billions of years. Social media are not only inextricably connected to the natural world, they tax it in multiple surprising ways across a spectrum that includes mining, manufacturing, transportation, energy consumption, and waste. Although we often look to digital technologies as sustainability solutions, another painful truth about social media (at least as presently constituted) is that they are increasingly contributing to widespread environmental degradation.

Taken on its own, each of these painful truths is

disturbing. When they are added up, they present a very bleak picture of our social and political reality, and an even bleaker forecast of our collective future. In combination, they can feel profoundly overwhelming, like a tectonic force that cannot be reversed. In part, that is why these truths are "painful." Examining each of their pathologies completely and unreservedly, understanding and appreciating their scope and scale, can leave one feeling exhausted and resigned. Perhaps that is why social media continue to grow in popularity in spite of the "techlash." Perhaps this explains why so many of us choose to remain in a state of blissful ignorance, never untethered for too long from our precious devices. But, as with the challenges of the climate crisis, fateful resignation to social media's disorders will only invite looming disaster. While the personal, social, political, and ecological implications of social media are profoundly disturbing, not doing anything to mitigate them will be far worse.

In the final chapter, I turn to the question "What is to be done?" The negative implications of social media are increasingly acknowledged and well documented. But what to do about them is a different matter. That's not to say that there are no proposed solutions. Indeed, those are abundant and multiplying, but they also lack an overarching framework that ties them together, and in some instances they are even contradictory. In the interests of pulling some of these partial solutions together, I make a plea for a single, overarching principle to guide us moving forward: *restraint*. The common-sense meaning of "restraint" is keeping someone or something under control, including our emotions, our habits, and our behaviours.

What may be less apparent to many readers is that restraint, while seemingly simple, is a concept with a rich historical legacy connected to a long line of political thinking and practice that reaches all the way back to ancient Greece. Restraints are at the heart of liberal political theory, and more specifically that family of liberal theorizing known as "republicanism," derived from the Latin *res publica* (and not to be confused with the party that goes by that name in the United States). Republican thinkers from Polybius to Publius and beyond have seen restraints as critical to checking the state to prevent abuse of power. Police put restraints on criminals, and we, in turn, put restraints on police. Restraints of the latter sort are sorely missing in some areas of life, and rapidly threatened by technological change in others. Drawing inspiration from some of the ways republican-inspired thinkers have conceptualized restraint mechanisms in the past, I put forward some suggestions for how we might think about restraint measures in our own times — as means to rein in the excesses of social media and guard against abuses of power, all the while preserving the great potential of our communications ecosystem. After our reset, I argue, we need to double down on *restraint*.

WHILE *RESET* IS WRITTEN in the context of the COVID-19 pandemic, its larger backdrop is the looming climate crisis and the existential risks it poses to human civilization. As environmental activist and author Naomi Klein has put it, "Humbling as it may be, our shared climate is the frame inside which all of our lives, causes, and struggles unfold." If it wasn't apparent before, it should be now: nature is an inescapable force and the foundation for our very being. Pandemics, rising sea levels, melting ice caps, and escalating surface temperatures show that we are all in this together: one species, one planet.

The many different applications that make up our communications ecosystem will be integral to environmental rescue and ensuring the continued habitability of planet Earth. The internet and even social media hold out the promise of peer-to-peer communications on a global scale, essential for sharing ideas and debating our collective future. The myriad of sensors that span the globe, from satellites in near-Earth orbital space down to biomedical sensors implanted in our bodies, will be essential to taking the pulse of the planet's vast ecology, our own habitat included. Machine-based calculations undertaken at quantum scale can help us solve complex puzzles, increase efficiencies, and help predict and weigh the benefits of alternative trajectories.

However, the time has come to recognize that our communications ecosystem — as presently constituted around surveillance capitalism — has become entirely dysfunctional for those aims. It's disrupting institutions and practices and unleashing new social forces in unexpected ways, many of which are having malign effects. Emergency measures now in place could turn superpower policing practices into totalitarian-scale population controls that quash individual liberties while creating unbridled opportunities for corruption and despotism. Runaway technological innovation for its own sake continues on a disastrous path of unbridled industrial consumption and waste, obscured by the mirage of virtuality. Leaving it as is, with all of its intertwined pathologies intact, will all but ensure failure. A reset gives us a rare opportunity to imagine an alternative, and begin the process of actually bringing it about. To be sure, it won't be easy, nor will it happen overnight. But fatalistic resignation to the status quo is no real alternative either.

ONE

THE MARKET FOR OUR MINDS

IT'S LATE 2013. BLOCKBUSTER reports of state surveillance are dominating the news cycle, courtesy of former National Security Agency contractor and whistleblower Edward Snowden.

I settle into a lounge in Toronto's Pearson International Airport and boot up my laptop. I click the "I accept" button for the Wi-Fi agreement and connect with a VPN (virtual private network) to Citizen Lab servers, effectively wrapping my internet connection in an encrypted tunnel. Reflexively, I pause to consider whether I've made any minor errors in my digital security routine that would inadvertently expose my sensitive communications.

Does this really protect me from a sophisticated threat actor? There is slight relief as the VPN flashes "connect" and the encryption is complete, but the anxiety never fully disappears.

Among the emails in my inbox is one from an investigative journalist from the Canadian Broadcasting

Corporation who wants to speak to me. I plug my headphones into my iPhone and call. He has a lead on the Snowden disclosures.

"Greenwald and company have shared with us some of Snowden's cache that relates to Canada's spy agency," he explains (referring to journalist Glenn Greenwald, one of a very small handful to whom Snowden entrusted his materials), "and we want to get your confidential input."

"Oh really? Sounds interesting," I reply. "Tell me more."

"It seems to be some kind of top secret program to spy on Canadians, *here in Canada,*" he says in hushed tones, as if whispering over the phone would shield us from unwanted surveillance.

"It's difficult to interpret the slides," he continues, "but it looks to be some kind of real-world proof-of-concept experiment in which CSEC [Communications Security Establishment, Canada's signals intelligence agency] is tracking travellers by hacking into Wi-Fi hotspots in domestic airport terminals and lounges, including Toronto's Pearson Airport."

Toronto's Pearson Airport. Hacking Wi-Fi hotspots in lounges...

I look around me with new apprehension: over my shoulder, down at my laptop, at the mobile phone in my hand. I focus on the ceiling above and survey the scattered Wi-Fi routers with their green lights and antennae. What once seemed innocuous suddenly feels ominous.

Situated between them, in numbers that start to feel very oppressive, are the many black-domed surveillance cameras. These cameras are omnipresent in just about every public space these days. Countless individuals pass underneath their constant gaze, seemingly oblivious to their very existence or purpose.

Except me, right now.

I scrutinize other travellers: nearly everyone has a mobile device in their hands or a laptop opened in front of them, or both. There's a couple comparing matching fitness trackers on their wrists. A young teen, thumbs tapping frantically, is immersed in a mobile game. His parents, meanwhile, are preoccupied with their respective devices. No one speaks to anyone else. Business people are pacing around, pinching their headset microphones close to their mouths, each of them siloed in a serious conversation. I imagine waves of data emanating from all their devices outwards in continuous pulses, filling the airport lounge with intersecting bits of information that only I can see: email addresses; usernames and passwords; IP addresses; time stamps; session IDs; device identification numbers; SIM card information.

"Are you still there?" he asks after an extended silence.

"Yeah..." I respond, now with trepidation. "I'll tell you what. Given that I'm sitting right in one of those very airport lounges as we speak, how about we pick up this conversation another time, in person?"

ADMIRE HIM OR NOT, almost everyone would agree that Edward Snowden is a thoughtful person, and he deliberated carefully over what to do with the enormous cache of top secret materials he had purloined from the U.S. government. Rather than publish them wholesale on the internet via WikiLeaks or another dump site, he chose to hand them over to a few select journalists for vetting. This arrangement created a safety check of sorts — a way to remove Snowden himself from the decision loop and publish only material that the journalists, their editors, and the experts they consulted concluded was in the public interest. It also created a unique opportunity for me and some of my colleagues at the Citizen Lab to review a substantial slice of the materials in their raw form, before they were subject to redaction. So began about a year of careful handover of sensitive documents, special access controls, "air-gapped" systems disconnected from the internet, and a general angst all around as to what minefields we might be stepping into.

From popular films and TV shows like *Enemy of the State*, the Bourne series, *Homeland*, and *The X-Files*, many of us have become accustomed to Hollywood portrayals of top secret, seemingly omniscient government agencies having special means to peer inside our lives, turn on cameras on street corners, or tap into phones at will. Given the secrecy that surrounds it all, however, very few without classified access could meaningfully separate fact from fiction. The Snowden disclosures helped demystify a lot of that, principally by verifying that much of what was presented in those fictional dramas was remarkably close to the truth. Snowden's trove of materials, released in slow-drip fashion, showed that government spy agencies had been quietly thriving in the shadows on an epic scale. They had studiously developed astounding capabilities involving bold operations to reap a harvest of intelligence data from across the planet's information and communications infrastructure, most of it behind our backs.

But there was also an important subtext, a more nuanced story, one that may have been easy to overlook. What seemed upon first blush to be principally about Orwellian state surveillance was about something far more complex and disturbing. It was a story not solely about a "deep state" apparatus — an unaccountable "other" that was pulling strings behind a veil of classification to monitor us unwitting victims. It was, rather, about something in which we were all complicit. The NSA and its allied agencies had not so much constructed an information gathering system of their own from scratch as piggybacked on an already existing, deeply entrenched, and widely dispersed system of surveillance spawned by private enterprises and fed by our culture of digital hyperconsumption. By 2013, commercial data collection efforts dwarfed what any spy agency could do alone, even one as well resourced as the NSA and its estimated $11 billion annual budget. In other words, the Snowden disclosures offered not only a window into secret state spying; as importantly, they offered a window into ourselves.

The top secret Canadian airport Wi-Fi program that I and my team first analyzed with the CBC is a case in point. Blandly titled "IP Profiling Analytics & Mission Impacts," the classified slides outlined an ingenious operation to track travellers as they passed through Canadian airports, stopped at lounges or coffee shops to check their emails or browse the web, or headed to hotels and places of business. All of the data described in the slides we reviewed were collected by third parties: large telcos, Wi-Fi hotspot service providers, and obscure data analytic companies. So sensitive were these arrangements that even in the classified documents a key corporation implicated in the program was not disclosed; instead, it was referred to obliquely as "Special Source," a tradecraft euphemism for businesses with whom the Five Eyes agencies have cultivated a close partnership. However, it didn't take a rocket scientist to guess which company was "Special Source" in these slides. "Probably Bell Canada," we all ventured, more or less simultaneously, as soon as we saw the reference. Bell Canada: the mothership of telecommunications infrastructure in Canada, through which the bulk of internet traffic passes. To this day, it's still just a guess. But it's a good guess.

Other companies *were* named. There was Boingo — the Wi-Fi hotspot service provider with which many airline travellers will be familiar from their overpriced and often frustratingly inconsistent airport Wi-Fi services. There was Quovo, a company that few outside of the cloud computing business would know. Quovo collects information on IP addresses — the numerical code assigned to an internet connection — including latitude, longitude, city, country, and network operator, and then sells that information to corporate customers, such as advertisers. There was Akamai, a company that caches websites for speedier retrieval so that your request doesn't have to travel to a server on the other side of the planet to fetch what you want from the web. The slides did not mention specifically *how* all this private data was acquired by CSEC, only that it had been.

The press coverage and reception of the airport Wi-Fi story was slightly confused in this regard. Headlines said "CSEC Used Airport Wi-Fi to Track Canadian Travellers." A casual reader might be excused for imagining that Canada's spies had secretly infiltrated the airport itself, perhaps disguised as janitors, jacking into the Wi-Fi routers with special data-gathering technology that they would later retrieve under the cover of darkness. In fact, Canada's spies had not planted any special equipment inside the airports at all. Their agents had not likely even set foot in Pearson Airport as part of this project, nor in any of the other airports, hotels, or coffee shops mentioned in the program's slides. In fact, the analysts likely never left their windowless cubicles in their dank Ottawa headquarters. Instead, all the data they used were gathered by the companies that own and operate the infrastructure we call "cyberspace." It is to them that we entrust our most intimate digital details. How it got into the hands of the spy agencies — and what exactly they were doing it with it — was (and still is) a serious question raised by the Snowden disclosures, to be sure. But how and why it was all collected from us in the first place was a different sort of question, requiring much deeper introspection.

Looking at it this way, you have to give credit to the NSA, CSEC, and their partners for their initiative and opportunism (however illegal, unethical, or otherwise wrong-headed it may have been — topics for another conversation). Buckets of data acquired in this manner are far more useful than anything the spies could do themselves on-site. As the IP analytics presentation showed, this approach allowed them to triangulate data points and follow targets across a much wider geographic scope — in this case, across just about all of Canada — than any sort of physical surveillance of their own could realistically accomplish. At least not, that is, without a huge investment in labour, technology, resources, and the risk of covert operations being exposed. Armed with data from these sources, they could even "travel back and forth in time," as the analysts boasted, following data trails into the distant past or fast-forwarding from an initial starting point up to the present. Powerful stuff indeed, all thanks to the always-on routines of our digital lives.

And it wasn't just this isolated case, either. It was the same story across almost all of the Snowden disclosures. There was the infamous PRISM program, the second Snowden-related bombshell reported by the *Washington*

Post and the *Guardian*, on June 6, 2013. The initial coverage of the PRISM program mistakenly described the NSA as "tapping into" the servers of Facebook, Apple, Skype, Microsoft, and other high-tech giants with some kind of "direct access." In fact, the data was turned over to the U.S. Federal Bureau of Investigation by the companies under lawful access procedures, *and then shared with the NSA*. That explains why the companies responded to the news reports with denials of knowledge of PRISM: the latter was a code name the NSA had given to the arrangement, not something the companies themselves would recognize. They just thought they were complying with a warrant. Regardless of the means by which it was acquired, the NSA reaped second-hand a regular crop of likes, contacts, calls, messages, and other details that the social media platforms themselves had first collected. PRISM was like a top secret tax on Silicon Valley data-harvesting practices.

Others followed the same convenient arrangement. Under the auspices of a top secret program called Dishfire, for example, the NSA was able to "take advantage of the fact that many banks use text messages to inform their customers of transactions" and thereby monitor international financial exchanges. Another NSA presentation showed how the agency had piggybacked on "the tools that enable Internet advertisers to track consumers, using 'cookies' and location data to pinpoint targets for government hacking and to bolster surveillance." A program code-named HAPPYFOOT showed that the NSA and its U.K. partner, the Government Communications Headquarters, were exploiting the location data "leaked" by popular mobile apps. To help locate targets of interest, the NSA collected hundreds of thousands of contacts from instant messaging and email applications. On and on the stories went, following the same pattern: an astounding digital vacuum-cleaning operation up and down the entire infrastructure of global communications networks owned and operated by the private sector.

To be sure, the NSA and its partners did still "tap into" and have "direct access" to a lot of networking equipment and infrastructure. Their hubris was remarkable. By partnering with or otherwise enlisting the cooperation of undersea cable providers, telecommunications companies, and cell service operators, they hoovered up massive volumes of data flowing directly through the arteries of the global communications ecosystem, storing it in giant data warehouses for later fusion (the process of integrating disparate data sources together) and analysis. They hacked into backbone routers (the equipment that connects large networks together) and the computers of technicians working at Internet Exchange Points (the physical locations where internet service and other network providers exchange their traffic). They even hacked into the pipes connecting Google's own private data centres. But the means were less significant than the overarching approach. The infamous "collect it all" mentality that guided post-9/11 signals intelligence gathering was a response to an epochal shift in communications technology and practices which had taken place outside the realm of international espionage. In but a few short decades, our everyday world had been thoroughly digitized and networked from the inside out. For the NSA and its partners, this revolution in personal data practices marked the dawn of the Golden Age of Signals Intelligence. They were reaping what all of us had sowed. And they still do.

In September 2013, the German newspaper *Der Spiegel* published an article about an NSA program to exploit unpatched vulnerabilities in Apple, Google, BlackBerry, and other smartphones. A line on the slide from an analyst seemed to sum up best this historic shift in state–society relations. Summoning up George Orwell's dystopian surveillance classic *Nineteen Eighty-Four,* the analyst asks, "Who knew in 1984 that this would be Big Brother [referencing a picture of Apple's then-CEO, Steve Jobs] and the zombies would be paying customers?"

Those paying customers? Those "zombies"? Turns out that's all of us.

"GOOD MORNING, ALEXA," you murmur, bleary-eyed. The sun peeks through the blinds that were automatically drawn to half-mast thirty minutes ago while you were still asleep — just how you like it. The smell and sound of the coffeemaker brewing down the hall make you salivate like Pavlov's dog. *Who's the one doing the programming here?* As the familiar chimes of the opening credits to BBC *World Report* drift in, you roll over and grab your mobile device off the bedside table. Accelerometers, gyroscopes, and other motion detectors buried in the hardware of your device confirm you're awake. As you bring it closer, its built-in camera and infrared diode scan your face and retina to automatically compare its stored biometric data against thousands of data points it can read. Satisfied within a split second that it has identified you, it then unlocks itself, passing no judgement whatsoever on your early-morning appearance.

While you may have been asleep for many hours, your device has been working relentlessly. Apps that you left open have been communicating "home," sending data in short regular bursts across the internet. Algorithms of many companies and platforms have been busy digesting the data you have shared with them, and which they in turn share with numerous other "third parties" — data brokers — all with the intent to know you better. You first open your Instagram feed, then Facebook, then Twitter. A screen roll of last night's boozy parties that you did not attend flickers to life. You swipe and move on, but the apps take note of how long you lingered. There's another toddler picture. *Is that my nephew or someone else's?* An obligatory funny cat video. A ridiculous Donald Trump tweet. An inspirational poem from your aunt. Another mass shooting. *Should I sign the petition?* And then an ad for a special on an exclusive Hawaiian resort.

Umm, weren't we just talking yesterday about going to Hawaii? I swear, Alexa's listening to everything we're saying...

If this — or something closely approximating it — is not your normal morning routine, it may soon be. It is already for hundreds of millions of your fellow humans. Make no mistake, the platforms that run it all want this to be your routine too, just as they want it to be universally extended to everyone else on the planet. A mere twenty years ago, this would have been the stuff of science fiction. Now it's becoming an everyday reality.

It seems like only yesterday that pundits fretted about how to make money off the internet. Throughout the 1990s, investors were shovelling billions of dollars at start-ups managed by twenty-somethings, and yet no one seemed to have a clear vision of a viable business model for the web. Everyone hoped that some kind of monetary magic would materialize out of technology that itself seemed to many to be magical. Analysts would later dub these hopes an "irrational exuberance" after it all came crashing down in the spectacular dot-com bust of 2000, when the value of internet companies plummeted suddenly after what seemed like unstoppable success. "Can the dot-com party go on forever? Not likely," wrote Bloomberg's Catherine Yang on April 3, 2000. Investors have been acting like "intoxicated college students on spring break," she added. The hangover was harsh. Between March and September 2000, the stock value of the Bloomberg U.S. Internet Index's top 280 internet companies had lost a combined $1.755 trillion.

However, the bust did not last long. Under pressure to earn money, principals at Google adjusted their strategy. Previously averse to monetizing their users' search behaviour, Google founders Sergey Brin and Larry Page did an about-face and started tying advertisements, displayed modestly at first on the margin of their website, to users' search queries. In doing so, they not only boosted Google's market value astronomically but helped to create a model of how to derive revenue successfully from internet connectivity and all of the services that were being given away online for free. Their experiment led to a massively successful initial public offering in 2004 and a market valuation of $23 billion.

Google's success would be quickly emulated by Facebook, Amazon, Twitter, and numerous other players in the social media universe. These innovations in personal data surveillance were initially restricted principally to business on the internet. But the model that Zuboff memorably helped christen "surveillance capitalism" would spread like wildfire to encompass and eventually dominate the entire global economy. At the core of surveillance capitalism is a relatively simple concept: in exchange for services given to consumers (mostly for free), industries monitor users' behaviour in order to tailor advertisements to match their interests. "This new form of information capitalism," Zuboff explains, "aims to predict and modify human behaviour as a means to produce revenue and market control."

Surveillance capitalism did not emerge out of nowhere, and it certainly did not just spring from the minds of Silicon Valley entrepreneurs like Page and Brin. There was a prehistory to the personal data surveillance economy, a social and historical context that reaches back decades and even centuries. Its ground was prepared long ago with the rise of the early modern bureaucratic state and its mass record keeping, which helped encode individuals as units of information that could be measured, compared, and socially sorted. Starting in the early twentieth century, birth certificates, social security numbers, real estate and financial records, educational scores, and psychological profiles were increasingly adopted and standardized, making informational elements key attributes that define a person. Of course, we could not have this latest variant of capitalism without the emergence and spread of industrialization and capitalism itself, and especially some of its central characteristics, such as private property, wage labour, individualization, consumer culture, and especially the science of advertising (about which more will be said in the next chapter). In a more immediate sense, the blast-off of social media could not have happened without innovations in telecommunications, digital computing, and networked services, particularly the invention of the internet itself and the radical redistribution of information and communication exchanges that it permitted. Policy decisions were critical too, especially decisions in the United States to deregulate and privatize the telecommunications sector and legally insulate tech platforms from liabilities that traditional media face. All of these touchstones were essential to the causal pathways leading to surveillance capitalism. It would be an overstatement to say Google's innovations were preordained, but it would be correct to say that they couldn't have happened without those prior developments. Many of us were socially and economically prepared to embrace the personal data surveillance economy years before it came to dominate our lives, and long before we started to fully appreciate its unintended consequences. This prehistory was like a pile of dry kindling waiting for a match to ignite the fire: the innovations of Brin, Page, and others like them — to see personal human experiences as the raw material for a new kind of business model — were just that spark.

It is the latter that makes surveillance capitalism distinct from prior forms of capitalism, according to Zuboff. The novelty is to see our private human experiences as free raw material that can be endlessly mined. On one level, it is the perfect sustainable resource: our habits, preferences, relationships, moods, and private thoughts are like constantly replenishing wells. On another level, as we shall see in chapter 4, it is entirely *un*sustainable, dependent as it is on toxic mining of raw materials, rising energy consumption, and non-recyclable waste. Under surveillance capitalism, social media drill into personal human experiences by whatever ingenious means may be derived from their proliferating sensors, and then turn them into what Zuboff calls "behavioral surplus"—proprietary data that is used for predictive signalling. The primary customers are not us, the consumers or users of social media; the real customers are other businesses that are interested in predictions of human behaviour generated by the social media platforms and the data analytics machinery that surrounds them. We are simply a means to a larger, commercial end. We're the livestock for their farms.

Social media, of course, do not openly describe themselves in the way social theorists and political economists do. Naturally, the platforms market themselves in much more anodyne ways. For example, instead of referring to its users as "raw material," Facebook refers to them as a "community." "All the world's information at your fingertips," a catchphrase trumpeted by Google executives, seems much more benign and empowering than what Google really does. An application that knows everywhere you want to go and tracks how you get there would likely freak people out, so instead Google Maps describes itself as a tool that "makes navigating and exploring your world faster and easier." Social media companies strive as much as possible to make all of the extraordinary surveillance of our personal lives seem, well, *normal*. As the product manager of Google's smart-home system, Nest, said, "You need different sensors and inputs and outputs across all the different rooms inside your house. And to the consumer, it needs to feel like one." *Feel like one.* In other words, all the sensors that envelop and monitor you are so blended into the taken-for-granted reality, the unquestioned environment that surrounds you, that they become, in effect, invisible. The less we question this environment, the more platforms can undertake extensive surveillance of our behaviour with as little friction as possible. Under surveillance capitalism, says Zuboff, our ignorance is their bliss.

THERE IS AN INERTIA, an inexorable logic, to surveillance capitalism. This logic, manifest in each and every new social media innovation, compels platforms to acquire data about consumers from ever more fine-grained, distributed, and overlapping sources of information. These sources dig deeper into our habits, our social relationships, our tastes, our thoughts, our heartbeats, our energy consumption, our sleep patterns, and so on. Each new source of data is like a door that opens only to present yet another door to be opened. Amazon is developing drones to deliver their packages. Why not equip them with cameras to map the houses to see if their customers might want to purchase some new gutters? And now that we have that imagery, why don't we market it to the local police too? Google's vehicles roam the streets collecting imagery for their Street View feature. Why not vacuum up internet data from open Wi-Fi hotspots while we're at it? Put simply, there is never too much data. Sensors are built upon sensors in an endless quest for yet more data about our lives.

One indication of this inexorable logic can be found in patent applications that Facebook has made, which effectively provide "a map of how a company thinks about where its technology is going." Facebook has taken out a patent for a process that would infer whether a user is in a romantic relationship, based on their gender, how often they visit friends' sites, and other indicators. Another prospective technology examines the content of your posts to mark your personality along each of the five basic dimensions of personality known as the "Big Five": conscientiousness, agreeableness, extroversion, openness, and emotional stability. Another uses a range of data points — credit card transactions, location data, etc. — to try to predict when a major life event (e.g., birth of a child, graduation) is going to occur; another proposes to use tiny scratches on camera lenses to create a unique "signature" for a user; yet another proposes to exploit electrical disturbances in the power cables of television sets to observe television shows being watched while a user is online.

The endless quest to acquire more data invariably leads down a path towards the unguarded, subliminal, and other sub-rational components of our behaviour — what the academic Jan Padios calls "emotional extraction." How long we linger on an advertisement or an image might reveal something about our state of mind. How long we stare at something, or conversely, how quickly we swipe past a suggested link, can be suggestive of some deeper personality trait or mood swing. "Mining the mind" for subtle affects is something the platforms can do without necessarily revealing overtly that they are collecting something from us. As new-media researcher Amanda Greene put it, "This information does not pass through a cognitive filter as it is created and stored, but instead emanates from physical rhythms and actions that are usually not consciously recognized in the moment of their appearance." Instead, platforms combine the talents of psychologists, neuroscientists, and engineers to develop interdisciplinary means of "unobtrusive monitoring" or "passive sensing and detecting" of our mental states based on data that come from their sensors. (The utility of these data for not only predicting but *shaping* human behaviour is extraordinarily valuable, and will be addressed in more detail in chapter 2. In chapter 3, we shall see how that imperative to shape human behaviour does not just remain restricted to commercial goals, but leads irresistibly to *political* ones as well — for customers that include powerful elites, autocrats, and despots.)

Consider an app called "Mindstrong Health," which describes itself as "transforming the diagnosis and treatment of behavioral health disorders through the ubiquity of mobile technology." Drawing on a user's normal interaction with their device — how long they perform certain routines like typing and swiping — their algorithms develop an "emotional profile" from which deviations can be registered. The app's founders claim the app can help diagnose depression and other mental illnesses, *before they happen*. They say "the app can even predict how a person will feel next week, or at least how a person will perform on the Hamilton Rating Scale for depression — kind of like a weather app for your mood." Think about that for a second: *a weather app for your mood*. You've heard of "Future Crimes." Get ready for "Future *Breakdowns*."

THE PERSONAL DATA SURVEILLANCE economy consists of the frontline service companies that most consumers recognize, but also a large number of secondary "analytic" companies that operate behind the scenes. Social media companies derive revenues by allowing third-party developers, applications, data brokers, and other services in their orbit to access their customer data, through either application programming interfaces (APIS) or other privately contracted data feeds. Analytic companies take the data harvested by the sensors of frontline companies, subject them to analysis, and then sell or trade business intelligence to advertisers and other companies. Orbiting further out are still other companies that provide the algorithms, software, techniques, and tradecraft used by the social media analytics firms. (Further out yet are those that supply the basic hardware, software, and energy required to keep it all operating.) Most users never hear of these companies in the outer orbits until there is a breach or a scandal, such as that involving Cambridge Analytica, or when their names surface in a leaked classified surveillance document, such as those we reviewed in the Snowden disclosures.

These partnerships can mean that users of one platform or application may be unwittingly sharing vast amounts of personal data with dozens of other services in a behind-the-curtain information-sharing bonanza. For example, according to a *New York Times* investigation, Facebook has data-sharing partnerships with at least sixty device makers — including Apple, Amazon, BlackBerry, Microsoft, and Samsung. After installing an app for one of them, the journalist undertaking the investigation found that the app was able to gain access to unique identifiers and other personal information of hundreds of his Facebook friends, and close to three hundred thousand friends of friends.

Most often the direction of the sharing bonanza starts with data collected by the social media goliaths and works outwards to smaller, less recognizable data brokers and applications operating in the shadows. But the flow can work in the opposite direction too. For example, in December 2018, the NGO Privacy International (PI) published a report in which they examined thirty-six apps and found that nearly two-thirds of them automatically transfer data to Facebook the instant a user opens the app — "whether people have a Facebook account or not, or whether they are logged into Facebook or not." PI found the data that was transferred included some highly sensitive and personally revealing information. The sharing happens as a consequence of application developers using Facebook's Software Development Kit (SDK), essentially a shortcut for developers to automatically embed Facebook's features in their product. By seeding SDKs to hundreds of thousands of developers, Facebook can effectively burrow its way into applications with implants that have nothing to do with Facebook directly, or are even used by individuals who want no part of Facebook's operations.

In one particularly egregious case, PI examined an app called Maya, which is marketed as a tool to help female users track their menstrual cycles. The PI study showed that upon activation, Maya sent detailed private health information to Facebook and other third parties, including contraceptive practices, period cycles, whether a user had unprotected sex or not, and details on blood pressure, swelling, acne, and even mood swings. PI's investigation also found that the Maya app automatically transferred this type of sensitive data upon start-up to wzrkt.com — which, after further investigation, turned out to be the web server operated by an analytics company called CleverTap. CleverTap describes itself as "a customer retention platform that helps consumer brands maximize user lifetime value, optimize key conversion metrics, and boost retention rates." Never heard of CleverTap? Chances are it's heard of you.

One of the best examples of the data-sharing bonanza that occurs over social media can be found on the principal tools we use to navigate the web: our browsers. Depending on their settings and how they are coded, browsers can tell a lot about a user, and the user's software and hardware: your CPU (central processing unit), GPU (graphics processing unit), and battery; your operating system; the IP address you are provided for each session; your geolocation; a detailed history of the websites you have visited; your mouse movements and clicks; whether your device has a gyroscope and a compass, and which orientation it is currently in; the social media accounts into which you have logged; which fonts and languages are set to default or are installed on your machine; and so on. All of these data points tell a story about you, your machine, and your habits that other data brokers can use to build profiles about you. Our browsers are not just portals to the web, in other words; they are portals into each of us: a digital fingerprint that follows us around wherever we go online.

One of the ways browser data harvesting is accomplished is through "plug-ins" or "browser extensions"—little programs that are added to browsers ostensibly to make our online navigation more "user friendly." While extensions can serve a variety of useful purposes, they can also siphon off data from a user's online habits and employ them for whatever purposes they want. Probably because these companies prefer to stay in the shadows, they tend to attract shady, unethical behaviour. Take Nacho Analytics, a data broker and self-styled "market intelligence company." Independent researcher Sam Jadali found that Nacho Analytics was behind a catastrophic privacy disaster because of the leaky browser plug-ins it operates, affecting at least four million users. Even though Nacho Analytics claimed to scrub personally identifiable information from the data they collect, by signing up for a free trial to a third-party service to which Nacho Analytics was selling its data, Jadali found that he could nonetheless access usernames, passwords, GPS coordinates, and medical records — including the names of doctors, their patients, and their prescriptions; airline reservation information, including passenger names, from carriers like United and Southwest Airlines; tax information from Microsoft's cloud storage service, OneDrive; and numerous documents marked "top secret" — *all in near real time.* If Jadali could pull off something like that, imagine what an agency like the NSA, or a criminal organization, could do.

While Jadali's study examined data collection undertaken by browser extensions, users' online activities are also collected at the receiving end: through tracking done by the web servers they visit. Most people are familiar with "cookies" — little programs that are attached to browsers when a user visits a website — but few truly appreciate the depth of the harvesting that is undertaken in this manner. Ironically, the best way to understand the scope and scale of this tracking is to install a tracker detector as a browser extension. One of these, called Privacy Badger (developed by the Electronic Frontier Foundation) exposes the web tracking that takes place when you visit a website. Using Privacy Badger, I visited the employment-oriented social media service LinkedIn and found fifteen separate trackers, including those operated by Bing, Google, Facebook, and DoubleClick (companies I recognize), and TripleLift, AppNexus, Cedexis, and DemDex (companies I had never heard of). I then visited the "Privacy Project," a special section of the *New York Times* that investigates many of the issues detailed here, and found the same number of trackers. Nacho Analytics, CleverTap, and DemDex, and countless other shady data brokers that almost everyone reading this chapter will have never heard of, are like social media bacteria: though largely invisible to the naked eye, they flourish in the cracks and crevices of our digital environment, parasitically living off our daily social media experiences and providing the nutrition that feeds surveillance capitalism.

THE SCALE OF THE ECONOMIC transformation unleashed by the personal data surveillance economy is hard to overestimate. One way to gauge the importance of this new mode of production is the way traditional industries are being transformed into vehicles of personal data surveillance, even if they did not start out that way. A commercial airline, for example, is in one respect simply a mode of transportation. In another respect, however, commercial airlines are also data-gathering and marketing firms embedded in a wide array of other data-gathering and marketing firms with which they are associated, such as hoteliers, taxi operators, and vacation companies. Loyalty rewards programs draw customers into company alliances, but they also collect information on customers' preferences, movements, and spending habits. It is now increasingly commonplace to download an airline's mobile app to book flights, check in, and receive a boarding pass (and if you haven't downloaded it yet, the airlines definitely encourage you to do so — budget airlines even make it difficult *not* to do so). These apps are not just about convenience. As noted in Air Canada's privacy policy, these programs and tools collect information about customers in order to allow the airline to "develop and recommend products and services based on an understanding of your interests and needs." As the policy stated at the time of writing,

> We and our marketing partners, affiliates, or analytics or service providers, use technologies such as cookies, beacons, tags, and scripts, to analyze trends, administer the website, tracking user's movements around the website, and to gather demographic information about our user base as a whole. We may receive reports based on the use of these technologies by these companies on an individual and aggregated basis.

There are also what we might consider hybrid mutations of old- and new-school data surveillance. Firms are employing social media tools to give a new look to well-established business practices, such as loan sharking. Take "FinTech" — it sounds high-tech and futuristic and refers to innovation around the digital delivery of financial services, but in practice FinTech can be about as grimy a tool of commercial exploitation as it gets. In Kenya, mobile banking FinTech apps have proliferated astronomically but have led to widespread debt problems and horrific tales of abuse. California-designed apps like Tala and Branch are given away to Kenyans for free, but then they scan their users' devices and social media accounts to evaluate their creditworthiness. The apps analyze how often you call your family, whether you go to the same workplace every day with consistency, and how fastidiously you maintain your network of contacts. Why the latter? Tala's CEO said that "repayment of a loan is more likely by someone whose contacts are listed with both first and second names." The apps do not rely on traditional forms of collateral, like money deposited in a bank or property ownership, but rather on the metrics derived from the harvesting of users' behaviours — what historian Keith Breckenridge calls "reputational collateral." The apps take advantage of the fact that they are literally in the pockets of their debtors and can send unsolicited text messages throughout the day, enticing users to borrow at cutthroat rates — sometimes as much as 100 percent annualized. Since the apps know your habits and location, they can send these messages when you're at your most vulnerable and open to suggestion. Many Kenyans report receiving them late at night on weekends, when their defences might be down because of alcohol consumption. An app called

OKash even goes so far as to harvest users' contacts to then call bosses, parents, and friends to shame defaulters into repaying.

ALL SOCIAL MEDIA HAVE a higher- and a lower-level function. The lower-level function is the apparent one. An application that you use to tease your brain is, for most people, nothing more than a game. But the game is just the window dressing for a higher-level, more important function: to observe and acquire data about you, your device, your other applications, your contacts, your pictures, your settings, your geolocation, and so on. To take just one example, Zynga, the mobile app developer behind the popular *Words with Friends*, gives its games permission to access first and last name, username, gender, age and birthday, email, contacts from the address book, in-game purchases, the contents of chats between players and everything they post on the game's message boards, and approximate physical location. They also use cookies, beacons, and other digital tags to gather information on your IP address, your device's media access control (MAC) address, the type of device you are using as well as its operating system, and your browser information. While you and your friends are busy playing word games over the internet, Zynga is busy sweeping up everything it can about you to sell to data brokers. I suppose that is what Zynga means by its tagline "connecting the world through games."

Sometimes there are even higher-level functions than merely mining your experiences. Zuboff provides the illuminating example of *Pokémon Go*, the "augmented reality" mobile game application that spread wildly, to the point that by the end of the year it was introduced (2016), it had been downloaded five hundred million times. On the surface, the aim of *Pokémon Go* is to encourage users to locate and acquire as many *Pokémon* characters as they can, using their maps function. While *Pokémon Go* apps routinely requested as many permissions as they could to monitor users, their social networks, their devices, locations, and so on, they also herded them into the vicinity of other businesses, like McDonald's franchises, in the hope that they would consume products there, thus earning *Pokémon Go* additional advertising revenue. It's worth noting that Google Maps functions, more or less, in this manner too. Google solicits businesses to pay a premium to have their company logos, instead of plain icons, as identifiers on its maps. Seeing a familiar Starbucks logo, instead of a generic coffee cup, promotes brand recognition and drives up traffic to those outlets. One illustration of a higher-level function that most users will recognize is the "I'm not a robot" CAPTCHA tests, which ask users to identify all the images that contain cars, bridges, or street signs before they are allowed to proceed onwards to an online service. While the lower-level function is ostensibly to protect us from spam and malicious bots, the higher-level function is to use us as free labour to help train the company's artificial intelligence systems. Next time you're asked to complete one, consider sending an invoice for services rendered to Facebook or Google. You're working for them, after all.

In order to accomplish many of these higher-level functions, apps give themselves permission to access parts of your device, data contained on it, and its functional features — even your camera and microphone. Not surprisingly, the social media world is awash in boondoggles and horror stories in which company engineers voraciously overreach for permissions, through malign intentions, institutional inertia, laziness, or some combination of the three. For example, in 2014, Pew Internet undertook an analysis of over one million apps in Google's Android operating system and discovered that apps can seek 235 different kinds of permissions from smartphone users, with the average app asking for five. A study undertaken by the International Computer Science Institute's Serge Egelman found that more than one thousand Android apps harvested location data even after the user explicitly denied them permission to do so. For example, a photo-editing app called Shutterfly gathered location information from the metadata of pictures or Wi-Fi network connections. According to the study, apps that were denied permission to gather certain information would even go so far as to scan the device's memory card to locate and harvest data that other apps were permitted to gather but they were not. The app's own privacy restrictions, in other words, were seen as a temporary inconvenience for the engineers to eventually circumvent through a clever work-around. In one particularly egregious case, Egelman and his team of researchers discovered that the app for CVS, a pharmacy widely used in the United States, sent a user's GPS coordinates to over forty different third parties. Perhaps the most astonishing revelation of Egelman's team's research concerned data sharing among apps targeting children. According to Egelman,

> More than 50 percent of Google Play apps targeted at children under 13 — we examined more than 5,000 of the most popular (many of which have been downloaded millions of times) — appear to be failing to protect data. In fact, the apps we examined appear to regularly send potentially sensitive information — including device serial numbers, which are often paired with location data, email addresses, and other personally identifiable information — to third-party advertisers. Over 90 percent of these cases involve apps transmitting identifiers that cannot be changed or deleted, like hardware serial numbers — thereby enabling long-term tracking.

A group of researchers at Northeastern University, Princeton University, and technology website Gizmodo used real-world tests to show that Facebook used contact information, like phone numbers handed over for security reasons, for targeted advertising. Users submitted their phone numbers for enhanced two-factor authentication (2FA) security protocols, prompted by Facebook.

But unbeknownst to the users, Facebook then used that contact information to target users for advertising. The researchers also revealed that Facebook was collecting "shadow contact information": if a user shared their contact list and it included a phone number previously unknown to Facebook, that number would then be targeted with ads, without consent.

Facebook's "People You May Know" feature is yet another classic illustration of permission overreach driven by an insatiable lust for more user data. The feature, well known to social media users, suggests friends or colleagues with whom you might have some relationship, and whom you might want to befriend. However, the function started to raise alarm bells when users reported "creepy" or otherwise disturbing and possibly harmful recommendations — like sex workers having their clients recommended to them as friends, or psychiatrists being revealed as the missing link among patients who otherwise did not know each other. Turns out that Facebook had quietly scanned users' entire email contacts and kept all the addresses to which a user had sent an email, without disclosing that they would do so. Journalist Kashmir Hill, who researched the People You May Know functionality, discovered that the team developing it was aware of, and sensitive to, these potentially disturbing outcomes. According to Hill, "A person familiar with the People You May Know team's early work said that as it was perfecting the art of linking people, there was one golden rule: 'Don't suggest the mistress to the wife.'" Hill also reports that Facebook purchased a data analytic company called Octazen, based in Malaysia. "In a TechCrunch post at the time," she writes, "Michael Arrington suggested that acquiring a tiny start-up on the other side of the world only made sense if Octazen had been secretly keeping users' contact information from all the sites it worked with to build a 'shadow social network.'" Even if you don't use Facebook, it is through these shadow contacts that Facebook can still develop a profile of you — which explains why, when you first create an account, the platform readily serves up dozens of potential friends with whom to connect.

Our own research at the Citizen Lab has uncovered similar examples of bizarre and unsettling overreach combined with sloppy coding, at least one of them connected to our engagement on the Snowden disclosures. In one top secret document prepared in 2012 by Canada's Communications Security Establishment (CSEC), we noticed reference to the agency's collecting data for fingerprinting from a leaky mobile browser application developed in China, called UC Browser. At the time, few on our team were familiar with UC Browser. However, it was the fourth-most popular mobile browser in the world, used at the time by over five hundred million people. Given the possibility of vulnerabilities affecting a larger number of at-risk users, we conducted an independent investigation and discovered a gong show. As I described in a *Globe and Mail* editorial at the time of our publication, UC Browser

> leaks a huge torrent of highly detailed personally identifiable data about its users. Those leaks include the unique identification number hard-baked into the device (IMEI), personal registration data on the user's SIM card (IMSI), any queries sent over the browser's search engine, a list of the names of any WiFi networks to which the device has recently connected, and the geolocation of the device. Some of this data is sent entirely "in the clear" without encryption; others are sent using weak encryption that could be easily decrypted. Some of it is sent the moment the application is turned on, in an "idle state." None of it is sent with the explicit permission of its users.

Notably, CSEC didn't disclose the vulnerabilities to UC Browser, preferring to keep that knowledge to itself and use it for intelligence gathering. But we did. After a year of back and forth with the parent company, Alibaba, most of the problems were fixed. But the case was an interesting illustration of how poor software engineering combined with overzealous data harvesting can lead to significant risks for a sizable population of unwitting users — and yet another fishing hole for signals intelligence gathering agencies.

The "Internet of Things" towards which surveillance capitalism is now directed will turn the average home into a showroom for these split-personality higher/lower-level functionalities. Your dishwasher cleans the dishes, but it may also monitor your morning routine.

Your fridge keeps food cool, but also tracks what you eat. Your lightbulb illuminates your living room, but it also sends data on your day-to-day life back to GE. You watch television while the television, in turn, watches you. Roomba vacuums your bedroom but sends detailed maps of your house's dimensions to the company. It is noteworthy to reflect on just how the "home" and its relationship to our private lives is being thoroughly transformed through surveillance capitalism. Once the epitome of an individual's sanctuary and the primary metaphor for the concept of privacy (at least as it was mythologized in Western liberal political theory for privileged elites), the "home" has been turned completely inside out, the most minute details that go on behind closed doors exposed as raw material to be mined by thousands of data analytics companies across the globe.

THERE ARE COLOSSAL UNINTENDED consequences of surveillance capitalism, some of which we'll explore in later chapters. Some of them we may not fully reckon with until today's younger generations begin to age and grapple first-hand with the blowback of their always-on social media lives. Take the fact that today's social media–engaged youth have had their private lives documented, categorized, published, and subjected to algorithms from the moment they were born. Proud parents unwittingly splash their children's biometric data over social media platforms — something for which the children are, naturally, unable to provide consent. Looking over my own extended family's Instagram and Facebook posts, there's a steady stream of minors' lives under surveillance: here's Johnny doing something silly; cooking his first cupcake; having a temper tantrum; beginning his first day at kindergarten; learning how to ride a bike. Before Johnny reaches adulthood, he'll have millions of data points fed into a distributed machine whose aim is to shape the choices he makes — all before he's "of age." While most parents fret about their children encountering inappropriate content on the internet, perhaps they should be more concerned about what happens when the internet, because of their own actions, is constantly encountering their children?

A rash of unintended consequences surrounds DNA data, such as that collected by companies like 23andMe and Ancestry.com — a market that is exploding in popularity as genetic testing technology advances and curious customers want to know more about their lineage or health risks. Like all digital technologies, genetic testing services such as these have higher- and lower-level functions, including selling data they collect on their customers to third parties. For example, 23andMe and Airbnb have partnered to offer customers "heritage vacations" based on their genetic results. Large pharmaceutical companies could use genetic data to target users who have specific genetic markers with tailored advertisements for their drugs. That's no doubt why, in 2018, the pharmaceutical giant GlaxoSmithKline acquired a $300 million stake in 23andMe. Another obvious potential third-party client is law enforcement agencies, which can use genetic information to locate perpetrators of crimes (however those may be defined). And while specific customers of these services may inform themselves of the risks of handing over their genetic data to these companies, and all third parties to whom they might provide it, none of that due diligence extends to those who share their genetic fingerprints. When you hand over your DNA data, you're not just handing over your own genetic data, you are handing over your entire family's too — including those of future generations yet to be born. You might even be unwittingly selling out a brother or sister you never knew you had! Where is their "informed consent"?

Perhaps the most profound unintended consequences will emerge around the chronic, pervasive insecurity throughout the entire infrastructure of surveillance capitalism. Social media platforms are in a race to accumulate profits, corner market share, ship products and services before their competitors, and extract data from as many users as possible. Ensuring the security of their users, and of their users' data, is largely an afterthought. Facebook founder Mark Zuckerberg's flippant mantra "move fast and break things" fully embodies this negligence. To be sure, data security is not entirely ignored. But security is prioritized only to the extent that it makes sense from a business perspective, that it helps mitigate some kind of liability. Fortunately for many digital companies, liabilities are light and entirely manageable relative to the monumental revenues. The existing market structure allows them to pass the costs of most of their pervasive insecurity on to their users. Add it all up and you have the situation we see on a near-daily basis: massive data breaches and epic platform security failures.

One could fill an entire library with volumes that contained nothing but lists of data breaches and privacy scandals connected to surveillance capitalism. My inbox is full of them on an almost daily basis. Allow me to describe just three:

- A security researcher discovered that the popular video conferencing technology Zoom could actually be used to turn on the camera of any random laptop on which the program was installed, without the user's consent or knowledge. Calling the flaw "bananas," he estimated it could affect around 750,000 companies.

- Facebook admitted that a poorly secured online database exposed hundreds of millions of its users' phone numbers, a few short months after it was revealed that millions of its users' passwords were stored in a manner that made them accessible to more than twenty thousand Facebook employees.

- More than twenty million Ecuadoreans had their personal data — phone numbers, birth certificate

> information, tax identification and employment information, names of family members — fully exposed online as a consequence of poor security implemented by an Ecuadorean data analytics firm. The breach included personally identifiable information on seven million children. Ecuador has a population of 17.5 million, so the breach was more than the entire country's population — the difference explained by the number of deceased people's data included in the breach.

These are but a few examples from just the last couple of weeks of 2019 — a year in which a study found that 3,800 publicly disclosed breaches had exposed an astounding 4.1 billion individual records in the first six months of that year alone.

When situated in the context of the personal surveillance data economy, what appears to be a kind of feckless incompetence and criminal negligence around data security is actually quite easy to understand. These are not "bugs" but "features." We can't reasonably expect companies to prioritize privacy and users' data security when the entire ethos of innovation is oriented in precisely the opposite direction: to dig deeper, relentlessly, into as many areas of human life as their sensors can reach, as quickly as possible, before their competitors beat them to it. "Our privacy crisis is a crisis of design," as *New York Times* journalist Charlie Warzel puts it.

It is for this reason that social media companies'

promises to do more to "protect user privacy" ring hollow and are usually just flat-out ignored. For example, after a Consumer Reports investigation found that Facebook did not provide a simply explained "opt-out" for users for its facial recognition scanning technology, the company took eighteen months to alter its settings — and only after a U.S. Federal Trade Commission fine of $5 billion. Expecting social media companies to incorporate privacy by design on their own makes about as much sense as expecting the beef industry to protect the lives of cattle they slaughter.

"IS MY SMARTPHONE SECRETLY listening to me?"

It's the question I get asked more than any other. Years ago, the answer used to be: "No, at least not without your explicit permission." I felt pretty comfortable that was the case. There were always exceptions — like if your device was hacked and the operators turned on the microphone. We knew of plenty of cases like those. But surely companies themselves wouldn't go so far as to record users without permission. Or would they?

And then, over time, my answer became more qualified. There was Shazam, the popular mobile app that users can employ to detect the name of a song and its artist being played on the radio. Turn on Shazam, hold it up to the speakers, and within a few seconds, you get a match: Talking Heads, "Life During Wartime." Brilliant! You can even click on a link to purchase the song.

It turns out Shazam was not just recording what you wanted it to record, when you wanted to record it. A researcher who monitored the application's network traffic data discovered that it was drawing audio from its surroundings while it was on in the background, even when the app was set to "off." The company excused the behaviour by explaining it away as a convenience for the user: "If the mic wasn't left on, it would take the app longer to both initialize the mic and then start buffering audio, and this is more likely to result in a poor user experience where users 'miss out' on a song they were trying to identify."

Then I heard about Alphonso, the software analytics company whose application is embedded in thousands of seemingly unrelated innocuous gaming apps, including games targeted at children. Alphonso uses a device's microphone to pick up audio signals of television programs or movies in order to — you guessed it — *better target advertising at users*. It even works in the background, as long as one of the applications in which Alphonso is embedded is installed and open. In other words, Alphonso is an application embedded in thousands of other applications whose purpose is to "listen in" on what you are watching. It even has a partnership with Shazam (which Apple bought out in 2018).

Naturally the answer to the question became more complicated when personal digital assistants started showing up on devices and in homes as convenient appliances working in the background, awakened to action by the utterance of a few words like "Okay, Google" or "Hey, Siri." We were assured by those companies that the device's audio capture system would activate a connection to their cloud system only when a user would utter the exact phrase that matched a file stored locally on the device itself. No one was actually "eavesdropping." Rather, the company's artificial intelligence and natural language processing algorithms analyzed the audio to improve the quality of the responses provided to users' questions.

And then, one after another, news reports showed that those assurances were misleading. In fact, Amazon, Google, Microsoft, and Apple all retain human contractors to listen in on audio recordings to transcribe what's being said in order to improve the companies' AI systems. Moreover, an investigation undertaken by the Belgian news organization VRT showed that some of Google's audio recordings were activated without the trigger words being uttered, apparently by accident. VRT obtained and listened to more than one thousand recordings shared with them by an outside contractor used by Google, confirming that the recordings started without the activation words and included highly sensitive personal information, discussions about finances, conversations involving minor children, and even what sounded to the journalists like physical violence and distress.

Upon learning about the interception, a group of California citizens launched a class-action lawsuit against

Google, since California law prohibits the recording of oral communications without the consent of all parties. But for the overwhelming majority of other social media users, my guess is that any outrage (if there is outrage at all) will be limited and short-lived — at best, fodder for a few viral memes. There's a *Groundhog Day* quality to stories like these: a technology scandal is followed by shock, which is then followed by a company apology and a pledge to "do better," which brings us around to a new normal. Rinse and repeat. Whether it's a form of what Zuboff calls "psychic numbing" or what science fiction author Cory Doctorow has called "peak indifference" (problems seem so overwhelming that the only viable option is just to shrug and move on), it seems that no revelation about the practices surrounding surveillance capitalism is outrageous enough to separate users from their precious applications. Indeed, a recent survey of American attitudes undertaken by Georgetown University and NYU found that Amazon and Google were the second- and third-most trusted institutions respectively, ahead of even colleges and universities and courts.

The direct effects of such a profound transformation in modes of communication are enormous, but the unintended consequences are likely to be far more unsettling. Social media are spawning an extensive and deeply penetrating web of sensors whose boundary knows few limits. All of us users, in turn, are being unwittingly drawn into this vast enterprise as both consumers and something akin to domesticated livestock in a post-industrial data farming industry. Without any explicit debate, personalized, mobile, always-on, networked devices have allowed tech platforms to appropriate our personal information as something they can own, as if all our data was merely a *res nullius* (Latin for "nobody's thing")—there for the taking. Our likes, emotions, relationships, and thoughts have become *their property*.

Coincidentally, digitally herding and monitoring people in this manner turns out to be highly advantageous for government security agencies, as does the pervasive insecurity that provides them all with the keys to a seemingly endless number of convenient back doors, as the Snowden disclosures revealed. With no cages to keep us penned up, social media must rely on tools and techniques to attract and keep our attention instead. The tradecraft of the decades-old advertising industry—what media scholar Tim Wu calls the "attention merchants"—has been radically transformed into something approximating a real-time, continuous, and digitally enabled set of controlled experiments on billions of human subjects. But this environment has also enabled far darker and more insidious species to flourish as well, serving a different set of "customers" whose aims are not to sell lipstick or vacations, but to undermine public accountability, spread social division, and foster chaos.

TWO

TOXIC ADDICTION MACHINES

IN LATE 2019 AND EARLY 2020, as I was preparing this manuscript, the deadly COVID-19 virus broke out in Wuhan, China, and began to quickly spread around the world. Governments, NGOs, international health organizations, health officials, and others rushed to inform and prepare populations and contain the spread of the contamination.

In 2020, one might be excused for thinking that the lightspeed communication channels we have established across the planet, which we rely on for news and information, would greatly assist in the swift dissemination of accurate information and safety precautions. Think again.

In what has become commonplace around any major news event, the circulation of information about the coronavirus on social media was flooded with conspiracy theories, misinformation (false or inaccurate information), disinformation (deliberately propagated false information), racist memes, chat censorship and surveillance, and even viruses of another kind.

Official news, alerts, and health tips from groups like the Centers for Disease Control and Prevention (CDC) and the World Health Organization (WHO) competed with tweets and Facebook posts from conspiracy theory accounts that said, among other things, that drinking bleach could cure the virus. I wouldn't recommend that, but tens of thousands of those who reposted it did. The WHO went so far as to label COVID-19 an "infodemic," explaining that "the outbreak and response has been accompanied by . . . an over-abundance of information — some accurate and some not — that makes it hard for people to find trustworthy sources and reliable guidance when they need it."

Even a colleague of mine whose judgement I trust sent me an email from the news website CCN (yes, that's CCN, not CNN) claiming that the virus was the result of an accidental release of a secret Chinese military biological weapons test. Meanwhile, Russian propaganda outlets spread disinformation across social media that the virus is actually a *U.S.-made* bioweapon deliberately designed to target China. The latter had echoes of a much earlier, KGB-sourced disinformation campaign from the pre–social media age, codenamed Operation Denver, which propagated the false theory that AIDS was the product of a U.S. bioweapons experiment gone wrong. By April 2020, the Chinese Communist Party had so heavily promoted the same conspiracy theory over social media and state TV that journalists reported it was inescapable and widely accepted throughout Chinese society.

Meanwhile, a conspiracy theory linking the spread of COVID-19 to 5G cellular services sailed through global social media, with disturbing consequences. Promoted across Facebook, WhatsApp, and YouTube by far-right fringe groups and celebrities like Woody Harrelson and John Cusack, the conspiracy theory claimed that radio waves emanating from 5G cell sites cause molecular changes to people's bodies that make them susceptible to the virus. One YouTube video, which received close to a million views before it was taken down by the streaming service, falsely claimed that Africa was immune to COVID-19 because there were no 5G services on the continent (neither assertion was true). In fact, the ten most popular 5G COVID conspiracy videos posted in March 2020 were viewed over 5.8 million times in total. The conspiracy view would be but a ridiculous side note were it not for the way it spilled out of social media into the real world, with destructive consequences. In March 2020 in the United Kingdom alone, there were more than thirty incidents of arson and vandalism as anti-5G activists set fire to base stations and cell towers and harassed telecommunications technicians.

Alarmingly, disinformation spread through social media contributed directly to mob violence and armed clashes with police in Ukraine. An email designed to appear as though it was from an official Ukrainian health agency claimed that cases of the infection had begun to spread wildly in the country. The information was false and the email was a forgery. Yet that did nothing to stop a significant number of Ukrainians from believing it and circulating it widely through social media. A large, angry group of protestors gathered at an airport to confront a plane chartered to evacuate Ukrainians from China. The mob smashed the windows of buses carrying the evacuees, torched police barricades, and clashed violently with police. The entire melee — broken glass, fist fights, arrests, and all — was the result of what was, in essence, a doctored meme.

In Canada, racist tropes tinged with misinformed speculation flooded social media, some blaming Asian people, their culture, and their culinary habits for the virus. When a widely read Toronto blog profiled a new Asian restaurant, the comment feed on the blog's Instagram account quickly became a cesspool of ignorant claims and racist slurs. Not to be outdone, the *Toronto Sun* shared a video on its social media feed showing a woman eating a bat, underneath the caption "a woman dining in China was filmed taking several bites." Problem is, the video wasn't filmed in China at all, and not anywhere near the time of the outbreak. It was filmed in 2016 on the small Pacific Ocean archipelago of Palau. So much for fact-checking.

Meanwhile, across the world, computer threat intelligence companies (firms that research and provide information to clients about threats and threat actors causing harm in cyberspace) raised alarms about phishing emails sent out with malware-laden documents, links, and other lures as cybercriminals took advantage of the fear and paranoia to trick users. Researchers at the cybersecurity firm IBM X-Force spotted a rash of malware-laden emails sent to Japanese citizens early in the virus's spread, and warned that more was to come. Summing up the neuroses of our collective social media condition, the researchers concluded that "unfortunately, it is quite common for threat actors to exploit basic human emotions such as fear — especially if a global event has already caused terror and panic." As if on cue, it wasn't long before health agencies, humanitarian organizations, and hospitals worldwide were blitzed with ransomware, digital espionage attacks, and phishing schemes. Exhausted individuals working in the threat intelligence and cyberdefence industries with whom I spoke said the rash of attacks was like nothing they'd ever experienced before.

Social media companies responded to the "infodemic" in typically mixed and slightly confused fashion. At first, Facebook announced that it would remove posts containing misinformation about the virus, while YouTube, Twitter, and Reddit claimed that inaccurate information about health was not a violation of their terms-of-service policies, leaving the algorithms to surface content that grabbed attention, stoked fear, and fuelled conspiracy theorizing. After sending human content moderators into self-isolation, Facebook turned to artificial intelligence tools instead, with unfortunate results. The machine-based moderation system swept through, but mistakenly removed links to even official government-related health information. Gradually, each of the platforms introduced measures to point users to credible health information, flag unverified information, and remove disinformation — but in an uncoordinated fashion and with questionable results. The platforms' intrinsic bias towards speed and volume of posts made the measures inherently ineffective, allowing swarms of false information to circulate unimpeded.

As is customary in authoritarian systems, China was concerned less about preventing the spread of misinformation than about silencing criticism of their own ineptitude and potential culpability. China's police detained numerous people for their posts on social media, while medical personnel were instructed not to speak to the media. Doctors who dared to do so were arrested. One Wuhan-based physician, Dr. Li Wenliang, who after treating infected coronavirus patients was himself infected with the virus, was arrested for messages sent to an online chat group alerting his colleagues to the illness — among the very first warnings issued about the virus. The reason for Dr. Li's detention: "spreading rumours." On February 7, 2020, sadly, he succumbed to the virus.

At the Citizen Lab, we have built technical systems to monitor censorship and surveillance on China's social media applications, and as soon as we heard about the virus outbreak, we started to test for censorship on two platforms: YY, a live-streaming application, and WeChat, a popular China-based social media app used by over a billion people. We discovered that YY began to censor keywords related to COVID-19 on December 31, 2019, only one day after doctors (including the late Dr. Li) tried to warn the public about the then-unknown virus. By reverse-engineering the YY application, we found that keywords like "武汉不明肺炎" (Wuhan unknown pneumonia) and "武汉海鲜市场" (Wuhan Seafood Market) began to be censored weeks before central authorities publicly acknowledged the outbreak and prior to the virus's even being named.

Our tests showed that WeChat also ramped up censorship on topics broadly related to COVID-19, including criticism of the Communist Party of China and central government, and any discussions of China's leader, Xi Jinping, as well as general discussions of the death toll and government policies related to the outbreak. Perversely, even references to credible health authorities, like the CDC, were censored by WeChat. We found that censorship on both platforms lacked transparency and accountability: there were no public details about censorship regulations, and users were not notified if a message containing sensitive keywords was deleted from their chat conversations. Send a chat message with any number of banned keyword combinations, and it simply would not appear on the recipient's device, with no notice given to either the sender or the intended recipient. Although it's impossible to rerun history to see what might have been had China not taken such a heavy-handed approach, it is quite possible that the country's officials may have inadvertently contributed to needless confusion and even death by suppressing communications about the disease in the early days of the outbreak. What we witnessed in China, in other words, was a kind of cynical and self-serving experiment in information control that generated lethal consequences, which rippled across the globe.

The sorry state of miscommunication and information chaos around COVID-19 is not the first instance in which a major public health crisis has been exacerbated by social media. When the deadly Zika virus broke out in Brazil in 2015, health workers told reporters they felt overwhelmed by the false content deliberately seeded through social media channels. Propelled forward by algorithms that select content for its sensational content, Brazilians searching YouTube for accurate health information received instead disturbing claims that the virus was being spread by vaccinations and by insecticides meant to curb mosquito populations. The poorest communities (where literacy is low, time to fact-check is scarce, and access to more detailed content is constrained by mobile media) were most affected by the spread of inaccurate and inauthentic news, and they were among those the disease hit the hardest. A pediatric neurologist hoping to stem the Zika tide expressed his frustration: "Fake news is a virtual war... we have it coming from every direction."

In late 2019 and early 2020, the world watched in shock as devastating fires swept across Australia. Widely attributed to the global climate crisis, the fires caused massive devastation to property and wildlife, and even loss of life. But the crisis also provided an opportunity for climate change denialists to propagate disinformation, and for misinformed speculation to swarm and compete for people's precious attention. Conspiracy theories circulated across social media, claiming bushfires were deliberately lit to clear a path for a high-speed rail line down Australia's east coast, that they were the work of Islamic State militants, that they were caused by Chinese billionaires using lasers to map out new construction projects, or that they were lit by eco-terrorists trying to spur action on climate change.

At least one prominent politician bought into it all. Speaking in the U.K. House of Commons, Foreign and Commonwealth Office minister Heather Wheeler answered a question about the Australian bushfires by stating, "Very regrettably, it is widely reported on social media that 75 percent of the fires were started by arsonists," prompting a group of U.K. scientists to write an open letter condemning her for giving legitimacy to a widely debunked claim. Meanwhile, an article in the Rupert Murdoch–owned newspaper the *Australian* falsely claimed that 183 arsonists had been arrested in the "current bushfire season." Though false, the piece was widely circulated on social media channels by important influencers like Donald Trump Jr. and the right-wing conspiracy outlet InfoWars — the latter claiming that "authorities in Australia have arrested close to 200 people for deliberately starting the bushfires that have devastated the country, yet the media and celebrities continue to blame 'climate change' for the disaster." Australian opposition politician Anthony Albanese lamented the confusion. "What Australians dealing with the bushfire crisis need is information and support. What they don't need is rampant misinformation and conspiracy theories being peddled by far-right pages and politicians."

WE LIVE IN A SINGLE "global village" with numerous shared problems crying out for collective action, from immediate emergencies like COVID-19 to longer-term existential challenges, such as global climate change and nuclear weapons. What harbinger is it for the future when one of the principal means we have to communicate with each other is so heavily distorted in ways that propel confusion and chaos? What hope do we have to ever manage our collective future when our global public sphere has become such a poisonous brew of xenophobia, ignorance, and malice? One might reasonably ask: How is it that — with such awe-inspiring computer power and telecommunications resources at our disposal — we have arrived in such a dismal condition?

Even though a growing number of people are alarmed by social media, recognize the ill effects, and lambaste the various platforms as cesspools of hatred, racism, intimidation, and ignorance, the fact of the matter is—*we still rely on them*. Indeed, many of us even *like* them. To understand the roots of this apparent contradiction requires us to take a step back and examine not only our own uses of social media, but the way social media, in turn, *use us*, and what their engineering of us implies for the global public sphere.

Oxford Bibliographies defines the "public sphere" as "the social space in which different opinions are expressed, problems of general concern are discussed, and collective solutions are developed communicatively." According to the German political theorist Jürgen Habermas, arguably the topic's best-known thinker, the public sphere is intimately connected to the material circumstances of time and place. For example, Habermas argues, the combination of European coffee houses and salons, a high degree of relative literacy, and a print-based, vernacular media environment led to the flourishing of the "bourgeois" public sphere of the Enlightenment period.

We are living in the midst of a fundamental reordering of our communications environment, one that is unprecedented in its scope and scale. While there are some positive aspects of social media, there are also numerous negative by-products and externalities that seem to be spreading unhindered. To be sure, there has never been a particular place or time in history when we could say the media were decidedly unprejudiced or not biased in some manner. There's a reason Habermas referred to his conditions for the public sphere as "ideal." But almost everyone now senses a serious erosion in the quality of discourse online — a deterioration in the quality of our admittedly already flawed domain of public conversations; a complete inversion of the conditions that gave rise to Habermas's coffee houses. And yet, in spite of it all, this deterioration only accelerates, deepens, and expands as social media's popularity advances. How to explain it?

The answer lies in a series of linked causal relationships inherent to our communications ecosystem and emanating out of the dynamics of surveillance capitalism. At the lowest level is the most basic business imperative of the personal data surveillance economy: capturing and retaining customers' attention. As shown in chapter 1, social media companies need users, and they want the users to stay connected to their services as long as possible. To accomplish that objective, social media engineers use techniques from advertising and behavioural science to make the uses of social media more compelling — and more difficult to ignore. Human nature being what it is, our attention tends to be captured by sensational, extreme, scandalous, and even horrifying content that shocks us or pulls on our emotions. The systematic preference given to emotionally charged content, combined with the sheer volume of data, makes it increasingly difficult (or at least more time-consuming) for the average person to discern fact from falsehood. The personalization of social media, especially content targeted at individuals and small groups of people with shared interests, helps to divide mass audiences into specialized segments, which in turn reinforces social polarization. And it is here where opportunity knocks. A communications ecosystem that propels sensational, extreme, and polarizing content by design is a perfect fit for those actors who aim to foment chaos and cynicism.

Looking at it this way, it's clear how deeply embedded are the multiple causal mechanisms that together produce the surface phenomena we experience with social media on a daily basis. This outcome is not an accident or a minor by-product; it is a predictable behavioural outcome of the material properties of the communications environment in which we live. It also makes evident how solving the malign characteristics we associate with social media is not going to be simple. It won't be something that we can fix with a single policy, let alone a newfangled app. What we are experiencing, collectively, is a function of a linked set of deeply entrenched and mutually supportive social forces. Untangling these will be exceedingly difficult — a topic we'll address in more detail in the final chapter.

IN 2018, A NEW TERM CIRCULATED widely: "techlash" — not only a growing irritation with social media's ill effects but a major pushback against the entire roster of technology platforms. Let's face it: people are fed up with social media. Just about everyone has some kind of complaint, not just about the applications or the platforms, but also about the billionaire executives who run it all, people like Facebook's Mark Zuckerberg or Twitter's Jack Dorsey. I don't know how many times I've heard friends and family members complain, *Twitter is a Dumpster fire!* Or, *I can't stand Facebook! Zuckerberg is creepy!*

And yet, everywhere I look, I see the same people still glued to their devices. Numbers bear it out too. In February 2020, the *Economist* reported that "in the past 12 months the shares of America's five biggest technology firms have been on an astonishing bull run, rising by 52%." Facebook was notoriously fined $5 billion by the U.S. Federal Trade Commission in 2019 — a number that was widely described as equivalent to a "rounding error" for a company that makes three times that much in revenue every quarter, and has about ten times that amount in reserves. In fact, Facebook's stock jumped close to 2 percent on the day the fine was announced, adding $10 billion to its market value — double the value of the fine itself. (Although the big tech giants' share values took a hit alongside all other industrial sectors as the COVID pandemic shut down the global economy, the turn to social media as a lifeline has seen those share prices rebound considerably.)

Driving the increasing revenue is a seemingly never-ending supply of users waiting to get hooked. While Facebook and other platforms may have peaked in North America and Europe, they are just beginning to expand into untapped billions of customers in the global South. Facebook's $5.7 billion investment in India's Jio (the country's largest mobile network operator and the third-largest in the world) in early 2020 is just one example of the way tech platforms foresee enormous untapped revenue in the developing world's rising number of users. Travel to any major city in Asia or Latin America, and you'll see that just about everyone now has at least one mobile device, if not several, and a Facebook account to go along with it. The popularity of social media continues to grow unabated, in spite of spreading knowledge of the platform's many problems. To be sure, there are ups and downs. One social media platform is superseded by another. MySpace is replaced by Facebook. Facebook will undoubtedly be eventually overtaken by something else. But the economic system as a whole upon which they are all based — the personal data surveillance economy — continuously expands.

But is this popularity entirely *witting*? Here, the answer gets a bit more complex.

First, because social media are so pervasive, there are strong incentives for adopting them and strong disincentives against not doing so, including inconvenience and cost. Students of mine often remark that they cannot leave Facebook because they would face social ostracization, or at least miss out on parties. A growing number of companies offer convenient engagement with their services through social media or other digital applications, excluding customers who choose not to have accounts. Think of airline reservation or concert ticket apps — it's much easier to enjoy both without having to print out that ticket. Or consider Facebook's "Free Basics" program, marketed primarily to the global South as a low-cost way to get users online, which effectively locks them into Facebook as the entry point to the entire internet, a kind of "digital colonialism," as Global Voices' Ellery Biddle calls it. Siva Vaidhyanathan, in his book *The Googlization of Everything*, refers to this process as "infrastructural imperialism," in which companies like Google increasingly structure our choices through subtle but powerful incentives.

Then there is the issue of whether users fully understand the choices they are making when they sign on to social media. Most have by now become accustomed to downloading and installing numerous applications, each of which comes with lengthy terms of service that most users do not read, let alone understand. In fact, it would be physically impossible for the average user to read all of the terms of service to which they consent, and still be able to do anything other than spend all their waking hours reading them. One computer software diagnostic company did an experiment to prove the point: it put an offer to give away $100 at the very end of its terms of service, to see how many would read that far. Four months and three thousand downloads later, one user finally did. Add to the mix the boilerplate contract language used in terms of service, which most laypeople are poorly equipped to understand, and the veil of ignorance around contractual obligations becomes thicker.

As contract law experts Brett Frischmann and Evan Selinger put it, "Almost no one is discussing the negative impact the electronic contracting environment has on our habits and dispositions, and more generally, on who we are as human beings... [boilerplate contracts] condition us to devalue our own autonomy." The concept of "consent" is trivialized when users simply click "I agree" and then move on without so much as a second thought. Rather than informed agreement, the repetitious act of granting consent is more like a pest to be swatted down. It's more *performative* than substantial, an obligation companies undertake to protect their liability but that (more importantly) enables them to appropriate users' data — which effectively includes everything we do through social media and, in turn, all the information the platforms extract from us while we do so — as *their* property. It obscures rather than informs, creating a kind of "consent fatigue," all the while enforcing a kind of digital serfdom. And perhaps that's the ultimate intent.

WHILE MOST WOULD ACKNOWLEDGE the constraints on choice these incentives (and disincentives) create, a growing body of research points to a much more fundamental (and less witting) mechanism at work that explains our embrace of social media. According to a report published by the International Center for Media & the Public Agenda at the University of Maryland, students around the world who were asked to give up social media for a day all experienced the same striking symptoms. Said the report, "Most students from all countries failed to go the full 24 hours without media, and they all used virtually the same words to describe their reactions, including: Fretful, Confused, Anxious, Irritable, Insecure, Nervous, Restless, Crazy, Addicted, Panicked, Jealous, Angry, Lonely, Dependent, Depressed, Jittery and Paranoid." In short, social media are addiction machines.

Social media are addictive because they stimulate us in a powerfully subconscious and hormonal way. Social media affect brains like falling in love. Your level of oxytocin — otherwise known as the "love hormone" for the feelings it generates — rises as much as 13 percent when you use social media for as little as ten minutes. Studies are now convincingly showing that people addicted to social media "experience symptoms similar to those experienced by individuals who suffer from addictions to substances or other behaviors" — such as withdrawal, relapse, and mood modification. One research project showed that the mere presence of a switched-off smartphone significantly decreases a person's ability to focus on a task. Environmental stimuli, such as people, places, or routines, can stimulate and help reinforce the addictive behaviour, which might explain why many of us habitually pull out our phones every time we're waiting in a grocery line or using public transport. Is it accurate to describe our embrace of social media as wilful and voluntary when that embrace has the properties of an addiction?

In fact, the companies are not only aware of the addictive and emotionally compelling characteristics of social media, they study and refine them intensively and with extraordinary resources. In order to be effective, company executives understand, social media must generate a kind of consumer compulsion. To encourage continued engagement with their platforms, social media companies borrow basic psychological methods reaching back to American psychologist B. F. Skinner, such as operant conditioning. Operant conditioning is based on altering behaviour using a system of rewards and punishments. Behaviour that is followed by pleasant consequences or anticipation of future rewards is likely to be repeated. Behaviour that is followed by negative consequences is likely to be avoided.

A good example of operant conditioning in social media is what is known as a "compulsion loop." Compulsion loops are found in a wide range of social media, and in particular online games. Take a scan (discreetly, of course) of what people are doing with their devices as they ride your local public transit system, and you'll see a sizable number of them glued to their mobile device screens as they swipe and tap their way through the levels of brain teasers or primitively animated games of skill. These mobile games work by a process known as "variable rate reinforcement," in which rewards are sought after but delivered in an unpredictable fashion (e.g., through "loot boxes" containing unknown rewards). Variable rate reinforcement is most effective at shaping a steady increase in desirable behaviour, and it has effects on the release of dopamine, another hormone that plays an essential physiological role in reward-motivated behaviour. Game designers use variable rate reinforcement to entice players to continue playing the game repeatedly. The higher- and lower-level functions of social media outlined in the previous chapter are, as always, significant. While the player is moving through the game, slowly getting addicted, the game's application learns more and more about the player's device, interests, movements, and other factors. Social media platforms — and the devices that connect us to them — even sense when you are disengaged, and their designers have created techniques and tools to draw you back in: little red dots on app icons, banner notifications, the sound of a bell or a vibration, or scheduled tips and reminders. The typical mismatch between the actual information we receive after a notification and what we hoped to receive before we checked can in turn reinforce compulsive behaviour — all typical behaviour extensively studied by neuroscience.

The former president of Facebook, Sean Parker, recently made remarkable admissions about how Facebook employs such methods to hook people on its platform. Parker described how features such as "like" buttons were designed to give users "a little dopamine hit." He went on to explain: "It's a social-validation feedback loop... exactly the kind of thing that a hacker like myself would come up with, because you're exploiting a vulnerability in human psychology." Concluded Parker, ominously: "Our choices are not as free as we think they are." As the author of the book *Overconnected*, William Davidow, similarly put it, "Thanks to Skinner's work, brain MRIs, and more recent research by psychologists, neuro-scientists, and behavioral economists, we now know how to design cue, activity, and reward systems to more effectively leverage our brain chemistry and program human behavior." One case where these dynamics are clearly illustrated is Snapchat, the popular app in which users post and view "disappearing" images and videos. The fleeting nature of the content, combined with the app's promotion of "streaks," in which users review each other's feeds obsessively, encourages compulsive checks of the platform amongst its users to the point where many do so for thousands of days on end. Similarly, many social media feeds encourage obsessive scrolling, as a result of the feeds having no defined endpoint; the apps are "designed to maximize anticipation, rather than reward," a dynamic that is referred to in social psychology as a Zeigarnik effect.

As with other products where addiction is a factor (e.g., tobacco, casinos), the behavioural modification parts of the story are only dimly understood by consumers, but they are studied intensively by the people who run the platforms and by the social media analytics companies, marketing firms, and PR consultants that orbit around them. As New York University professor Tamsin Shaw put it, "The findings of social psychology and behavioural economics are being employed to determine the news we read, the products we buy, the cultural and intellectual spheres we inhabit, and the human networks, online and in real life, of which we are a part." Indeed, psychological experiments on consumers are essential to refining just about all social media and related digital applications. It's not just the platforms alone that zero in on these mechanisms of addiction and compulsion; huge numbers of marketers and PR firms do so as well. The appetite to gather and retain "eyeballs" has generated a massive value-added sector of start-ups, social psychology consultants, and boutique behavioural modification firms that provide services to platforms (and firms interested in exploiting platforms for revenue). These marketing and PR firms gather in large professional conferences (like the Traffic & Conversion Summit, advertised as "the premier gathering of digital marketers on planet Earth") to share best practices on how to "game" the platform's ad and content moderation systems in their clients' favour. According to one comprehensive study on the topic, "marketers use information about the customer to actively design more addictive offerings and employ information collected through digital experiences for further marketing." Digital technologies make these design choices inherently more effective too: "more data is available; experiments are easier and almost costless to run; and, thanks to programming, the cycle of testing and redesign can operate almost instantaneously." Social media, wearable apps, and digital games "are tenaciously designed for compulsive use." With the help of hired scientists, game developers (to give just one example) employ psychological techniques to make their products as "unquittable" as possible.

With so much precision data at their disposal, social media engineers can perform repeated, real-time statistical hypothesis testing (known as "A/B" tests) on their users. Engineers create an "A version" and a "B version" of some feature, then randomly send each of those out and observe which performs better according to a metric (such as "likes" or screen time or even users' facial expressions). Whichever of A or B works better against that metric can then be either deployed at scale or incrementally nudged up. Lacking ethical oversight, sometimes these experiments can go wrong. The most infamous example, though not the only one, was Facebook's admission that it had successfully modified over seven hundred thousand users' emotions in an experiment it undertook by hiding a small number of emotionally charged words from their daily newsfeeds. The experiment showed that such selective feeding of content worked, with users susceptible to the "emotional contagion" that comes with bad news. The experiment was conducted without informed consent, for which it was widely condemned by the academic community.

An even more disturbing example is an experiment Facebook undertook in 2010, just before the U.S.

midterm elections that year. Facebook researchers placed an "I Voted" button at the top of the users' news feeds, along with the locations of polling stations and details on whether their friends had clicked the button. Facebook researchers then checked public voting records to determine which users actually voted, and found they were more likely to click the "I Voted" button if they noticed their friends had done so as well. In other words, Facebook discovered it could subtly encourage people to vote. Although that experiment may seem banal (perhaps even socially beneficial), it's but a short step from "encouraging people to vote" to "encouraging people to vote for *this party,* and *not that one.*" With such capabilities in hand back in 2010, imagine what can be done now, or a few short years from now. In 2019, Facebook announced a breakthrough in its research into machine learning algorithms capable of turning brain activity into speech, while Neuralink, a company owned by Tesla founder and inventor Elon Musk, is reportedly developing "a high bandwidth brain-machine interface" to connect people's minds directly to a computer and to "read" the activity of neurons. University of Washington cyberlaw expert Ryan Calo has ominously warned where these experiments might lead, noting we are entering into a new era of digital market manipulation, whereby "firms can not only take advantage of a general understanding of cognitive limitations, but can uncover, and even trigger, consumer frailty at an individual level." Such awesome power to manipulate the emotions of billions of users, in the hands of a few small platforms, should give everyone serious cause for concern.

While social media's engineers develop their platforms in subtle ways to grab and keep our attention, they also aim to make their products as unintrusive as possible. The goal of the developers is to have social media recede into the background, to wash from our minds the fact that they are, indeed, always there, lurking, probing, and shaping. The design of the "informed consent" process (which is more accurately a means to acquire consent without users actually being informed) is a case in point. As Evan Selinger put it, social media "instill trust by getting 2.2 billion users to forget about the platform and make trusted 'friends' (and, of course, 'friendly' brands and organizations) the center of attention." It perfects, in other words, "intimacy by design." It leverages the trust around information sharing among friends to manipulate us into sharing information with advertisers. That design is meant to lull customers into a sense of complacency, to ignore the intense surveillance that is shaping their lives, and the vast machinery that supports it all. Judging by the continued popularity of social media, it works.

AS WITH ANY OTHER COMPULSION, too much of what at first seems like a good thing can lead to very bad results. It's already clear that this type of addictive compulsion to use social media and other digital technologies associated with them can amplify numerous psychologically and socially negative traits, including along gendered lines. For example, because of societal expectations and a multitude of other factors, adolescent girls tend to engage in forms of indirect aggression such as mean-spirited gossip, social exclusion, relational aggression, and covert bullying. Whereas in previous times, these activities would be limited in scope and scale, with social media they have been amplified a thousandfold as the terrain has moved beyond school grounds. Now adolescent girls' social media feeds tell them who's "in" and who's "out," who has been invited to party and who hasn't. And though the posts may be fleeting, they don't disappear. Instead, they are archived and recycled and used repeatedly to shame and belittle, leading to increased depression and other mental health risks.

With respect to adolescent boys, on the other hand, social media — especially online first-person shooter games — tap into their craving for adrenaline rushes and their attraction to pack behaviour with an artificial and sedentary alternative to the real thing. (A 2018 meta-analysis of twenty-eight separate studies confirmed that there's a higher prevalence of internet addiction among adolescent males — possibly related to their greater susceptibility to developing addictions altogether — than there is among the population overall.) It's become familiar to hear about boys who go to school (where they sit most of the day) and then return home to sit in front of a screen to which they are hopelessly attached.

The compulsive overuse of digital technologies of all sorts and the ensuing harms they cause individuals are the subject of research in a wide range of scientific studies, driving the establishment of numerous treatment facilities in the United States, Europe, China, and elsewhere. In 2019, both the World Health Organization and the American Psychiatric Association added "internet gaming disorder" to their classification of diseases and addiction. About two billion people worldwide play video games. That number includes about 150 million Americans (half the country's population), 60 percent of whom do so daily. Some studies have shown that higher levels of screen time among adolescents, both girls and boys, may be linked with increased symptoms of depression (although ruling out other causes is challenging). A comprehensive 2019 summary of the existing research on the negative effects of "addiction to digital experiences" listed psychological, physical, societal, and economic harms, such as low self-esteem, mood swings, anxiety and depression, sleep disturbances, relationship problems, accidents caused by distracted driving, and impaired childhood socialization, among others.

Beyond the negative impacts on individual segments of the population, the dynamics of surveillance capitalism at the core of social media are clearly also having an impact on the quality of public discourse. Consider the most basic feature: the problem of information overload. The phenomenon of information overload is not new to the social media age. The concept has a long history dating back at least to the time of the printing press and accelerated by the advent of radio, television, and other modes of communication. It has its modern genesis in the mid twentieth-century research of American engineer Vannevar Bush, who was concerned about data deluge and how it would impede rational exploration of problems. The concept is closely tied to a particular view of the human mind as an information processing machine, then just gaining widespread acceptance.

Ironically, the solutions Bush and others proposed to mitigate information overload may have led to some of the very technologies that would evolve into social media. For example, in 1945 Bush proposed a "memex" machine, an imagined personal device used to access information and build connections among disparate bits of data. Similarly, in the 1960s, biologist and academic administrator James Grier Miller, who coined the term "behavioral science," proposed dealing with information overload by the creation of what he called EDUNET, which was conceived of as a "knowledge bank" and a "network of networks."

While the concept of information overload may not be new to the social media age, we are arguably entering an era in which sheer quantity is producing a qualitative shift. According to Twitter's own usage statistics, "Every second, on average, around 6,000 tweets are tweeted on Twitter, which corresponds to over 350,000 tweets sent per minute, 500 million tweets per day and around 200 billion tweets per year." On average, 1.47 billion people log onto Facebook daily, and five new Facebook profiles are created every second. Facebook videos are viewed eight billion times per day. Every minute, more than 3.87 million Google searches are conducted and seven new articles are added to Wikipedia. The fact that we typically carry with us devices that are always on and connected further exacerbates information overload. The vast amounts of information produced by individuals, by businesses, and even by machines operating autonomously, twenty-four hours a day, seven days a week, is unleashing a constantly swelling real-time tsunami of data. While it is certainly true that the volume of information expanded rapidly in prior eras (e.g., the advent of mechanized printing), what makes our communications ecosystem different is that the overall system is designed to both push that information in front of us and simultaneously entice us through addictive triggers (pull us, in other words) to stay connected to it at all times.

The overall dynamic systematically tilts public conversations into a kind of discursive gutter — the "cesspool" with which we have all become familiar. Part of the reason for this dynamic is what Stanford cybersecurity expert Herb Lin calls our "human cognitive architecture," which has remained unchanged for millennia but has unique characteristics that turn into major shortcomings in an information environment such as our own ("shortcomings," that is, for us; for the platforms, they're vulnerabilities to be exploited). Human cognitive processing capabilities are not unlimited; they are finite, and can reach their limits, especially under stressful conditions. Our reasoning is affected by certain "hard-wired" cognitive biases that deviate from ideal conditions of rational judgement. Our rationality is bound in various ways, in other words, and we think differently in different types of situations.

Thanks to the pioneering work of Nobel Prize–winning psychologist Daniel Kahneman, it has become commonplace among cognitive psychologists to break down human reasoning into two general systems: System 1, in which short-term, visceral, and emotionally influenced reasoning takes place; and System 2, which is more deliberate, patient, and analytical. System 2 reasoning is what most of us have in mind when we think of the classical, utilitarian "homo economicus" version of reasoning. However, it is System 1, with all its cognitive shortcuts, ingrained biases, and emotional reflexes, that reigns supreme in the social media ecosystem. Social media engineers are well aware of System 1's more beneficial effects for their platforms' popularity. According to a major study by marketing psychologists Ezgi Akpinar and Jonah Berger, who combined controlled laboratory experiments with systematic analysis of hundreds of online ads, it is clear that "emotional appeals (which use drama, mood, music, and other emotion-eliciting strategies) are more likely to be shared" than "informative appeals (which focus on product features)." As attention merchants have known for decades, emotional appeals sell better than rational ones.

Social media's flood of content also amplifies other cognitive biases in ways that uniquely allow false information to root itself in the public consciousness. Consider "the availability heuristic" and "the illusory truth effect" — terms describing cognitive traits that explain how collective beliefs are reinforced regardless of their veracity or merit, as a result of their repetition. Social psychology experiments have demonstrated that repeated exposure to information increases the likelihood that observers will believe that information, even if it is false. It doesn't take a Nobel Prize winner to appreciate how social media's continuous surfacing of sensational content feeds into and reinforces these biases. It might also help explain why Donald Trump's firehose of obvious Twitter lies about "witch hunts" and "fake news" reinforces (rather than drives away) his diehard supporters.

While we are on the topic of the self-proclaimed "stable genius," it is worth pausing and reflecting on just what an epitome of social media's syndromes Donald Trump's Twitter account represents. His online bullying, petty name-calling, and patent falsehoods rain down daily on his nearly one hundred million followers from one of the most popular accounts in the world. (As an aside, in what has to be one of the greatest ironies of all time, First Lady Melania Trump has made cyberbullying prevention her personal cause.) Trump is, in many ways, the dystopian embodiment of all that is social media — revolting but compelling, both a product of and a major contributor to the poisoned well of public discourse.

It is also worth noting, with respect to Trump's social media presence, how social media and more traditional broadcast media interact dynamically. Like other sectors, social media have impacted traditional broadcast media in critical ways. It is important to underline that many people still receive the vast majority of their information from traditional news, but traditional news organizations do not operate in isolation from social media. News organizations increasingly analyze the popularity of their stories over social media, and adjust their production process accordingly. The more an audience "likes" a topic or editorial approach through social media channels, the likelier broadcast news organizations are to focus on and amplify them. Social media provide a resource for journalists to "crowdsource" stories and sources, but research has also found that doing so can distort their priorities. According to one survey study, for some journalists "Twitter has become so normalized that tweets were deemed equally newsworthy as headlines appearing to be from the AP wire."

Then there are the physical characteristics of digital interactions that affect the nature of discourse, a topic in which Marshall McLuhan would be right at home. Hidden behind screens with relative anonymity, lacking the physical and other cues that come from face-to-face interaction, users are less inhibited online than off. Their utterances are more likely to be emotionally charged and stripped of the usual decorum that comes from speaking in front of intended recipients. Text-based forms of communication, especially those that are composed and sent while multitasking, or just without proper time for care and consideration, can in turn be easily misunderstood by the recipients, leading to unnecessarily heated conflicts. Multiply these dynamics a billionfold, and you get the idea: what one group of researchers calls "online firestorms." Huge waves of outrage that spread virally in a few hours are now endemic to our global public sphere, as are pointless spats between friends. Who among us hasn't felt the pang of anxiety that comes after sending a message that might be misunderstood? It's imperative to note that these "waves of outrage" do not affect all users evenly. Women, minorities, and people of colour may be particularly prone to self-censorship out of fear of harassment and "doxing" (the practice of researching and publicly broadcasting private or identifying information about an individual or organization). Social media ignite the passions, and vulnerable groups dive for cover.

The impact on public deliberation of all these dynamics is profound, and part of a building strain on democratic institutions that goes back decades. As Siva Vaidhyanathan puts it in his book *Antisocial Media,* because social media are "designed to favor content that is high emotional power, is quick to digest, is image-heavy and preferably video-graphic, and flows through a person's field of vision among a weird mixture of decontextualized social, personal, and entertainment-based items, it is the worst possible forum through which we could conduct our politics." Consider the implications for just one major democratic institution: legislative assemblies. Legislative assemblies were designed as forums for thoughtful debate, rational deliberation of pros and cons, and careful reflection. In theory, to work effectively, they need to encourage patient consideration of all sides of a debate. (I know, sounds quaint, doesn't it?) Framers of the U.S. Constitution, such as James Madison, were acutely aware of how heated, emotional debates could lead to rash decisions, and so they constructed various mechanisms to guard against that — to artificially slow things down. The separation of the House from the Senate, the introduction of staggered term limits of unequal length, even the vast geographic expanse over which the republic was spread, were all explicitly designed or incorporated to introduce friction and foster an environment conducive to slow, careful deliberation.

Political theorists who study legislative decision making worry that the speed and volume of information, which increased in the nineteenth century with advances in telecommunications but exploded in the internet age, have increasingly overwhelmed these institutions, which all the while are being torn apart by partisanship and polarization. Among other consequences, this situation has led to increasing delegation of powers (including a growing volume of "emergency powers") to executive branches, which have more flexibility to make decisions at high speed, but are also less accountable democratically. (As an important aside, during the early twentieth century one of the reasons Italian fascism and the so-called Futurist movement with which it was associated embraced "velocity" and the "aesthetic of speed" was the way they clashed with the checks and balances of modern liberal democratic institutions.) Close to a hundred years ago, American philosopher and psychologist John Dewey remarked that the "acceleration and mobility" of the telecommunications age disturbs social relationships necessary to formation of the public sphere. Said Dewey, "without abiding attachments associations are too shifting and shaken to permit a public readily to locate and identify itself." One imagines him being gobsmacked at just how extreme these conditions have become in our highly polarized, fast-moving social media age.

ANY PARTICULAR ECOSYSTEM can become a breeding ground for parasites or other invasive species, and so it is with our existing social media ecosystem. An environment already biased towards content that is sensationalistic, emotional, and divisive is perfectly suited to those who wish to bend the rules to their advantage. Just as mosquitoes breed in a warm, humid climate with lots of standing water, those who seek to foment chaos, mistrust, and fear as smokescreens for their corrupt aims are flourishing in our communications environment. Even those who are more inclined to "play by the rules" (and let's be blunt, there are few rules in the targeted advertisement industry) feel the pressure to get on board or be left behind when it comes to capitalizing on the System 1 effects of social media. As a consequence, we are seeing an explosion of social media–enabled PR, disinformation, "psy-ops," and "influence" operations — some open, commercial, and seemingly above board, but many others inhabiting a subterranean underworld of illicit acts, "dark money," and state subterfuge.

Propaganda, mass advertising, psychological operations — terms and concepts all linked to manipulating people's thoughts and thus behaviours — have a long history that goes back to ancient times. In the early years of the twentieth century, the twin engines of commercial advertising and military propaganda took off simultaneously, and not coincidentally. Edward Bernays, widely considered the father of modern public relations, drew from the theories of his uncle Sigmund Freud to tap into subconscious, erotic, and emotional human traits and push (among other products) cigarettes to women. Those whom he influenced and who came after him, like John Hill, founder of the international PR firm Hill & Knowlton, developed more ambitious and even less ethical "issue management" campaigns to undermine advocacy groups and push flawed science to confuse consumers about the adverse health effects of smoking. At the same time that Freudian theories were being used to play on people's emotions on behalf of big corporations, the U.S. government was clandestinely experimenting with techniques around "mind control," tapping into the expertise then emerging among civilian researchers.

According to Tamsin Shaw, "Much of the classic, foundational research on personality, conformity, obedience, group polarization, and other such determinants of social dynamics — while ostensibly civilian — was funded during the cold war by the military and the CIA." As part of a project code-named "MK-Ultra," for example, the U.S. Central Intelligence Agency used LSD to experiment with prisoners' cognition and behaviour, in some cases injecting them with overdoses on a daily basis, for days on end. Some of these experiments were undertaken on Canadians at a clinic at McGill University. Although extreme in nature, MK-Ultra was in fact but one part of a major complex of "psy-ops" programs run by the U.S. government (such as those associated with the still-functioning Fourth and Eighth Psychological Operations Groups of the U.S. Army), and which were executed as part of clandestine regime change and other military and intelligence programs throughout the Third World.

As happens today, commercial and nation-state disinformation campaigns periodically overlapped. In the 1940s, the United Fruit Company hired Edward Bernays, who later used his public relations expertise to help foment a coup in Guatemala after the election of a president who was unfavourable to the company. Bernays helped mount a multi-pronged disinformation campaign designed to discredit the democratically elected president, Jacobo Árbenz, as a communist puppet and to motivate U.S. lawmakers and thought leaders to support an overthrow. Eventually, the CIA did just that, launching a covert coup d'état, code-named Operation PBSUCCESS, which replaced Árbenz with the military dictatorship of Carlos Castillo Armas. Bernays's Freudian-inspired techniques of thought persuasion not only inspired the coup, they became instruments in the arsenal of the CIA.

To think that covert ops such as these are the dark arts of a distant time is naive in the extreme. While the early pioneers may be gone, the precedents they set, and the techniques and tradecraft they innovated, have all now been passed down to social media–enabled descendants superpowered by computing resources, finances, and seemingly endless pools of behavioural data from which to draw. Psychological operations have become a highly profitable market, and so, not surprisingly, a huge industry is sprouting up to serve the interests of dozens of autocrats, despots, and unethical business executives.

Herb Lin summed it up: "In the new information environment, exploitation of human cognitive architecture and capabilities — which are largely unchanged from what existed millennia ago — provides the 21st century information warrior with cyber-enabled capabilities that Hitler, Stalin, Goebbels, and McCarthy could have only imagined." Social media platforms, data brokers, and "analytics providers" have spent the past decade monitoring, analyzing, and "actioning" trillions of bits of data points on consumers' interests and behaviours. It is but a short pivot, but one with ominous consequences, to turn the power of this vast apparatus away from consumer interests and towards nefarious political ends. Not surprisingly, we are now seeing the early glimpses of how social media–enabled psychological warfare will present itself, from Russian troll factories to the Dr. No–like antics of shady private intelligence companies funded by the likes of Trump ally and fellow billionaire Peter Thiel. Most of these operations are hidden in the shadows, protected by the secrecy conferred on them by black budgets and national security agencies. What glimpses we do get emerge in bits and pieces, thanks to investigative research, lawsuits, data breaches, or leaks.

Probably the most well-known provider of these new types of commercial psy-op services is Cambridge Analytica, thanks to its prominent and controversial role in the U.K. Brexit and in the U.S. 2016 presidential election, as exposed in the documentary *The Great Hack*. Cambridge Analytica is very much representative on a number of levels of this type of emerging and dangerous marketplace. It applied the rigour and computing resources of social psychology, neuroscience, and engineering and computing sciences, but lacked any consideration whatsoever of the ethical rules that constrain bad behaviour around research on human subjects. Cambridge Analytica also tapped into the reservoirs of our digital exhaust, thanks to the freewheeling philosophy of social media platforms, like Facebook, that all too readily opened their vaults to third parties, who in turn readily shared that data with Cambridge Analytica. Before it was kicked off Facebook's platforms for breaching the company's terms of service (and let's face it, Facebook probably kicked it off only because of the bad publicity), it vacuumed up data on hundreds of thousands of unwitting users and 87 million of their even less witting networks of friends to fine-tune precision messaging and behaviour manipulation of tiny segments of target populations.

Cambridge Analytica had the support of a group of wealthy but highly dubious backers, including conservative muckraker and Trump supporter Steve Bannon and billionaire right-winger Robert Mercer. More ominously, it also had links to the U.K. and U.S. defence establishments. These political and financial supporters helped the company recognize that their psychometric profiling expertise, normally applied to digital marketing, could easily be repurposed for political campaigns, however unethically or illegally. Their client base was seeded in the U.K. and North America, but it didn't stop there. Cambridge Analytica, alongside its parent company, Strategic Communications Laboratories (later SCL Group), voraciously sought clients for its services in the developing world, where it could experiment on live populations with real-word consequences, but without any type of meaningful oversight from local government authorities.

Cambridge Analytica itself was destroyed by its own sloppy hubris, and the conscience of a few whistleblowers. But countless other companies like it roll on, following variations on the same successful model. BuzzFeed News, which has studied online disinformation campaigns extensively, discovered that "since 2011, at least 27 online information operations have been partially or wholly attributed to PR or marketing firms. Of those, 19 occurred in 2019 alone." Their investigation profiled the Archimedes Group, an Israeli "black PR firm" that boasts it can "use every tool and take every advantage available in order to change reality according to our client's wishes." Among its clients are individuals and organizations in states vulnerable to sectarian violence, including Mali, Tunisia, and Nigeria. In the case of the latter, the company ran both supportive *and* oppositional campaigns against a single candidate, former vice-president Atiku Abubakar (it was speculated that the supportive campaign was a ruse meant to identify his supporters so that they could then be targeted with anti-Abubakar messaging).

Not surprisingly, those inclined to authoritarianism around the world are actively taking advantage of the already propitious environment that social media present for them and their strategic interests. A recent survey by the Oxford Internet Institute found that forty-eight countries have at least one government agency or political party engaged in shaping public opinion through social media. Authoritarian-minded leaders like Donald Trump, Russia's Vladimir Putin, Turkey's Recep Tayyip Erdoğan, the Philippines' Rodrigo Duterte, and numerous others lambaste "fake news" while simultaneously pushing — often shamelessly — blatant falsehoods. Supporting their efforts are a growing number of black and grey companies, ranging from sketchy start-ups to massive consulting ventures, all of which stand to make millions engineering consent, undermining adversaries, or simply seeding dissent. We are, as a consequence, witnessing a dangerous blending of the ancient arts of propaganda, advertising, and psychological operations with the machinery and power of AI and big data. These efforts have helped transform the nature and character of information control among authoritarian regimes. In the early days of the internet, authoritarian governments (many using Western-made surveillance and censorship technologies) tried to prevent their citizens from accessing undesirable content. Now, thanks to social media, an environment of information abundance, and the opportunities for disinformation, these regimes are following a strategy that author and journalist Peter Pomerantsev, in his book *This Is Not Propaganda*, calls "censorship through noise." If you can't beat them, join in and *flood them*.

Of course any discussion of disinformation is not complete without mention of Russia. In Russian, "*dezinformatsiya*" refers to the manipulation of information in the service of propagation of falsehoods. It has a long history, going back to pre-Soviet times, and developed into a kind of dark art under the Cold War–era KGB. For decades, "professional, organized lying," as political scientist Thomas Rid calls it, has been used by Kremlin-backed agents to discredit, intimidate, and silence political opposition both domestically and abroad.

As with all authoritarian regimes, the aim of Russia's influence operations is less to convince people, or nudge them towards a particular point of view, than it is simply to inflame pre-existing prejudices, stoke grievances, and pit groups against one other: "to add heat but no light to political discourse," as Herb Lin puts it. The point of much Russian-backed disinformation is to make people cynical about *all* political institutions, to encourage a postmodern fatalism succinctly encapsulated in the title of Pomerantsev's other book on the subject, *Nothing Is True and Everything Is Possible.*

Russia has been a pioneer in the use of social media for autocratic control, what I and my colleagues referred to more than a decade ago as "third-generation" techniques (distinguished from first- and second-generation controls, such as internet filtering and content regulation). Third-generation techniques are mostly covert in nature and rely on surveillance and targeted espionage to mount "counterinformation campaigns that overwhelm, discredit, or demoralize opponents." One of the oldest methods of Russian-style *dezinformatsiya* is the use of "*kompromat,*" which is defined as the public release of stolen data intended to embarrass or discredit adversaries — a technique to which most of the non-Russian world was introduced with the 2016 hack of the U.S. Democratic Party establishment and the leaking of stolen emails to WikiLeaks. Our own research has shown similar Russian hack-and-leak operations being used as a way to discredit local opposition figures, as when emails stolen from the journalist David Satter and the George Soros–founded philanthropy Open Society Foundations were acquired by hacking, doctored, and then strategically amplified by social media companies and patriotic state media to make it appear as if Russian opposition figure Alexei Navalny was on the payroll of the CIA.

In recent years, Russian disinformation efforts have become more "professionalized," but not in the sense of staying within the bounds of decency or the rule of law (and not necessarily in the sense of being tidier or more effective either). Russian disinformation is undertaken by organized criminal groups acting as proxies alongside independently operating, overlapping, and sometimes competing spy agencies and security services, all of which work within a culture of barely concealed corruption. A representative example is the St. Petersburg–based Internet Research Agency (IRA), an infamous hacking and social media trolling company that itself is but one among a large portfolio of companies controlled by Yevgeny Viktorovich Prigozhin, an associate of Vladimir Putin, also known as "the chef" for his catering businesses. As described in detail by U.S. special prosecutor Robert Mueller in 2018 alongside indictments handed down to numerous Russians associated with the IRA, Russians travelled to the United States to conduct research, employed hundreds of personnel to manufacture social media posts to "ensure they appeared authentic," and organized political protests *both in support of and against* Donald Trump, while simultaneously denigrating his opponents. They also stole "social security numbers, home addresses, and birth dates of real U.S. persons to open accounts at PayPal," which were then employed to register fake social media accounts and website domains. Operations such as these are like a portal into a dystopian future, whose aperture is getting wider and wider with each passing day: unethical, illegal, not bound by norms of respectable behaviour, willing to do whatever it takes to discredit, intimidate, and silence, and finding a highly propitious — indeed, almost tailor-made — social media environment within which to do so. Although it is not clear whether the IRA's operations swayed Americans' attitudes enough to influence the 2016 election outcome, there is some disturbing evidence that IRA accounts purporting to belong to Black activists received a high level of engagement, a finding that will undoubtedly prompt further experimentation and refinement of such malicious techniques the next time around.

Russia is by no means alone in treating social media as a real-life workshop in which to experiment on disinformation techniques. Take the Philippines, which is a good case study of what is likely to become more common across the global South. As with many developing countries, traditional internet connectivity is still a challenge for many Filipinos, but cheap mobile devices and free social media accounts are growing in leaps and bounds. As a consequence, Filipinos principally get their news and information from Facebook and other social media platforms, prioritizing headlines they skim through over the lengthier content that accompanies them, and fostering the type of cognitive biases outlined earlier, which appear endemic to social media consumption. But they enjoy it nonetheless, spending as much as ten hours per day online.

Meanwhile, dozens of sketchy PR companies have sprouted up, openly advertising disinformation services barely disguised as benign-sounding "identity management" or "issue framing." Political campaigns routinely make use of these consulting services, which in turn pay college students thousands of dollars a month to set up fake Facebook groups designed to look like genuine grassroots campaigns and used to spread false, incriminatory information. The situation has devolved to the point where Facebook's public policy director for global elections said the Philippines was "patient zero in the global information epidemic." Spearheading it all is the country's right-wing president, Rodrigo Duterte, who has been widely criticized for harnessing Facebook to undermine and demonize political opposition and independent journalists, and to fuel a lethal drug war. His organizers marshalled an army of cybertrolls, called Duterte Diehard Supporters, or DDS, that openly mocked opposition leaders and threatened female candidates and journalists with rape and death.

In March 2019, Facebook took down two hundred pages, accounts, and groups linked to Nic Gabunada, the social media director for President Duterte. In announcing the takedown, Facebook said that a "total of

3.6 million Filipinos follow at least one of the 'inauthentic' pages, and at least 1.8 million Facebook accounts are involved in one of the identified groups." These types of campaigns cut across political lines. Joyce Ramirez, who ran social media for one of Duterte's political rivals and at one time controlled an army of fifty social media loyalists who together had forty-five million Twitter followers on accounts with fictitious names, bragged that with a simple nod she could make any topic she desired trend on Twitter in the Philippines. Her loyalists are paid in cash, cellphones, and other gifts.

The rabid social media–fuelled disinformation wars are degrading the political environment in the Philippines, but since virtually everyone in a position of power has bought into it, there is little will or incentive to do anything about it. Disinformation operations are run with impunity. PR start-ups are thriving, while everyone else is mildly entertained, confused, or frightened by the spectacle of it all. As the *Washington Post* summed it up, "Across the Philippines, it's a virtual free-for-all. Trolls for companies. Trolls for celebrities. Trolls for liberal opposition politicians and the government. Trolls trolling trolls." The *Post* report, which profiled numerous companies that paid trolls to spread disinformation, also warned that what was happening in the Philippines would likely find its way abroad. "The same young, educated, English-speaking workforce that made the Philippines a global call center and content moderation hub" will likely help the internationalization of Philippine's shady PR firms, which will find willing clients in other countries' domestic battles.

The story of the Philippines is one that could be told in more or less similar terms the world over. In sub-Saharan Africa; throughout Southeast Asia, India and Pakistan, and Central Asia; spread across Central and South America; across the Middle East, the Gulf and North Africa — the same dynamics are playing themselves out, with a spice of local flavour and entrepreneurial variation. In Indonesia, low-level military personnel coordinate disinformation campaigns that include dozens of websites and social media accounts whose operators are paid a fee by the military, and whose posts routinely heap praise on the Indonesian army's suppression of separatist movements in Papua. Taiwan is like a petri dish of disinformation, given the long-standing tensions between it and China, which sees Taiwan as a renegade separatist province. According to the *New York Times*, "So many rumors and falsehoods circulate on Taiwanese social media that it can be hard to tell whether they originate in Taiwan or in China, and whether they are the work of private provocateurs or of state agents." In India, racist disinformation on WhatsApp groups and other social media platforms has incited mass outbreaks of ethnic violence and public lynchings, including the horrific "Delhi Riots" of February 2020, during which mostly Hindu mobs attacked Muslims, leading to dozens of deaths. The list of examples could go on to fill volumes.

Governments are not the only ones exploiting the opportunities of social media to experiment in psy-ops. It should come as no surprise that big corporations are getting into the game too. Perhaps the most alarming are the well-funded corporate disinformation campaigns around climate change, which have roots going back decades but are now multiplying in the chaos of the communications ecosystem. Big oil, chemical, and other extractive-industry companies have hired private investigators to dig up dirt on lawyers, investigative journalists, and advocacy organizations. They've employed hackers-for-hire to target NGOs and their funders and leak the details of their strategic planning to shady media outlets on corporate payrolls. They have built entire organizations, think tanks, and other front organizations to generate scientific-looking but implausible reports, which are then seeded into disinformation campaigns and targeted advertisements meant to disorient and distract audiences from the real science of climate change. The consequences for global public safety are disturbing, to say the least. As one author presciently put it, "Manufactured doubt is everywhere, defending dangerous products in the food we eat, the beverages we drink, and the air we breathe. The direct impact is thousands of people needlessly sickened." The social media space has become a giant "disinformation laboratory" (as my Citizen Lab colleague John Scott-Railton put it) for sketchy PR firms and their unethical and corrupt clients.

AN ALWAYS-ON, REAL-TIME information tsunami creates the perfect environment for the spread of false narratives, conspiracy theories, and leaks. Hard-wired cognitive biases and mental shortcuts are primed to push them along. Individual users may not have the expertise, tools, or time to verify claims. By the time any of them do, the falsehoods may have already embedded themselves in the collective consciousness. Meanwhile, fresh scandals and outlandish claims are continuously raining down on users, confusing fact and fiction. Worse yet, studies have found that attempts "to quash rumors through direct refutation may facilitate their diffusion by increasing fluency." In other words, efforts to correct falsehoods can ironically contribute to their further propagation and even acceptance. The constant bombardment of tainted leaks, conspiracy theories, and other misinformation in turn fuels cynicism about the media and all institutions. Citizens become fatigued trying to discern objective truth as the flood of news washes over them hour by hour. Questioning the integrity of all media can in turn lead to fatalism, cynicism, and eventually paralysis. In the words of social media expert Ethan Zuckerman, "A plurality of unreality does not persuade the listener of one set of facts or another, but encourages the listener to doubt everything."

Contributing to this problem are the actions (or inactions) of social media companies themselves, who appear either unwilling or unable to weed out malicious or false information. That's not to say the companies are sitting idle. They are feeling the pressure to react, and have taken several noteworthy steps to combat the plague of disinformation, including shutting down inauthentic accounts by the thousands, hiring more personnel to screen posts and investigate malpractice on their platforms, "down-ranking" clearly false information on users' feeds, and collaborating with fact-checking and other research organizations to spot disinformation. These efforts intensified during the COVID pandemic.

But in spite of these measures, social media remain polluted by misinformation and disinformation, not only because of their own internal mechanisms, which privilege sensational content, or because of the speed and volume of posts, but also thanks to the actions of malicious actors who seek to game them. For example, in spite of widespread revelations of Russian influence operations over social media in 2016, two years later researchers posing as Russian trolls were still able to buy political ads on Google, even paying in Russian currency, registering from a Russian zip code, and using indicators linking their advertisements to the Internet Research Agency—the very trolling farm that was the subject of intense congressional scrutiny and indictments by Robert Mueller. In similar fashion, despite all the attention given and promises made to control misinformation about COVID-19 on its platform, an April 2020 study by the *Markup* found that Facebook was nonetheless still allowing advertisers to target users who the company believes are interested in "pseudoscience" — a category of roughly 78 million people.

In testimony before the U.S. Congress, Facebook CEO Sheryl Sandberg made a startling admission: that from October to March 2018, Facebook deleted 1.3 billion fake accounts. In July 2018, Twitter was deleting on the order of a million accounts a day, and had deleted 70 million fake Twitter accounts between May and June 2018 alone. The revelations caused Twitter's share price to drop by 8 percent — a good indication of the type of business disincentives working against digging too deep into one's own platform in the search for fake accounts. Put simply, removing accounts and cleaning up your platform is also bad for business.

Social media's inability to track inauthentic behaviour seems destined to get far worse before it gets better, as malicious actors are now using altered images and videos, called "deep fakes," as well as large WhatsApp groups, to spread disinformation virally. These techniques are far more difficult for the platforms to combat and will almost certainly become a staple of discrediting and blackmail campaigns in the political realm. In spite of all the deletions, fact-checking, and monitoring systems they produce, social media will remain easy to exploit as a tool of disinformation as long as gathering subscribers is at the heart of the business model.

IN WHAT IS CERTAINLY an ominous decision, but one with which it is hard to argue, in January 2020 the esteemed Bulletin of the Atomic Scientists set their widely referenced Doomsday Clock (a symbol representing the risk of human-caused existential catastrophe) twenty seconds closer to midnight. Although they cited a number of factors, one that stood out was their concern about the toxic information environment in which we find ourselves, which they concluded had deteriorated to the point of being a public safety hazard. Said the Bulletin's editors, "Continued corruption of the information ecosphere on which democracy and public decision making depend has heightened the nuclear and climate threats." It's hard to argue with them on that point.

What happened here? Information and communications technologies are in theory supposed to help us reason more effectively, facilitate productive dialogue, and share ideas for a better future. They are not supposed to contribute to our collective demise. Writing at the cusp of the Second World War, and terrified by the awesome destructive military power the Great Powers were about to unleash on each other, H. G. Wells described an imaginary "World Encyclopedia," or "World Brain," that humans might one day engineer, which would greatly contribute to resolving our endemic conflicts:

> The whole human memory can be, and probably in a short time will be, made accessible to every individual. [The World Brain] need not be concentrated in any one

> single place. It need not be vulnerable as a human head or a human heart is vulnerable. It can be reproduced exactly and fully, in Peru, China, Iceland, Central Africa, or wherever else seems to afford an insurance against danger and interruption. It can have at once, the concentration of a craniate animal and the diffused vitality of an amoeba...
>
> And its creation is a way to world peace that can be followed without any very grave risk of collision with the warring political forces and the vested institutional interests of today. Quietly and sanely this new encyclopaedia will, not so much overcome these archaic discords, as deprive them, steadily but imperceptibly, of their present reality. A common ideology based on this Permanent World Encyclopaedia is a possible means, to some it seems the only means, of dissolving human conflict into unity.

The essay has always fascinated me. It's hard not to see what Wells describes as something we have, indeed, already accomplished. What is Wikipedia if not the very World Encyclopedia that Wells envisioned? Always on, accessible to virtually anyone living anywhere on the planet who has internet access. The "whole human memory"—the storehouse of our collective wisdom—"accessible to every individual."

But Wells was clearly mistaken about how the World Brain would effect change. Rather than "dissolving human conflict into unity," our World Brain seems to be tearing us apart. Rather than facilitating the emergence of a common ideology based on science, social media are spreading ignorance and falsehoods, polluting the public sphere, and subjecting us to wholesale surveillance. As I write this book, the nerves of our World Brain are vibrating with full-on assaults on truth, science, ethics, and civility.

It's a perfect storm — tools that enable precise details about people's preferences and habits; sophisticated machines that can swiftly analyze and then manipulate data as points of leverage around human emotions; unethical companies willing to do anything for a profit; and clandestine government agencies that lack public accountability but do have big budgets and a blank cheque to use social media as an experimental laboratory for their dark arts. The potential implications of this perfect storm should be profoundly unsettling for everyone concerned about democracy, the public sphere, and human rights.

To be sure, we need to avoid mythologizing an imagined state of affairs where truth and democracy reigned supreme; this never actually existed. Media throughout history have been biased in important ways and manipulated by outside actors, and have served the interests of powerful elites at the expense of democratic engagement. Information and communications technologies have perennially held out hope for more reasoned deliberation and a more informed citizenry, but rarely rise to the occasion. Elites have for centuries deliberately spread false information to serve their narrow political aims, and have used whatever communications technologies were at their disposal to do so.

However, social media are uniquely architected in such a way that these types of practices can easily flourish and thrive. Thanks to their attention-seeking algorithms, social media platforms propel sensational and extreme content by design. Using methods that are refined to tap into deep-seated cognitive traits, social media feed on our emotions, biases, and other mental shortcuts, creating roadblocks to effective reasoning and rational public discourse. The overall environment turns out to be one that can easily be "gamed" by those whose aims are to foster social divisions and public chaos, now a dark money-making venture of its own. It's clear who stands to benefit from this environment: despots who fear scrutiny and public accountability and who gain when citizens grow complacent with exhaustion from trying to separate fact from fiction. Here we see the power of unintended consequences in technological development perfectly illustrated: a vehicle designed to capture and retain people's attention while serving up a socially useful and entertaining platform has turned out to be a cesspool in which authoritarian practices can prosper unhindered.

THREE

A GREAT LEAP FORWARD . . . FOR THE ABUSE OF POWER

TUESDAY OCTOBER 2, 2018, 4:09 P.M. TORONTO / 10:09 P.M. DEN HAAG / 12:09 A.M. (+1) ISTANBUL

"I'm not freaking out but Mr. Jamal Khashoggi was kidnaped [sic] *this morning. So I'm not pretty sure about what is going on!"* — WhatsApp message

I looked down at Omar's text as I checked into my hotel room for a cybersecurity conference in Den Haag, Netherlands. At that precise moment, nearly three thousand kilometres away in Istanbul, Turkey, a macabre, premeditated act of murder was being covered up by the butchers responsible.

Earlier that day, exiled Saudi journalist Jamal Khashoggi entered the Saudi Arabian consulate in Istanbul, hoping to pick up papers related to his upcoming marriage. His fiancée waited outside, dutifully holding his phones for safekeeping. Later, as the hours ticked by without his return, she paced back and forth apprehensively, checking the phones repeatedly, but to no avail. She would never see her beloved again.

As Khashoggi walked through the front doors of the consulate, captured in CCTV footage subsequently seen worldwide, little did he realize that waiting in hiding for him were fifteen Saudi intelligence agents. A kill squad, as if straight out of *Mission Impossible,* had been specifically assembled and flown into Turkey from Saudi Arabia on separate private jets for a carefully planned execution.

Electronic interceptions made by Turkish intelligence and shared with special UN investigators revealed what happened next.

A large group of men surrounded and apprehended him roughly.

"I can't breathe," Khashoggi gasped, repeatedly, before eventually succumbing altogether.

Next, one of the Saudi agents — Salah Muhammed Tubaigy, the "chief of forensic evidence in the security division of the Saudi interior ministry" — coolly proceeded to take out his headphones. Pressing "play" on his favourite music stream, he advised the others around him to do the same. "I find it helps," he said nonchalantly.

And then he proceeded to systematically dismember Khashoggi's body with a bone saw.

A bone saw. A macabre example of what Hannah Arendt once called "the banality of evil."

According to the timelines published by the UN's special investigation into his execution, at the precise moment I received Omar's text in my Netherlands hotel room, Khashoggi's dismembered body parts were likely being secretly transported in plastic bags and suitcases to the Saudi consul general's Istanbul residence to be disposed of. To this day, the location of his remains is unknown.

But at that time, like just about everyone else in the world, I had no clue about the gruesome murder. My pressing concern was the urgent text message glowing up at me from my phone as I looked out my hotel room window into the night.

Jamal Khashoggi is missing? I asked myself. *What does this have to do with Omar? Why is he so frightened?*

OMAR ABDULAZIZ IS A CANADIAN university student and a prominent Saudi activist who sought and received asylum in Canada in 2014, after Saudi Arabia revoked his scholarship for his outspoken criticism of the regime. Prior to the Khashoggi execution, Omar was most well known for the popular satirical talk show he hosts on YouTube, and for his Twitter account, followed by a half a million. Thereafter, he has been forever linked to Khashoggi's murder.

Like many other authoritarian regimes, Saudi Arabia has aggressively pursued extensive social media manipulation, digital subversion, and cyber-espionage. While some of it has been directed at regional rivals like Iran and Qatar, the bulk of it is intended to thwart political opposition and dissent, both at home and abroad. For despots like the crown prince, Mohammed bin Salman ("MBS," as he's widely known), the principal "national security threat" is anything that undermines his own regime. Political opposition? Out of bounds. Criticism of MBS himself? Treason. Assertion of women's rights? Not unless we men permit it, and don't even dare try to mobilize women around it. Strictly taboo.

As is the case with despots the world over, MBS has had to contend with digital-enabled opposition, including criticism of his rule swirling unimpeded around Twitter, Facebook, and YouTube. Although the domestic sources of such criticism are easier to squelch, for the obvious reasons of proximity and the omnipresent threat of arbitrary arrest or torture, the Saudi diaspora presents a much more complex challenge. Digital influencers like Omar who are sheltered in foreign jurisdictions like Canada are the greatest risk — relentlessly trumpeting their disrespect for all to see and hear. But social media and the digital devices that connect to them are double-edged swords. Fortunately (for MBS, that is), the dissidents' reliance on social media and their related accessories also happens to be their Achilles heel: highly invasive by design, often unintentionally revealing of their most intimate details, persistently plagued by insecurities, and therefore easy to exploit.

One of the key figures overseeing Saudi Arabia's

offensive counter-dissent cyber-operations was Saud al-Qahtani, reportedly a close friend of MBS and an individual who rose through the ranks based on his experience and enthusiasm for the tools of digital repression. Al-Qahtani circulated through various minor state media posts early in his career, but as MBS's authority grew and he was looking for digital expertise, al-Qahtani became his "go-to guy," and thus Saudi Arabia's digital enforcer.

Early on, al-Qahtani spent hours on obscure cybercrime forums using a range of half-baked pseudonyms. Archives of those forums reveal he was eager to purchase the latest hacking tools to crack the devices and private accounts of targets, even requesting and offering to pay for "technical support" when the tools didn't work. Eventually he graduated to reaching out to more professional surveillance vendors, his name showing up repeatedly in the leaked corporate documents of the Italian spyware company Hacking Team.

Al-Qahtani also helped to refine a sophisticated counter–social media campaign. In Saudi Arabia's strictly controlled traditional media environment, Twitter and other social media platforms are the closest thing to a "public sphere." Instead of filtering access to the platform, which can be easily circumvented, al-Qahtani instead chose to *flood it* with artificial accounts and trolls. Widely followed account holders were either bribed or extorted to push hashtags and narratives favourable to the regime while bombarding and intimidating opposing views.

Saudi dissidents and opposition figures referred to these pro-regime Tweeters as "flies," earning al-Qahtani the terrifically appropriate nickname of "Lord of the Flies."

He also shrewdly saw dissidents' reliance on these open and (in some cases) insecure devices and platforms as a means to sow fear. In what is truly becoming a new normal in the playbook of digital authoritarianism, al-Qahtani employed at least three separate but linked tactics. First, he contracted with the prestigious consulting firm McKinsey & Company to prepare an internal brief identifying key social media "influencers." Left unsaid but obvious nonetheless, the aim of such a report was to help prioritize targets of al-Qahtani's cyberwar on opposition. He simultaneously managed to secretly infiltrate Twitter itself, paying a number of Saudi-born, Silicon Valley–based engineers to find employment at the company and then clandestinely acquire confidential data on users, such as real names, private direct messages, geolocations, and IP addresses. One of the targets of the Twitter infiltration operation happened to be one of the "influencers" tagged by McKinsey: Canadian permanent resident Omar Abdulaziz.

Al-Qahtani then contracted with a Saudi PR company called Smaat (whose ownership has close ties to Saudi security services) to flood Twitter and other social media with pro-regime narratives connected to Smaat-controlled Twitter accounts. While Smaat used standard social media tactics to grow audiences and maximize its reach, it also concealed its true aims and identities, violating Twitter's terms of service. In December 2019, Twitter suspended eighty-eight thousand accounts connected to Smaat for "platform manipulation" in support of Saudi-backed information operations. But by then, damage had long since been done.

The contextual data drawn from McKinsey, combined with the more precise details acquired clandestinely from Twitter, were almost certainly used to calibrate the more advanced spyware technology that al-Qahtani employed. In the summer of 2018, research by the Citizen Lab and Amnesty International showed that numerous Saudi activists, journalists, and others were sent private SMS messages containing malware-laden links manufactured by one of the world's most sophisticated spyware companies, Israel-based NSO Group. In Omar's case, a fake DHL courier notification was the "ground zero" source of his infection; it had been sent in June 2018, only hours after he made a purchase on Amazon. Clicking on the link allowed al-Qahtani and others in Saudi intelligence to use NSO's flagship Pegasus spyware to silently commandeer Omar's device and acquire an unprecedented, intimate window into his private life. Thanks to Pegasus, they could observe his every movement; they could see his Twitter posts, emails, and SMS messages *even while they were being composed*. They could turn on the camera and microphone to record his meetings or gather incriminating pictures of Omar's private affairs that in turn could be used for blackmail. But most insidiously, they could silently observe, as if looking over his shoulder, while Omar and his friend Khashoggi hatched plans to mobilize opposition to MBS and the Saudi regime.

For weeks, Saudi operatives vacuumed up and analyzed everything that Omar communicated, including his regular interactions with Khashoggi. They eavesdropped as Omar and Khashoggi heaped disdain on the Saudi regime, and on MBS personally. "The more victims he eats, the more he wants," Khashoggi sent in a WhatsApp message—referring to MBS, whom he also described as a "beast." They monitored Omar's and Khashoggi's plans to counter the "Lord of the Flies" with what they called "an army of bees"—Khashoggi even offered to finance it, transferring thousands of dollars to Omar to seed the campaign. In the eyes of the Saudi despots, such plans amounted to treason punishable by death. And that's just what happened to Khashoggi on that fateful October day in the Saudi consulate in Istanbul.

Autocrats are not averse to combining digital and physical surveillance. At one point in the summer of 2018, Saudi officials visited Omar in person in Canada to try to persuade him to give up his activism and return to Saudi Arabia. (Presciently, Omar secretly recorded those conversations and later turned them over to the press.) They brought Omar's brother along, dangling him as a putative threat. *Drop your social media nonsense, return home, and everyone will be fine.* They even tried to encourage him to come to the Saudi embassy in Ottawa, a terrifying prospect in light of what would later befall his friend Khashoggi.

"Don't do it," advised Khashoggi to the younger Omar. "I wouldn't trust them." Omar took this advice to heart. Khashoggi himself apparently did not.

While the Saudis were using Israeli-made spyware to watch dissidents abroad, we were, in turn, watching them. The Citizen Lab's team, led by senior researchers Bill Marczak and John Scott-Railton, had been using a mix of fairly refined network monitoring methods to document NSO Group's infrastructure, and we had (unbeknownst to either the company or its clients) a real-time bead on the number of infected devices worldwide, as well as the likely government operators behind them. In the summer of 2018, we could observe that someone based in the Montreal region had their device hacked by Saudi operatives using Pegasus, but we didn't know who. In what must rank for our team as one of the most unlikely discoveries of a needle in a haystack, we did the virtual equivalent of going "door to door" against a shortlist of known Saudi dissidents based in Canada, one of whom was Omar. After Marczak spoke to him and checked his device's SMS messages, we confirmed he was indeed the target of the Saudi hacking operation. To say Omar was surprised would be inaccurate, as he suspected Saudi spies would be doing everything in their power to watch his every move. But even he didn't fully appreciate the capabilities NSO's spyware afforded to his Saudi adversaries back home.

"God help us," Khashoggi replied to Omar on WhatsApp when Omar informed him of the news of our discovery.

Like many other refugees who have fled persecution by authoritarian regimes, only to be hunted abroad, Omar was continuously on guard for his personal safety. Like many others whose accounts have been compromised, leading to harm in their communities, Omar felt both traumatized and guilt-ridden for what happened to others, like Khashoggi, because his phone had been hacked. Although it is impossible to say for sure, the surveillance we uncovered on Omar Abdulaziz may have been one of the principal motivating factors in the decision to kill Jamal Khashoggi. Our report detailing our discovery of the Saudi operation against Omar was published on October 1, 2018. On October 2, Jamal Khashoggi would enter the Saudi consulate in Turkey, and he would never be seen again.

THE 2011 ARAB SPRING. It was only nine years ago, but in internet years that's a lifetime. How long ago — and in another world — does it now seem that we all watched in shock as long-standing dictators succumbed to the "people power" of the social media age.

It's a Twitter rebellion! A Facebook revolution!

Geographic distance? No matter. We are wired together in a movement too strong to resist. Power hierarchies are a thing of the past.

Or so it seemed for that brief, sparkling moment.

While most of the Western media and policy world was drawing such sweeping "people power" conclusions, the autocrats watching it all unfold were asking themselves a much different question: *How do we prevent something like this from ever happening again?*

It was not long before they and their security agencies began to realize just how useful it is to have their adversaries plugged in, networked, and online communicating. How convenient it is to see who their friends and family members are. How easy it is to track their movements, to see their planning in progress as it unfolds from the very device they hold in their hands, and that they carry with them as they go about their daily business. How different it is from the time when moving to another country would shield them from the dictator's totalizing gaze and iron grip.

Thanks to social media and spyware, we're in your chats. We're in your Skype calls. We're in your bedroom. We're in your mind...

Whetting the appetites of autocrats, while simultaneously educating them on means and methods, have been the private intelligence and surveillance contractors, most of them based or originating in the West. While states do develop surveillance systems in-house, the reality is that most surveillance services are outsourced to private industry. No better illustration exists than the United States itself. Its mammoth annual expenditures on military and intelligence activities are well known, as is the dizzying array of private contractors orbiting Washington, D.C.—what journalist Dana Priest called "Top Secret America."

Boosted by the emergency response to 9/11 and the perceived need to "connect the dots" by fusing together disparate data sources, and capitalizing on the digital exhaust we all leave behind us as part of our always-on, mobile-connected daily routines, the cybersurveillance industrial complex has ballooned astronomically over the past two decades. There are products and services that monitor and manipulate the enormous masses of data flowing at lightspeed through telecommunications networks, from "deep packet inspection" systems to those that enable hacking of devices, through to the higher-level fusion and analytic platforms that turn it all into "actionable intelligence," and a virtual bonanza of surveillance wizardry of all sorts in between. This massive, expanding market knows no boundaries, and it is proliferating globally in response to the insatiable appetites of government law enforcement, intelligence, and military clients.

Although commercial, these are not the type of services anyone can just order up through Amazon. Surveillance technologies are bought and sold in a dark market shielded by classification, featuring secret contracts, shell companies, and closed military and intelligence trade fairs in places like Dubai or Panama City. Described as a kind of "dating service" for governments and surveillance contractors, one of the more well known of these is ISS World, whose CEO, Jerry Lucas, has openly bragged about how the Arab Spring boosted sales at his event. "At our upcoming March ISS 2013 World MEA in

Dubai," said Lucas, "we have scheduled over 20 technical training and product demonstration sessions addressing social network monitoring and intelligence gathering tools," which he said were "must-have . . . for countries . . . in the Middle East, Africa and Asia." Lucas was particularly enthusiastic that the number of non-Western vendors of surveillance technologies at his trade show had grown from none a few years earlier to around 30 percent by 2013: "from China (ZTEsec and Semptian), India (ClearTrail and Vehere), Saudi Arabia (Creative TeleSoft), South Africa (iSolve, Seartech, and VASTech), Turkey (C2Tech), Poland (Macro-System) and United Arab Emirates (Advanced Middle East Systems and Global Security Network) to name a few," said Lucas proudly.

Sales of surveillance and intelligence equipment are considered national secrets, but an occasional glimpse is revealed by public interest research, insider leaks, or spilled secrets that come from data breaches of the surveillance companies themselves. For example, a 2017 joint Dutch-U.K. investigation uncovered that the U.K. defence giant BAE Systems marketed a mass surveillance system, called Evident, to Saudi Arabia, the United Arab Emirates, and several other Middle Eastern and Gulf countries in the immediate aftermath of the Arab Spring. Said an anonymous whistleblower, "You'd be able to intercept any internet traffic [with Evident]. If you wanted to do a whole country, you could. You could pin-point people's location based on cellular data. You could follow people around. They were quite far ahead with voice recognition. They were capable of decrypting stuff as well."

The type of system sold by BAE, though sophisticated, is hardly unique. For well over fifteen years, the U.K. NGO Privacy International (PI) has doggedly tracked the commercial surveillance industry. According to PI, more than five hundred companies now "sell a wide range of systems used to identify, track, and monitor individuals and their communications for spying and policing purposes." In spite of Lucas's enthusiasm about non-Western firms, PI found that the bulk of the companies in the surveillance industry were "overwhelmingly based in economically advanced, large arms exporting states, with the United States of America (USA), United Kingdom (UK), France, Germany, and Israel comprising the top five countries in which the companies are headquartered."

The lucrative business opportunities and close collaboration between government agencies and private industry have created a revolving door as employees with security clearances and sophisticated tradecraft move back and forth between them. One notorious example that hit particularly close to home comes from the United Arab Emirates, where security services recruited former spies from the U.S. and Israel as contractors for an espionage start-up called DarkMatter. One of DarkMatter's activities was an offensive hacking operation called Project Raven, the aim of which was to get inside the devices of human rights defenders, journalists, and other enemies of the regime based within the UAE and abroad.

Although we didn't know it at the time, a report the Citizen Lab published in 2016 that uncovered a UAE-run targeted espionage operation against the U.K.-based journalist Rori Donaghy, to which we gave the name Stealth Falcon, was actually detailing the work of DarkMatter. A former NSA contractor who was employed by DarkMatter and later became a whistleblower revealed that the intelligence start-up had even tried to hack the Citizen Lab in response to our investigations. To this day we do not know if they were successful or not.

This type of targeting is no surprise. The Citizen Lab's research into mass surveillance, censorship, and targeted digital espionage has pulled back the curtain on the quiet proliferation of the tools of digital repression. By far our most alarming discoveries have involved targeted digital espionage of the kind that entrapped Omar and Khashoggi. Although some countries, like China and Russia, undertake cyber-espionage using "in-house" security service personnel or cybercriminals moonlighting for the state, many can now purchase sophisticated espionage services "off the shelf."

Typically, these services (also known as "commercial spyware") give government clients the capability to surreptitiously hack into the devices of targeted persons. Over a decade, our research has revealed how the wares of companies like Gamma Group, Hacking Team, Cyberbit, and NSO Group have been deployed in countries with brutal track records of repression, like Bahrain, Saudi Arabia, the UAE, Turkmenistan, Rwanda, Malaysia, Mexico, Morocco, and others.

These tools are marketed benignly as a way to assist law enforcement, anti-terror, and other national security investigations. What we have found is that they are widely abused instead. In the hands of despots and autocrats who define "crime" and "terrorism" as including virtually anything that challenges their right to rule, spyware has been used to hack into the devices of journalists, activists, human rights defenders, humanitarians, exiled political opposition figures, lawyers, and academics. This "Wild West" of abusive targeting is not surprising, considering that controls on the market are virtually non-existent.

Perhaps the most notorious of the spyware companies we have been tracking is widely considered to be among the most sophisticated: Israel-based NSO Group, also known as Q Technologies, a company closely aligned with the Israeli Ministry of Defence. (Far from taming abuses connected to the spyware market, Israel's Ministry of Defence routinely grants export licences for NSO's sales, as well as those of other Israel-based surveillance companies.)

NSO Group first came onto our radar in August 2016, when award-winning UAE-based human rights activist Ahmed Mansoor received two text messages on his iPhone, purporting to show evidence of torture in UAE prisons. As a human rights defender, Ahmed might have been tempted to click on those links. Instead, he forwarded them to the Citizen Lab for analysis. Clicking on those links in a laboratory setting allowed us to infect an iPhone we controlled and inspect a copy of NSO Group's custom Pegasus spyware. The spyware was extraordinarily sophisticated; it included exploits that took advantage of three separate flaws in Apple's operating system that even Apple was unaware of at the time. (Known in the industry as "zero days" — or "open doors that the vendor does not know it should lock," as University of Toronto professor Jon Lindsay put it — a single one of these exploitable software flaws in Apple products can fetch as much as $1 million for those who discover it.) After disclosing the vulnerabilities to Apple, which pushed out a security patch to more than one billion users, and publishing our report on the targeting of Mansoor, we reverse-engineered Pegasus and began scanning for and monitoring NSO's infrastructure and government client base. (Regrettably, the UAE authorities promptly arrested Mansoor and, for insulting the regime, sentenced him to ten years in prison — where he remains to this day.)

The monitoring paid off. Throughout 2017 and 2018, we partnered with Mexican human rights investigators at organizations like SocialTIC and R3D to follow up on technical leads from our network scanning to identify abusive targeting in Mexico. Eventually we unearthed research scientists, health advocates, journalists, lawyers, and even international investigators into mass disappearances whose phones had received text messages embedded with NSO-laden links. We found that the Mexican government operators of the spyware would even attempt to infect the devices of targets' friends and family members. In a particularly egregious case, after failing to trick prominent Mexican investigative journalist Carmen Aristegui into clicking on malicious links, the operators pivoted and started sending them to her minor child, Emilio, who was attending boarding school in the United States at that time. A message sent to Emilio was crafted to appear as if it came from the U.S. embassy, with a warning that there were problems with his visa and he should click on the link to get more details. Imagine: a minor child in a foreign country, for whom English is a second language, receiving such a text.

Most disturbing for us have been the cases we have uncovered in which spyware infection attempts have been linked to, or associated with, targeted killings, such as Khashoggi's. Two days after Mexican investigative journalist Javier Valdez Cárdenas was gunned down in the streets of Mexico in a cartel-linked murder, we confirmed that his wife and colleagues had received SMS messages tainted with NSO spyware links, purporting to show evidence of who was responsible for the killings. Similarly, we discovered that the devices of a group of international investigators looking into a grotesque 2014 mass disappearance of forty-three Mexican students were all targeted with NSO's spyware.

Probably the most alarming cases that we uncovered involved the targeting of exiled political opposition figures by Rwandan death squads. We discovered these cases as part of an investigation into a particularly sophisticated attack that was discovered by WhatsApp's security team in May 2019, and which they attributed to NSO Group. NSO had developed an insidious "no click" version of their spyware in which operators could take over the devices of targets simply by calling the phone number. After WhatsApp issued a patch and blocked the attack, the Citizen Lab volunteered to identify the targets. WhatsApp shared about a thousand phone numbers with us, reflecting a two-week period of targeting for which they had data. After months of investigations, our research team was able to positively identify more than one hundred individuals in twenty countries, who were neither terrorists nor criminals but rather journalists, lawyers, human rights activists, and opposition figures, whose phones had been compromised in this manner.

Among the targets were about a half dozen exiled Rwandans who had fled the country in fear for their lives. These included Faustin Rukundo, whose name was on a widely circulated list of enemies of the government of Rwanda under the heading "Those who must be killed immediately." Other exiled Rwandans who were targeted, like Frank Ntwali, said that their private conversations had started to appear in pro-government Rwandan newspapers. Until our notification, he had no idea how it occurred. "We would read them, and we would wonder — how do they know? At least now we know," Ntwali told the *Financial Times*.

Others, like Belgium-based opposition leader Placide Kayumba, reported that people with whom they thought they were having private communications had suddenly turned up murdered or had gone missing, and that our discovery of the spyware seemed to provide the missing link. "I can't say whether or not those killings are linked to the hacking of my phone," says Kayumba. "But it is clear that the discussions that we have with members of the party, notably those in Rwanda, are certainly monitored in one way or another, because we see the reaction of the state."

The combination of Rwandan death squads and NSO's sophisticated spyware is about as noxious a nightmare brew as one can imagine of uncontrolled surveillance technology in the hands of unaccountable elites. It is astonishing to think that a company could bald-facedly claim that their product is strictly controlled to fight "terrorists and criminals," knowing full well that one of their clients, Paul Kagame's Rwandan government, has a notorious track record of sending death squads abroad to murder those who oppose his rule.

THE POWER OF THIS TYPE of technology explains why this marketplace for spyware is so lucrative. In the past, for Saudi Arabia to spy on someone like Omar Abdulaziz, they would have had to travel to Canada. To listen in on his phone calls, they would have had to somehow wire-tap his landline, something almost certainly out of their reach, both technically and legally, as long as he lived abroad. At best, they might be able to put some hidden microphones and cameras in his apartment, but even that would work only if he was discussing something sensitive while sitting in the room that happened to be bugged. And all of it at significant personal risk for the agents, who would have to undertake a break-and-enter operation in a foreign country. It's as if, armed with this type of spyware, Saudi agents are practically inside a target's head. They don't even have to set foot in a foreign country, let alone undertake risky physical surveillance operations. From the comfort of an air-conditioned bunker in Riyadh, Saudi agents can take turns listening in, or scoop up a massive load of data and then store it all for later analysis.

Social media, and our entire communications ecosystem as a whole, profoundly transform the cost-benefit ratio and the opportunity structures for political elites to undertake surveillance: *they radically erase the distance between those who exercise authority and the human objects of their control,* both domestically and abroad. The very tools that civil society relies on to organize, educate, and publicize have become its most vulnerable points of insecurity, the pathway its adversaries exploit to get inside and neutralize it. Omar, like most millennial activists, spends a great deal of his life online. His Twitter account and YouTube videos have generated millions of followers, with whom he interacts on those platforms, leaving a trail of data along the way. As an activist, he engages in a multitude of conversations, some that he might reasonably assume are either private or secure, many through his desktop computer, others through his mobile device.

The "intellectual property" of a spyware company like NSO Group consists of methods for taking advantage of these multiple networked connections, and finding and exploiting weak points in the constantly mutating and highly insecure digital infrastructure on which people like Omar depend. Surveillance companies employ thousands of well-paid, highly trained engineers to constantly scour operating systems, software, applications, hardware, platforms, routers, and networks for insecurities (in the case of NSO Group, many of them are veterans of Israel's sophisticated Unit 8200 signals intelligence group). For their part, targets like Omar lack capacity and resources to defend themselves. They are entirely dependent on consumer products made by technology companies for whom security is often an afterthought, intentionally designed to extract as much data as possible from their customers and follow them around wherever they go.

The extraterritorial reach provided by commercial spyware, in turn, creates a chilling effect even for those who are not targeted. Research has shown that diaspora activists feel overwhelmed about social media and digital technologies, unsure about what technologies to use or not, or whether to use them at all. When a network's weakest link can expose an entire community, community members start to feel paranoid and frightened that their communications and plans are exposed. Meanwhile, for those who find out their devices have been hacked, the revelation can be traumatic. Clinical psychologists Brock Chisholm, Sarah Whittaker-Howe, and Clara Usiskin conducted an extensive set of interviews with immigrant and refugee victims of spyware; study participants reported they felt they were under a current and immediate threat after the discovery of the spyware on their devices, and reacted fearfully. Targets with a prior history of torture and persecution, "regardless of whether they were in a safe country," had "symptoms synonymous with PTSD retriggered." Individuals also reported being afraid of communicating with friends and family members back home.

It may be hard for someone who hasn't been targeted by a despot abroad to appreciate how such attacks foment an insidious and inescapable *fear*. Fear of being watched and listened to. Fear that you or your loved ones are exposed. Fear that your life could be taken away at any moment. For dictators and despots, that may be the most valuable effect of them all. Writing in the eighteenth century on the topic of despotism, the political theorist Baron de Montesquieu famously described fear as "the principle of despotic government." According to Montesquieu, fear undermines the exercise of reason and any other morally based civil action; it induces a kind of paralysis, depresses the spirits, and extinguishes "even the least sense of ambition." It seeks to isolate individuals from each other and thus neuter civic associations that may hold despots to account.

Although Montesquieu would no doubt have his mind blown by the instant global reach of social media, he'd be sadly familiar with the way despotic fear has insinuated itself into the mix, gumming up the machinery of organized civil society, terrorizing people like Omar with the prospect that someone, somewhere, might be looking over their shoulder, or worse yet, peering back at them from the device they hold in their hand. While social media may be new, the type of political repression they facilitate is ancient. For despots across time, says Montesquieu, "whatever inspires fear is the fittest spring of government."

The practical consequences of this type of fear are, sadly, growing. As one Egyptian activist remarked, "All the time when we talk in our online meetings we don't know if we can speak freely or not. We have no alternatives, we are between two options: to be practical or to be secure. Every discussion is a test for us, to mention a name, to say something or not . . ." Ten years after the Arab Spring, facing an onslaught of persistent targeted attacks and the spectre of mass surveillance, the movement that brought despots and dictators across the Middle East to their knees has been largely stifled. Says Yahya Assiri — a Saudi activist exiled to the U.K. and himself a person we verified was targeted by Saudi intelligence using NSO Group's spyware—"I wouldn't be exaggerating if I said more than 90% of the most active campaigners in 2011 have now vanished."

It is a reminder, often overlooked, that while we may perceive our devices and social media accounts as our windows to the world, the flow of communications over the internet works in both directions. Those devices and accounts are also a window *into* our lives for those *on the outside* looking in. Far from being the existential threat that many observers of the Arab Spring assumed, social media have turned out to be a dictator's best friend.

WHEN ONE CONSIDERS "digital authoritarianism," the first thing that probably comes to mind is China, and for good reason. China has embarked on a massive experiment to exploit big data in the service of Big Brother. A major concern among those who value civil liberties and privacy is to what extent, and under what legal conditions, the state can access customer data from digital platforms. China offers a peek at what it looks like when most, if not all, prior restraints are removed. China's Cyber Security Law requires private companies to police their users, censor communications on their platforms, and hand over user data to authorities on request. The public–private relationship in China is, in important respects, largely seamless, at least from a formal regulatory perspective; anything to the contrary is either informal or a by-product of mismanagement.

China's relationship to the internet and social media has come full circle. When the first internet connections were established in China and the technology began to take off, many predicted the one-party state would face major hurdles in preserving the regime's control over public information. In social science terms, the Communist Party's ability to control the internet was a "hard case," meaning least likely to succeed. Over time, however, as social media have transformed the internet and technology use has ballooned (China is home to the largest number of internet users in the world), the situation has reversed. China has now become an "easy" case: a demonstration of how surveillance capitalism can work hand in glove with an authoritarian regime, combining rapid technological innovation, economic growth, and consumerism with comprehensive information controls.

China's censorship and surveillance over the internet and social media are broad and sweeping. The backbone is the so-called Great Firewall, which filters access to foreign-hosted websites, undertakes mass surveillance, and is occasionally used to inject malicious code into network traffic or repurpose web requests into distributed denial-of-service attacks (the latter a phenomenon we identified in 2015 and dubbed the "Great Cannon"). China's information control system has banned many popular foreign social media platforms, which has allowed domestic alternatives like WeChat, Weibo, and others to flourish. These are required by Chinese laws and regulations to undertake surveillance of their users and filter keywords related to a broad range of "taboo" topics, such as Tiananmen Square, Tibet, Falun Gong, Taiwan, and so on. Using a variety of technical methods, including reverse-engineering China-based social media apps, our researchers have peered beneath the hood of these information controls. We have found censorship and surveillance to be pervasive but highly decentralized (app developers vary widely in terms of the content they censor) and quite sloppy (exhibiting both under- and over-blocking of sensitive conversations). However, this distributed system is also very effective, less like a brick wall that would be easy to circumvent and more like a series of overlapping trawling nets that screen communications while fostering a climate of self-censorship.

China's information controls have evolved far beyond mere defensive measures into more proactive uses of social media for large-scale social and economic engineering. The so-called "social credit system" is a nationwide experiment to draw on data related to individuals, businesses, and government agencies, and then track and evaluate them all for their "trustworthiness" (守信, shouxin). Some of the Western media coverage of the social credit system has been sensationalistic: there is not one single massive database that ranks every single Chinese citizen with a score (at least not yet). Instead, and in line with China's overall approach to information controls, it is unevenly distributed across business sectors, with rewards and punishments varying from region to region. However, the prospects of the social credit system for authoritarian control are daunting. As it stands now, data from social media posts, credit card transactions, bank records, debt and employment history, and even statutory violations, like skipping public transit fares or spitting, can theoretically affect a citizen's trustworthiness score. A provocative social media post on a sensitive topic might contribute to a lower score, which can then affect an individual's ability to get a loan, purchase luxury goods or an airline ticket, or obtain a visa to travel abroad. While the system is uneven in various ways, it's also quickly streamlining, with industry and government agencies sharing databases of "blacklisted" individuals to more efficiently police behaviour. For example, TikTok, the massively popular video streaming app, has partnered with local authorities in some Chinese provinces to show photographs of blacklisted people in between video streams, even offering rewards for information on their whereabouts. In Shijiazhuang, the capital city of Hebei Province, local authorities have developed a plug-in to WeChat that displays the names and locations of nearby debt defaulters, urging users to either avoid or shame them.

The most salient feature of the social credit system is that it is highly attractive to both businesses and government — the latter for obvious reasons of social control, the former for the way it opens up new and highly lucrative revenue streams. In China, facial recognition systems have been deployed almost completely, in the absence of any privacy protections or other legal restraints, as part of a dystopian, science fiction–worthy project called "Skynet." The cameras are now commonplace all over China — an estimated one camera for every seventh person, which turns out to be roughly two hundred million of them. Combining the imagery with artificial intelligence systems has helped local authorities root out "uncivilized behaviour" — which apparently includes wearing pajamas in public or jaywalking. Images of such transgressions are then projected onto large billboards to shame people. The widespread deployment of the cameras has helped energize the tech sector that orbits around it. One Chinese AI start-up called SenseTime, which specializes in facial recognition systems, raised $700 million in venture financing in 2018, giving it a valuation of about $7 billion.

But as with social media companies the world over, SenseTime's security is poor. In 2019, a researcher discovered that SenseTime's database had inadvertently exposed the names, ID card numbers, birth dates, and location data of more than five hundred million people. The poorly secured database was disturbing in other ways, too. It showed 6.7 million location points linked to people, tagged with descriptions such as "hotel," "internet cafe," and "mosque."

Tagging "mosque" in a surveillance database highlights another, deeply disturbing side of China's experiment in social control: the way it has been employed as part of a massive genocidal campaign to police, incarcerate, and "re-educate" its Muslim minority populations. In the western region of Xinjiang, home to the Muslim Uyghur population, Chinese authorities have used vague "counterterrorism" laws to justify the mass internment of upwards of one million people. Digital technologies are integral elements of the repression, and include widely deployed surveillance cameras paired with AI-enabled facial recognition systems trained to spot and track ethnic minorities, both within and beyond Xinjiang. Xinjiang locals (as well as visitors to the region) are required to download and install mobile surveillance apps, which track sensitive conversations while alerting local police to "unlawful" behaviour. Authorities also require locals to install QR barcodes on the doors of their homes; these contain details on the residents and are routinely scanned by local authorities and cross-checked against centralized databases. According to Human Rights Watch, Xinjiang authorities have started systematically collecting biometric data too, "including DNA samples, fingerprints, iris scans, and blood types of all residents between the age of 12 and 65." Even voice samples are recorded and archived. Reports of arrests without due process are legion, as friends, family members, and minor children disappear into re-education and forced-labour camps; those left behind live in a Kafkaesque state of perpetual fear of algorithm-driven, omnipresent, and unaccountable surveillance.

The massive investment in social media–enabled information controls in China has helped fuel a burgeoning public security market valued in 2017 at roughly

$80 billion, attracting both foreign companies and a local surveillance industry that is spreading its wares abroad. The export of China-based surveillance technologies features prominently in the country's ambitious Belt and Road Initiative, which involves development projects in more than seventy countries throughout Asia, Africa, Europe, and Latin America. Political scientist Steven Feldstein, who has studied the use of AI for digital repression, found that "China is a major driver of AI surveillance worldwide," and that "Chinese companies — particularly Huawei, Hikvision, Dahua, and ZTE — supply AI surveillance technology in sixty-three countries, thirty-six of which have signed onto China's Belt and Road Initiative."

Fuelled with low-interest, state-backed loans and other subsidies, Chinese companies are spreading quickly through corrupt, fragile, or failed states looking to emulate China's information control regime. An archetypal example is Brazil. After a group of Brazilian lawmakers visited China, where they were feted and given demonstrations of China's showcase surveillance technologies, they returned to Brazil and introduced legislation that aims to make facial recognition systems mandatory in all public places. With street crime plaguing many neighbourhoods, and with the right-wing regime of president Jair Bolsonaro promising to fight it with expanded police resources, China's AI-enabled social media and facial recognition surveillance companies have proven to be a popular solution.

For the Chinese companies, on the other hand, Brazil represents a perverse kind of special appeal because monitoring its ethnically diverse population can help train AI algorithms. Pilot programs using Huawei-developed facial recognition cameras combined with a social media monitoring system and biometric databases have been rolled out in Brazilian cities and used to identify suspects and alert nearby authorities via mobile phones. Brazil's adoption of the "China model" has, in turn, become a regional advertisement. Both Argentina and Ecuador have purchased Chinese surveillance technology systems for their public safety programs as well.

To be sure, China's digital authoritarianism is not foolproof or comprehensive. There are numerous flaws throughout the entire system, as evidenced by the breach of SenseTime's facial recognition database. The censorship embedded in China's social media applications, though thoroughly opaque, is prone to under- and over-blocking, and it can be sidestepped by savvy citizens in a game of cat and mouse. In spite of restrictions and fears of prosecution, citizens are not averse to criticizing those in power, and routinely use social media both to do so and to organize collective resistance. However, it is important not to mistake accidents like poor software design and flawed implementation, or occasional bursts of resistance to authority, for genuine and legally implemented constraints on the abuse of power. Absent deliberate checks and balances, or laws that protect civil liberties, China's experiment in digital authoritarianism can develop largely unhindered, in turn providing a model for other autocrats and despots the world over to emulate. That's a fairly predictable outcome for an "easy" case like China. What's happening closer to home is another matter of concern.

IN JANUARY 2020, *NEW YORK TIMES* journalist Kashmir Hill broke the story of an obscure facial recognition AI start-up called Clearview AI. Invented by Hoan Ton-That, a young software developer among whose previous little-known accomplishments is "an app that let people put Donald Trump's distinctive yellow hair on their own photos," Clearview's system works by mathematically matching photos of persons of interest to billions of online images the company has scraped from social media. (After Hill's report, some platforms have banned Clearview AI from further harvesting—but the horses [images] have already left the barn [platform]). As a start-up, Clearview had the financial backing of, among others, Peter Thiel, a conservative ally of President Trump and an early investor in both Facebook and the data fusion company Palantir (precisely the type of ownership one needs if you want your product in front of potential security and intelligence clients).

There were definitely some troubling details Hill unearthed about Clearview AI that suggested a serious lack of transparency and accountability right from the get-go. Citing vague security concerns, Ton-That wouldn't disclose to Hill his customer list. When she persuaded a law enforcement client to run her own facial image through the system, they told her Clearview had then reached out and warned them not to speak to journalists — a clearly inappropriate abuse of Clearview's own face-matching capabilities.

A more detailed picture of Clearview AI's sketchy business practices soon came to light. Not surprisingly, it all started with the now all too common data breach, which in the case of Clearview exposed the entire database of customers. It wasn't long before the shocking information contained in the breach was leaked to journalists. On February 27, 2020, the news organization BuzzFeed provided a detailed overview. The breach showed that people associated with 2,228 law enforcement agencies, companies, and institutions in twenty-seven countries had created accounts and had collectively performed almost half a million searches, all of them tracked and logged by Clearview.

Among Clearview's clients: numerous federal agencies in the United States, including the Department of Homeland Security (DHS); Immigration and Customs Enforcement; Customs and Border Protection; the Department of Justice; the Federal Bureau of Investigation; the Drug Enforcement Administration (DEA); the Bureau of Alcohol, Tobacco, Firearms and Explosives; and numerous so-called fusion centres run by DHS and spread across the United States. Hundreds of regional, state, county, and local law enforcement agencies across the United States queried its databases as well.

Surprisingly, the client list went beyond law enforcement agencies to include dozens of high schools and universities, as well as hundreds of private companies, including Walmart, Best Buy, Albertsons, Kohl's, Bank of America, and Wells Fargo. Numerous companies in the entertainment, gaming, and sports industries were also clients — even the National Basketball Association used Clearview's system. Several private intelligence firms were paying clients of Clearview AI and had queried the system thousands of times each. The *New York Times* reported that investors in the start-up even abused the app on dates and at parties, to identify unwitting members of the public for fun or just to demonstrate its power. But it didn't end there. Documents obtained by *HuffPost* in March 2020 revealed that Ton-That had close ties to several prominent alt-right extremists, white supremacists, and neo-Nazis dating back to 2016, and had included them in Clearview AI's operations but had gone to great lengths to conceal their involvement. One of those associates remarked that they hoped Clearview's technology could be used to "identify every illegal alien in the country."

Meanwhile, the leaked documents obtained by BuzzFeed showed Clearview AI had ambitious plans to expand its customer base globally. Already its clients included "national law enforcement agencies, government bodies, and police forces in Australia, Belgium,

Brazil, Canada, Denmark, Finland, France, Ireland, India, Italy, Latvia, Lithuania, Malta, the Netherlands, Norway, Portugal, Serbia, Slovenia, Spain, Sweden, Switzerland, and the United Kingdom." Several of these countries are known to engage in systematic human rights violations, but that didn't seem to concern Clearview AI's CEO, who sidestepped whether the company does any due diligence around whether it will sell to government clients in countries in which being gay is a crime. The breach also showed that Clearview's system was being queried by a sovereign wealth fund in the UAE, local police in India, and a think tank in Saudi Arabia.

BuzzFeed's analysis revealed a callous disregard at Clearview AI for legal or other guardrails against misuse. According to BuzzFeed, "Clearview has taken a flood-the-zone approach to seeking out new clients, providing access not just to organizations, but to individuals within those organizations—sometimes with little or no oversight or awareness from their own management." The company promoted the product to individuals in agencies and companies with free trials and encouraged them to search as many times as possible within the free trial period. They even recommended users share their access with others in their organizations. As a consequence, lower-level employees were using Clearview's system without clearances from upper management, leaving those in positions of authority oblivious to the fact that the technology was being used within their agencies. This may help explain why some agencies, like the City of New York Police Department and the Royal Canadian Mounted Police, officially denied they were using Clearview when the documents revealed that police officers were routinely conducting thousands of free searches. In fact, at least thirty Canadian law enforcement agencies used Clearview's system, including the RCMP and the Toronto Police Service, which ran "3,400 searches across about 150 accounts." A follow-up investigation by the *Toronto Star* found that nine law enforcement agencies that had initially denied using the system were in fact customers or employed individuals who were using the system. Even Via Rail's private security services used Clearview AI.

Summing up the frightening consequences of the Clearview AI story, Santa Clara University's Eric Goldman said, "The weaponization possibilities... are endless.... Imagine a rogue law enforcement officer who wants to stalk potential romantic partners, or a foreign government using this to dig up secrets about people to blackmail them or throw them in jail."

ALTHOUGH THERE ARE MANY lessons to be drawn, the Clearview AI case shows how police and other security agencies are experiencing a profound "great leap forward" in the capabilities of remote control, but without any compensating measures to prevent abuse. As recently as twenty years ago, CCTV cameras were rare, had primitive resolution and archiving features, and required manual review. "Real-time" identification boiled down to whether or not someone just happened to be there watching at the right time when something happened. "Facial recognition systems" (if they could even be described as such) were entirely analogue in nature — mugshots, family pictures, or opportunistic photos of suspects snapped from a distance. There was a lot of manual sorting, and cops carrying photographs to neighbourhoods where suspects might have passed, asking shop owners and bartenders: "Recognize this person?" A shot in the dark.

Today, high-resolution digital surveillance cameras are omnipresent, scattered throughout our cities, sprinkled through public transportation systems, mounted on the exteriors of buildings and entrances to residences, worn on the bodies of police officers, peering back at us from our ATM machines, and installed on freeways and city streets. Layered underneath those fixed cameras are the billions of consumer devices that nearly everyone carries with them at all times, the standard features of which include a built-in digital camera. Multiplying the effects is a widespread "selfie" culture of auto-surveillance, in which digital images of people's faces are frequently snapped and then shared on social media platforms with a mere click. Thanks to parental pride, unwitting children are given a head start as the evolution of their facial features is recorded with digital precision from birth and then uploaded to social media platforms, where it is analyzed and archived. From practically the moment a baby is delivered, and on through that child's young life, recording, tagging, and uploading their digital images to social media is now considered routine.

As the images are digitized, they can be easily converted into a matrix of data points that algorithms and artificial intelligence systems can sift through and sort. A person's unique biometric features become the equivalent of a digital fingerprint. Systems measure features on a person's face based on dozens of nodal points, like the distance between the eyes, the width of the nose, the shape of the cheekbone, the depth of the eye sockets, and so on. For example, Apple's Face ID system projects thirty thousand infrared dots on a user's face, and then deploys an infrared camera to fingerprint the unique features to securely unlock a device.

A huge industry has sprouted along each step of the way of these processes, including a bewildering array of companies like Clearview AI that scrape, archive, analyze, and instrument facial images in a way that is "customer friendly." The result is that we are all living in a vast distributed web of digital sensors, the data from which are readily available and marketed to law enforcement, intelligence, and security personnel, from the highest-level national security organs down to your local private eye — all within the time frame of basically a decade. Thanks to Clearview and other companies like it, your average cop no longer has to slip into bars and hotels with a crumpled old photo to look for a suspect; they just hit "enter." As Andrew Ferguson, the author of

The Rise of Big Data Policing, has said, the combination of facial recognition and AI is like a "superpower that we haven't seen before in policing."

A recent *New York Times* investigation demonstrated just how fast, easy, and cheap it would be to identify specific individuals in a crowd, thanks to the digital matrix in which we all now live. The reporters built their own bespoke database of people (and images of their faces) who work in the vicinity of Bryant Park, by scraping public social media platforms and other online sources. They then gathered data from the open feeds of several live CCTV cameras facing the park and ran one day's worth of footage through Amazon's commercially available facial recognition service. The experiment detected thousands of matches and allowed the researchers to identify at least one person by name: Richard Madonna, a professor at the SUNY College of Optometry, who had casually strolled through Bryant Park during his lunch break at the time the investigation was being undertaken. The whole experiment, based entirely on publicly available sources, cost only sixty dollars and did not violate any known U.S. laws. Said the journalists, "The law has not caught up. In the United States, the use of facial recognition is almost wholly unregulated." It's worth pointing out that the New York Police Department boasts that its Domain Awareness System, developed jointly with Microsoft, "utilizes the largest network of cameras, license plate readers, and radiological sensors in the world." In Lower

Manhattan alone, police have access to more than nine thousand camera feeds.

While the prospect of superpower policing using AI-empowered facial recognition systems is certainly unsettling, this is but one example of dozens of new technological applications fuelling this giant leap forward in remote control. For example, a 2016 Axios investigation found that Baltimore police had quietly deployed a pilot program for aerial surveillance undertaken by a small start-up called Persistent Surveillance Systems, whose CEO bragged the company's sophisticated wide-area imaging technology could "watch entire cities at a time." Each of the aircraft is outfitted with a camera system that has a capacity of 192 million pixels, which the CEO claims is equivalent to about eight hundred digital video cameras, and can capture thirty square miles every second. Live images are fed down to the ground, where they are analyzed by staff and shared with clients. Customers can scroll back and forth in time to monitor suspects as they flee buildings or drive away in cars. In a 2016 video, the CEO boasted that the company had done prototype missions in Philadelphia, Charlotte, Indianapolis, and Compton in the United States, and Nogales and Torréon in Mexico. For a year of surveillance services, the company charges local police about $2 million.

As futuristic as this all may sound, the company's fleet of piloted aircraft is both expensive and relatively primitive compared to a technology that is quickly superseding it: unmanned drones. One of the most popular drones used by law enforcement is sold by DJI, a China-based company. The company advertises its Zenmuse Z30 as "the most powerful integrated aerial zoom camera on the market with 30× optical and 6× digital zoom for a total magnification up to 180×." All in, a high-end drone of this sort runs about $6,000, whereas a typical police helicopter or Cessna can cost anywhere from $1.5 million to $3 million, not including hourly operating and maintenance costs. As one report put it, "With this cost differential, a department could potentially purchase a fleet of 500 drones in lieu of a single police chopper."

One company that provides high-tech cameras on drones, called PreVision, says the company's goal is to blanket entire cities with them. And their marketing appears to be working. Research conducted in 2018 by the Center for the Study of the Drone at Bard College says at least 910 state and local public safety agencies have purchased drones. Of those, 599 are law enforcement agencies. One vendor of drones has bragged about a 518 percent growth in use by U.S. agencies in just the past twenty-four months, including 347 sheriffs, local police and fire departments, and city and state officials. The same vendor brags about how drones can be used to undertake crowd monitoring "in situations such as large gatherings, concerts, or protests." Hypothetically, data feeds from a small fleet of drones outfitted with high-resolution, infrared, and thermal night-vision cameras could record an entire city twenty-four hours a day, seven days a week, archiving the data to be rewound at a later time, or constantly scrutinized by artificial intelligence and machine learning programs to look for signatures, patterns, or suspect behaviour, with barely a human in the loop.

CCTV cameras, AI-enabled facial recognition systems, and remote sensing technologies are but the tip of the iceberg in technologies of remote control. There are automatic licence plate readers, cell phone tower simulators, and mobile data extraction systems. Installed at choke points throughout the internet and telecommunication networks are deep-packet inspection and content filtering devices. Thousands of apps routinely installed on mobile devices harvest masses of data points as we go about our daily lives, uploading them to platforms for archiving and analysis, and then selling the data to third parties, many of whom now see government security services as a highly lucrative crossover market. Among the many political effects of the past couple of decades' worth of innovations in digital technologies, the sudden rise of technologically enabled superpower policing may be among the least appreciated but most consequential.

AS WITH SURVEILLANCE CAPITALISM in more consumer-oriented spheres, it's natural (and irresistible) for companies that service law enforcement and security agencies to try to integrate various data sources into a single system — known as "fusion" in industry jargon. The concept of fusion speaks volumes about the broader implications of our communications ecosystem. Whereas checks and balances aim to divide government agencies against each other to guard against abuses of power, "fusion" aims to bring them together.

Examples of data fusion around policing and intelligence are legion and have been growing ever since 9/11. The imperative to "connect the dots" has opened up otherwise siloed databases across government agencies to seamless integration while simultaneously injecting billions of funds into policing, intelligence, and military service start-ups. Hundreds of DHS-run fusion centres now blanket the United States and serve as hubs for data sharing among local, state, and federal police; military and intelligence agencies; and private contractors. Probably the most notorious of the data fusion services used widely by the government is sold by Palantir, a company that has its origins in PayPal's fraud detection unit (and was founded by the previously mentioned right-wing libertarian Peter Thiel). Palantir's data fusion and analytics platforms are widely employed by U.S. security agencies both at home and abroad. The same fusion system that helped pinpoint targeted assassinations as part of counterterror operations in Afghanistan and Iraq is now deployed in domestic U.S. policing efforts, such as those undertaken by Immigration and Customs Enforcement. Palantir technology "allows ICE agents to access a vast 'ecosystem' of data to facilitate immigration officials in both discovering targets and then creating and administering cases against them" and provides ICE with "access to intelligence platforms maintained by the Drug Enforcement Administration; the Bureau of Alcohol, Tobacco, Firearms and Explosives; the Federal Bureau of Investigation; and an array of other federal and private law enforcement entities."

The trends towards data fusion have helped blur military and civilian applications; technologies developed for commercial purposes are easily cross-purposed for public security, intelligence, and military functions. For their part, security agencies of all sizes have voracious appetites for data acquisition, fusion, and analytics services; many at the higher end (e.g., departments of defence, signals intelligence agencies) have deep pockets for contracting. National security regulations also conveniently shield many of these agencies from public transparency and accountability, meaning experiments in social media monitoring and other techniques of information control can be undertaken without much meddlesome outside scrutiny. This also makes it challenging to assess the efficacy of the tools: Do they actually accomplish useful goals? Who's to say? Meanwhile, private security contractor services that start out in shadowy "black ops" abroad (like those offered by Palantir) gradually seep into civilian and domestic policing operations, carrying the culture, norms, and ingrained secrecy of their military roots with them.

The clearest and perhaps most concerning area where

military and civil applications are blurred, leading to widening gaps in public accountability, is around social media surveillance at border controls. According to research undertaken by the U.S.-based Brennan Center, the U.S. government began checking social media feeds for immigration vetting in 2014. What started out as manual and ad hoc quickly became both routine and systematic. Since the summer of 2019, the U.S. State Department requires around fifteen million foreigners who apply for U.S. visas each year to disclose all social media handles and usernames, while the Department of Homeland Security has proposed a similar initiative for all other visitors. (It's worth noting that these assessments are often flawed: cultural slang is misunderstood, racism abounds, and when/if passwords are compelled, there is a good chance that U.S. government agencies won't properly protect them, putting people at risk, as well as increasing the chances of officers snooping in personal information they shouldn't be.)

Customs and border officials at most international border crossings have enormous scope of authority, making these increasingly heavily monitored and policed areas "rights-free zones." As pressures have mounted to gather social media data on travellers as they transit through checkpoints, and to monitor large stretches of territory, border officials have turned to technologies originally developed for military and intelligence purposes. For example, as the wars in Afghanistan and Iraq wound down in the 2010s, huge defence contractors like Raytheon, Northrup Grumman, and General Electric began lobbying for legislation that would bolster border security and open up new markets for their technologies. Border regions and international crossings alike have become heavily militarized as a consequence, with customs and border patrol agencies now outfitted with intelligence-grade surveillance equipment.

In a report released in April 2017, *Forbes* journalist Thomas Brewster detailed that "just three days after President Trump signed off his second attempt at a travel ban from Muslim-majority countries, U.S. Immigration and Customs Enforcement...ordered $2 million worth of what's believed to be some of the most powerful phone and laptop hacking technology available from the Israel-based company Cellebrite." Armed with a Cellebrite UFED Touch2 mobile extraction system, which is about the size of an iPad, a border agent can take a seized device, plug it in, and within a matter of seconds copy all of the relevant data they need. What does that include exactly? The company's advertising describes providing authorities with cloud-based private data from "over 50 of the most popular social media and cloud-based services." It says officers can "use login credentials provided by the subject, extracted from digital devices or PCs, retrieved from personal files or via other discovery means to gain access to time sensitive data." It goes on to say that it can help "gain insights into the subject's intentions and interest by pulling out the history of text searches, visited pages, voice search recordings and translations from

Google web history." Clients can "capture and review public data" like "location information, profiles, images, files and social communications from popular apps, including Facebook, Twitter, and Instagram." They can also "explore location history, and track online behavior."

Collecting all that data is one thing; making sense of it is another. The acquisition of masses of big data has pushed the agencies to find contractors who specialize in social media analytics (of which there are many—thanks to surveillance capitalism). One typical company that has benefited from the new marketplace for policing contracts is Giant Oak, which has its roots in the U.S. Defense Advanced Research Projects Agency (DARPA)—a Cold War–era "hothouse" whose aim is to spur on the development of military technologies. Giant Oak is led by CEO Gary Shiffman, a former chief of staff at the U.S. Customs and Border Protection agency and a U.S. Navy Gulf War veteran. The company's core product offering is something called "Giant Oak Search Technology," or GOST (pronounced "ghost"), which can create "a dossier on each individual with everything you need to know." GOST is especially designed for large triaging tasks, such as ranking thousands of people at once by relevance depending on an investigator's use-case and priorities, or what the company calls "continuous evaluation." The latter identifies patterns of behaviour over time and sends urgent alerts to law enforcement clients for follow-up.

DUAL-USE APPLICATIONS WORK in both directions, with companies that start out in civilian or consumer-based marketplaces then expanding to service policing, intelligence, and military needs. Consider Amazon, which began as a mere website selling books and DVDs and is now one of the largest tech companies in the world, specializing in cloud computing, streaming media, e-commerce, and artificial intelligence, among other services. Not surprisingly, Amazon has made inroads into the law enforcement and security marketplace in recent years. In June 2019, investigative reporters noted that Amazon had pitched its facial recognition technology to ICE at around the same time the company announced it had developed a new algorithm to better detect "fear" and improve "age range detection." Coming at a time when ICE was rounding up undocumented immigrants and refugees and separating children from their parents, the prospective sale of such a technology to the agency was sinister, to say the least.

Amazon also markets Ring, a personal home security service that features a camera, a floodlight, and an app so that homeowners can remotely view who is approaching their front door. Ring is bundled together with Neighbors, an app designed as a kind of virtual neighbourhood watch where subscribers can upload the footage to a forum-like system and comment on each other's feeds. But Amazon's client outreach does not stop with homeowners. In the United States, Ring has nurtured partnerships with more than six hundred local police forces, who agree in exchange to promote the product based on "talking points" provided to them by Amazon. Amazon also offers tips on how police can obtain footage from Ring customers without a warrant. Meanwhile, Ring and Neighbors customers (who tend to be more affluent) have reflexively undertaken racial profiling while using the platforms, with video posts disproportionately depicting people of colour and posts routinely making and sharing racist assumptions. In a similar vein, records obtained by the Northern California American Civil Liberties Union (ACLU) revealed that in 2015 a Fresno police department used a social media monitoring firm that boasted it could "avoid the warrant process when identifying social-media accounts for particular individuals," and could "identify threats to public safety" by monitoring terms including "police brutality," "we want justice," "Dissent," and "Blacklivesmatter."

Another typical example is Banjo, a small AI startup that began as a service scraping Facebook and other social media platforms to inform users about what other people were doing "nearby." The 2013 Boston Marathon bombing served as a revelation for the company, which quickly pivoted away from the consumer to the law enforcement market. Banjo landed a five-year, $20 million contract with the state of Utah, which gave Banjo real-time access to state traffic cameras, CCTV and other public safety cameras, 911 emergency systems, and location data for state-owned vehicles. Banjo uses its proprietary AI system to combine this data with information collected from social media posts, apps, and even satellites to "detect anomalies" that would be of interest to law enforcement. Like a lot of these algorithm-based, social media–scraping, crime-fighting companies, Banjo undergoes no real, rigorous oversight over how the data are used, or what counts as an alert. It advertises itself as a "solution for homelessness" and says its system can detect "opioid events" — whatever that means.

THE EXAMPLES OF AMAZON "coaching" police on how to acquire footage without a warrant, and Banjo promoting its services as a solution for "homelessness" and drug addiction, illustrate another major issue with the sudden turn to superpower policing: how laws and regulations designed to guard against abuse of power will fare in the face of this profound leap forward in technologies of remote control. A wave of high-tech surveillance applications has flooded policing and security agencies, from the national level down to the smallest municipalities. These tools are encouraging new policing practices to which it is unclear whether existing laws and regulations even apply. Some of these new practices are routinely and indiscriminately subjecting masses of otherwise innocent people to wholesale dragnet surveillance. They also carry with them, and even amplify, existing racial and other prejudices endemic to many local police forces. On top of that, the dizzying array of private contractors, from start-ups to mammoth corporations, vastly increases the challenges of ensuring proper oversight and accountability. The blurring of military and civilian applications makes these challenges even worse. The result is a volatile mixture of elements that threatens to overwhelm the safeguards we have traditionally relied on to preserve civil liberties and check against the abuse of power.

One of the most disturbing examples of this volatile mixture is location tracking. Nearly every one of us now carries at least one GPS-enabled mobile device twenty-four hours a day. Mobile apps, cellular service providers, and telecommunications networks all routinely collect detailed information on our locations and sell or share those data to third parties, such as advertisers or police. A *New York Times* investigation found that at least seventy-five companies receive "anonymous, precise location data from apps whose users enable location services to get local news and weather or other information." It determined that several of the companies claim to track up to two hundred million mobile devices in the United States, which is about half of those in use last year. The investigative journalists reviewed a slice from 2017 of a database held by one company, which showed "people's travels in startling detail, accurate to within a few yards and in some cases updated more than 14,000 times a day."

As that investigation suggests, the market for location data acquired by social media applications and telecommunications companies is poorly regulated. Data collected by apps and telcos are routinely sold or shared with third-party aggregators, which in turn sell them to a variety of customers, including advertisers, data analytics firms, police, private security, prison wardens, and even bounty hunters. (In one appalling case, journalist Joseph Cox was able to locate a phone by paying $300 to a bounty hunter, who easily found the phone through a location tracking service provider.) Those third parties may not have the appropriate legal or technical safeguards in place to protect the data they collect. For example, an investigation by Robert Xiao, a security researcher at Carnegie Mellon University, found that the portal for one location tracking service, called LocationSmart, was improperly secured, allowing him to determine the precise whereabouts of virtually any individual's device. "I stumbled upon this almost by accident, and it wasn't terribly hard to do," Xiao said. "This is something anyone could discover with minimal effort. And the gist of it is I can track most people's cellphones without their consent."

Even if they secure their databases, the companies may not have professional experience sharing with law enforcement and other security agencies that request access to their customer data. For their part, lacking official guidance to the contrary, law enforcement and intelligence agencies may see all these newfangled sources of data as "fair game" — information that is in the "public domain" anyway and thus not subject to privacy laws or warrants. For example, many U.S. prisons use a service provided by a company called Securus

Technologies to monitor inmates' calls. The *New York Times* discovered Securus was also providing access to thousands of law enforcement officials who were using the company's API without proper judicial authorization, to track suspects, judges, and even spouses. Illustrating the legal void around such a new and powerful system, a spokesperson for Securus said the company "is neither a judge nor a district attorney, and the responsibility of ensuring the legal adequacy of supporting documentation lies with our law enforcement customers and their counsel." A study by the ACLU found that cell phone tracking laws vary widely in the U.S. from state to state, with warrants required in some jurisdictions but no protections whatsoever in others.

Examples of "legal voids" such as these are spreading across the social media policing space. For example, as part of its Project Wide Awake, Canada's RCMP use a social media monitoring system sold by a D.C.-based contractor called Carahsoft. The company's marketing brochure nicely encapsulates the great leap forward in remote control technologies: "Ever wished you could be a fly on the wall in the homes of consumers?" the brochure asks. "That's kind of what social media monitoring is." (Just ask MBS and al-Qahtani.) In spite of the advertisement's nod to its own privacy-eroding potential, however, the RCMP maintain it is no big deal, since all those data are in the public domain. Said an RCMP spokesperson, "a search warrant would not be required to use this off-the-shelf tool, which queries and analyses publicly accessible information, where there is no reasonable expectation of privacy, such as public Twitter or Facebook posts."

The same type of "legal voids" surround the use of cell site simulators, variously known as DRT boxes, Stingrays, or IMSI catchers. Cell site simulators are typically about the size of a suitcase (although there are some larger variations) and can be remotely deployed at target locations in police vehicles, on top of vans, or even on low-altitude Cessnas or transport aircraft. When powered on, the simulators broadcast strong radio signals and thus "compel" devices in the vicinity to connect to them by default, bypassing legitimate cell sites. This allows the boxes to collect hard-coded device identification data, like IMSI identifiers, which can then be combined with other location data and access points to track targets. Some even advertise the ability to intercept and archive voice, text, and other traffic.

Although the tool is obviously effective, the way it operates inherently increases the risks of dragnet surveillance of innocent people. For example, a *Toronto Star* investigation, which analyzed RCMP logs of their use of the devices over a two-month period, found that "as officers targeted 11 suspects, they swept up cell phone data on at least 20,000 and as many as 25,000 bystanders." The investigation found that devices were used in busy Toronto neighbourhoods like Yorkville, Chinatown, Kensington Market, and the Dufferin Mall. More disturbing, however, was that both the RCMP and local police forces across Canada had used cell site simulators for years without acknowledging they did so. Some agencies flat-out lied to journalists and investigators when asked whether they did (including to several of us at the Citizen Lab). Although the Canadian Criminal Code requires police forces to list the number of warrants they have sought for wiretaps, cell site simulators have traditionally not been included in the requirements. Some forces went so far as to withhold evidence obtained by cell phone tower simulators in court proceedings so as not to reveal the investigative technique, leading to the dismissal of serious criminal cases.

It's not just Canadian police either. An investigation by the ACLU found seventy-five federal, state, and municipal agencies in the U.S. that used cell site simulators, although the ACLU also said its research was hampered by lack of disclosure. Another investigation discovered that local police in Maryland had been using cell site simulators for over a decade before publicly disclosing them. It said the secrecy was at least in part due to non-disclosure agreements passed down from the FBI to local police forces, which required them not to divulge the use of the technology for fear of exposing investigation techniques. The same investigation also found Maryland police were using them for routine investigations, including burglaries, assaults, and — in one case — "a Pizza Boli's employee who reported being robbed of 15 chicken wings and three subs while out on delivery."

AS PART OF THE BATTLE against the COVID pandemic, governments enacted extensive, exceptional, and in some cases far-reaching (and disturbing) emergency powers. The city (Toronto), province (Ontario), and country (Canada) in which I live all declared states of emergency (although, at the time of writing, prime minister Justin Trudeau had so far refrained from exercising the War Measures Act, which his father did in response to threats of domestic terrorism in the 1970 October Crisis, during which the separatist group Front de libération du Québec set off bombs, undertook kidnappings, and murdered a British diplomat). If there was ever a time that warranted such measures, during the COVID pandemic it definitely felt like we were in the midst of one.

But some of the measures many countries adopted or proposed were deeply unsettling. As if right on cue, not missing any opportunity to strengthen their grip, autocrats have used the "war on COVID" as an excuse to silence dissent, muzzle independent news, eliminate checks and balances, and extend their personal rule. In the Philippines, President Duterte instructed police, when they came across those who had violated isolation orders, to "shoot them dead." In Israel, Prime Minister Netanyahu ordered Israel's parliaments and courts to shutter (conveniently delaying his own corruption trial). In Turkmenistan, dictator Gurbanguly Berdymukhammedov went so far as to ban the mere mention of the disease. In Thailand, the government used the excuse of a crackdown on "fake news" to enact draconian media laws. In Hungary, the far-right leader Viktor Orbán ordered a sweeping emergency law that gave him carte blanche to bypass parliament and the courts and rule by personal decree, suspending all elections indefinitely and imprisoning opposition members without due process. The emergency law has no end date.

Not surprisingly, officials turned to technology to help combat the pandemic and assist in contact tracing and quarantine enforcement. The latent capabilities of social media and surveillance capitalism were too obvious to ignore as governments struggled to mitigate the spread of the virus and control the movement of populations. Many officials proposed turning to cellular, telecommunications, and social media providers to provide location data. At the time of writing, there were at least thirty-six government-sponsored applications proposed as either voluntary or mandatory for citizens to download and install as part of a biomedical surveillance regime. Even drones were being offered up and used as part of COVID mitigation efforts; in China, UAVs equipped with loudspeakers bellow at citizens who violate quarantine and distancing rules. One company, Draganfly, was developing a "pandemic drone" to fly over crowds of people and monitor temperature, heart rates, coughing, and even blood pressure. While there may be some beneficial uses of these sorts of systems, there are also questions about both the efficacy of such data and (more importantly) the potential for abuse of power. Although some companies that gather location data promise anonymity and confidentiality, experiments have shown how easy it is to unmask real identities contained in large personal data sets. As if unintentionally signalling these very risks, surveillance vendor NSO Group jumped into the ring, offering its services to trace the movements of known COVID-19 patients against those with whom they might have crossed paths, even back in time. (NSO's definitely not alone: a Reuters investigation found "at least eight surveillance and cyber-intelligence companies attempting to sell repurposed spy and law enforcement tools to track the virus and enforce quarantines," including the aforementioned Cellebrite.) NSO's platform would ostensibly draw data from cellular and telecommunications companies — data sharing that had already started among telcos and governments in numerous countries. NSO's campaign has the support of the Israeli defence minister, Naftali Bennett, who said all this would form part of an Israeli-backed global AI system that would give every citizen on the globe a score of between one and ten to determine how likely they are to spread COVID-19. (A more disturbing illustration of the risks of government-enforced and privately run biomedical surveillance I can hardly imagine.)

Meanwhile, as much of the world moved into work-from-home rules and self-isolation, technology became an essential lifeline. Applications and systems that were originally designed for more banal uses all of a sudden vaulted into areas of life and work for which they were never designed, including confidential communications, sensitive and classified government deliberations, and interactions among high-risk groups — including health workers and their patients. This sudden dependence on remote networking opened up a whole new assortment of security and privacy risks while simultaneously creating an irresistible smorgasbord of sitting ducks for government spies, police, and criminals. As the Citizen Lab's John Scott-Railton put it, "the world's business has slid into a world of personal devices, personal chat & calling apps, and un-administered, unpatched home wifi routers and networks."

Take Zoom, the popular video teleconference application that went from a relatively boutique corporate communications tool to something approximating a global essential service in a mere few weeks. Zoom had been plagued by security issues for a number of years, including vulnerabilities in its screen sharing feature, and privacy concerns around data sharing with Facebook, among others. Zoom's easy nine- or ten-digit code required to join a meeting created with default settings led to widely reported and highly disturbing instances of "Zoom-bombing," in which people were able to insert themselves uninvited into improperly configured conference calls. In March 2020, our Citizen Lab team reverse-engineered Zoom and discovered that it employed non-industry-standard cryptographic techniques with identifiable weaknesses that allowed attackers to intercept video and audio traffic. We also discovered that its sessions were encrypted with a single cryptographic key that was sometimes sent to users from servers in mainland China. (China requires all companies operating inside its jurisdiction to cooperate with law enforcement on demand, meaning Chinese security agencies could conceivably insert themselves into any conference call surreptitiously.) The insecurity of Zoom (which, to the company's credit, was improved upon in response to our findings) is but a symptom of a much larger disease: the devices, networks, and cloud computing systems on which nearly everyone is now forced to rely while in isolation were never built with complete security in mind, and they provide a gold mine of intelligence data for states and other nefarious actors. The risks of abuse are legion.

These public safety and health emergency measures are a good example of what I have elsewhere referred to as "event-based" information controls. Major anniversaries, sudden protests, incidences of mass violence, outbreaks of armed conflict, major health crises, and sporting events like the Olympics typically prompt governments to introduce special powers or emergency measures. While these may be justified in the short term, they are also opportunities for unaccountable elites to consolidate their rule and justify extreme measures over time. As political scientists Steven Levitsky and Daniel Ziblatt explain, "crises are a time-tested means of subverting democracy." They allow authorities to cast aside the frustrating straitjacket of constitutional safeguards and rule by executive decree. Once introduced, however, emergency measures are very difficult to walk back. Citizens, meanwhile, are more likely to accept these measures when their safety and security are at stake. They readily sacrifice their liberties and allow exceptional powers, which before long can become a "new normal."

"IF YOU'VE GOT NOTHING to hide, you've got nothing to fear." I can't say how many variations of this phrase I've read or heard. It most often comes up as a question after one of my talks. But while intuitively appealing and simple, the phrase is misleading and inaccurate.

Contrary to the saying, *many people do indeed have something to hide,* and for good reason. Moreover, even if they are not doing anything "wrong," they can still have something to fear. For those living in autocratic states, for example, the simple exercise of the most basic human rights enjoyed elsewhere can cost them prison time, or worse. Recall that Ahmed Mansoor — a victim of multiple targeted espionage attacks by his own government — was ultimately thrown in an Emirati prison for "insults to the regime."

What the "nothing to hide" argument overlooks, in short, is the potential for the abuse of power. Corruption, authoritarianism, and despotism are not practices neatly compartmentalized within sovereign boundaries, with some "good states" over here and the "bad ones" over there. They are pervasive throughout all societies and cut across all territorial boundaries. We forget that these practices are endemic to human societies, and they can easily reappear even in countries that have safeguards in place to defend against them.

It is worth reminding ourselves how numerous and recent abuse-of-power episodes have been within ostensibly liberal democratic societies. It was only several decades ago that J. Edgar Hoover's FBI illegally wiretapped American citizens, including civil rights advocates, members of Congress, and Supreme Court justices, without any concern for properly authorized judicial warrants. It was barely more than a generation ago that the CIA undertook secret LSD experiments on prisoners and mental health patients. It was barely fifty years ago that Canada's RCMP broke into hundreds of residences without a warrant, and went so far as to burn a barn to prevent what they suspected was going to be a meeting between Quebec separatists and the Black Panthers. It was only within the past ten years that the NSA secretly subverted encryption standards meant to protect the public's communications, hacked into the data networks connecting major cloud computing platforms, and installed massive data trawling equipment on the backbones of the U.S. telecommunications systems. A list of abuses such as these could fill an entire library.

It's also worth reminding ourselves that recent years have brought about a disturbing descent into authoritarianism, fuelled by and in turn driving income inequality in grotesque proportions and propelling the rise of a kind of transnational gangster economy. There is today a large and influential class of kleptocrats spread across the globe and supported by a professional service industry of lawyers, shell companies, accountants, and PR firms, the members of which move seamlessly between the private sector and agencies of the state. These are people who don't care whether or not someone "has nothing to hide" or is "not doing anything wrong." They thrive by victimizing innocent others, undermining individuals and organizations that seek to hold them to account, and using the power and machinery of the state for personal gain. There is no jurisdiction that is immune to corruption and authoritarian practices — only greater or lesser degrees of protection against them.

While it's become common to acknowledge the way these technologies are enabling a new type of "digital authoritarianism" to flourish, it would be a mistake to conclude that the effects of social media are limited to a group of bad actors "over there." In fact, the most disturbing dynamics are playing themselves out within nominally liberal democratic countries. Hyper-militarized policing practices that draw on big data and AI-enabled surveillance tools are creating states on steroids. Just look around next time you pass through any airport border crossing. Meanwhile, the constraints on abuse of power seem quaint and old-fashioned, as if constructed for a different time and context. We now have twenty-first-century policing practices with nineteenth- and twentieth-century checks and balances.

In its 2019 annual report, the U.S. NGO Freedom House, which measures indicators of democracy worldwide, recorded "the 13th consecutive year of decline in global freedom." Its report, titled *Democracy in Retreat*, noted that "the reversal has spanned a variety of countries in every region, from long-standing democracies like the United States to consolidated authoritarian regimes like China and Russia." The report noted that authoritarian regimes had become more nakedly authoritarian, absent outside pressures to reform, while countries that had recently transitioned to democratic rule had stagnated and slid backwards. But most remarkable was its observation that "even long-standing democracies have been shaken by populist political forces that reject basic principles like the separation of powers."

It would be an error to claim social media are the sole cause of this disturbing descent. But it seems increasingly indisputable that the environment of social media is dramatically facilitating it. Absent specific constraints or measures to the contrary, digital authoritarianism is taking root in China, with its exports acting as a transmission belt to spread those practices abroad. That may not be a surprise to many. But it is also taking root elsewhere, leapfrogging over constraints and countermeasures and putting liberal democratic institutions to the test. As University of Toronto political scientist Seva Gunitsky has put it, "The political uses of the internet in autocracies and democracies are becoming harder to distinguish." What we are therefore witnessing is not "a widening gap between open and closed regimes but an increasing blurring of the two." Thanks to superpower policing, we all now suddenly find ourselves looking over a precipice into a dark abyss of unconstrained abuses of power.

FOUR

BURNING DATA

OCTOBER 2019. I ARRIVE IN DELHI, India, and as I always do when travelling abroad, I spend my first day walking the streets to shake off jet lag. Delhi is a microcosm of all the themes that are laid out in this book. Social media use is skyrocketing: everywhere I look, someone has a mobile device in their hand; many people have several. There are countless advertisements for low-cost wireless plans. A new upstart entrant to the cellular provider field called Jio, launched in 2016 by India's richest man, Mukesh Ambani, and infused in 2020 with multi-billion-dollar investments from Facebook and other privacy equity firms, has undercut its competitors with basement-floor subscription rates, boosting social media's popularity even further.

But India also exhibits all the downsides, unintended consequences, and negative externalities of social media. Under the reign of prime minister Narendra Modi and his Hindu nationalist right-wing party, the BJP, the country has rapidly descended into authoritarianism. Disinformation and misinformation run rampant through social media, sparking frequent outbreaks of mob violence and ethnic animosity — the most recent of which was horrific sectarian violence unleashed principally by Hindu mobs against Muslims in northeast Delhi in February and March 2020. WhatsApp groups, which are end-to-end encrypted, making it more difficult for the platform to moderate content, are especially prone to these spikes of panic- or violence-inducing disinformation.

Like those in many other countries, Indian authorities have rolled out technologically enhanced surveillance and other information controls. Upon arrival at the airport, I (along with all other travellers) submit to a biometric scanning system. India has implemented the world's largest biometric identification program, called Aadhaar, but it is riddled with privacy and security problems. As in just about every other country to which I travel, CCTV cameras are seemingly everywhere (though it's hard to tell whether they're functional or not). The China-based IT company Huawei, whose 5G equipment has been banned in the United States and other jurisdictions for security reasons, has made quiet inroads in India. Indian journalists with whom I have spoken speculate that it is in exchange for China's Communist Party elites' remaining unusually silent over the Indian government's crackdown in Kashmir (the region's borders are disputed by India, Pakistan, and China, which have gone to war several times over the territory; exchanges of gunfire and artillery are still a common occurrence). As I arrive in India, Kashmir is in turmoil. Local authorities have shut down the internet and cellular connections, and they have combined those digital controls with a physical curfew — both of which have left citizens confused and afraid.

One of the reasons I'm in Delhi is to further our research on targeted digital espionage. The Indian connections to our cyber-espionage research go back over a decade. Our very first report on cyber-espionage (indeed, the first major public report on the subject at all), published in 2009 and called *Tracking GhostNet*, had its origins in fieldwork conducted at the Office of His Holiness the Dalai Lama (the Dalai Lama fled China in the 1950s for Dharamsala, India, after a violent crackdown on Tibetan protests against China's hardline anti-religious policies of the time). Since the GhostNet investigation, our researchers have made numerous trips to Dharamsala to work with Tibetans exiled there. While there, I am able to have a rare private audience with the Dalai Lama himself. I thank him and his community for their willingness to share data on the torrent of digital attacks originating in mainland China that they face on a daily basis, which has helped us and others understand and help mitigate them. When it comes to cyber-attacks, Tibetans are like canaries in the coal mine.

Although we will not announce it publicly until I leave India, we are finishing up an investigation into the

Indian civil society targets of NSO Group's sophisticated "no click" WhatsApp exploit, which allows operators of their spyware to clandestinely take over a mobile phone simply by calling it. We have identified over forty victims in India who were targeted in this manner, by far the most of any country in the world. The victims range from lawyers representing ethnic minority activists to journalists, environmental defenders, and opposition figures. That means Indian police and security agencies are heavy users (and abusers) of NSO's spyware, and undoubtedly are irritated that our research helped expose the abuses they have been conducting behind the scenes.

When the story eventually breaks (thankfully, for my safety, after I've left the country), the name "Citizen Lab" is splashed repeatedly over the chyrons of cable television news programs, and we are blitzed with requests for comment from Indian journalists, public officials, and citizens who suspect their phones have been hacked. India's mainstream mediasphere is a hyperbole machine. Vicious on-air arguments are not only common, they seem to be encouraged by the show's hosts and producers to grab attention—like the U.S.'s Fox News on amphetamines. Seeing our research lab's name splashed on the screen, set overtop heated arguments among Indian pundits, is surreal.

While these concerns are all uppermost in my mind as I begin my first day in Delhi, there's something else that is too overpowering to ignore: the noxious air. Delhi has recently overtaken Beijing as the most polluted capital city in the world. It is often said that Westerners visiting India are overwhelmed by the sights and sounds, especially the incessantly loud backdrop of vehicle horns — cars, buses, taxis, scooters, and auto rickshaws, all jockeying for position while signalling to each other via a symphony of incessant honks, toots, and beeps. But what is most in your face, what is instantly most overwhelming on my first day, is that it's difficult and unpleasant to breathe. The pollution in Delhi is like nowhere else on earth. Literally.

Air quality is measured by sensors that determine the levels of ozone, carbon monoxide, sulphur dioxide, nitrogen dioxide, aerosols, and particulate matter like smog, dust, smoke, and soot. An air quality index (AQI) of zero to fifty is considered good. As I am writing this chapter, the AQI in Toronto is seventeen. The day I arrive in India, the AQI in Delhi is over two hundred, which is categorized as "very unhealthy," meaning everyone is at risk of adverse health effects simply by stepping outside and breathing. As the days go by it gets worse, compounded by annual Diwali celebrations, in which Indians ring in the new year with fireworks that fill the air with yet more smoke and soot. By the time I leave Delhi, the AQI is off the charts in the five hundred range, officially described as a "severe-plus emergency" (as if they have run out of extreme adjectives). Delhi's chief minister, Arvind Kejriwal, tweets that Delhi has "turned into a gas chamber." The dust is so thick that, in combination with the heat, it makes walking outside for any period of time difficult. (I love to run wherever I travel, but doing so outside in Delhi is asking for potential long-term respiratory problems.)

Although India has made some pledges to improve its environment and green its power infrastructure, the pledges are continuously pushed back by the ongoing reliance on — indeed, further development of — coal-fired power plants. As an energy source, coal is very dirty, linked to pollutants such as mercury, sulphur dioxide (a component of acid rain), and the particulate matter that filters through my nostrils as I walk about the city. Regardless of the climate science, coal is still the primary source of electricity generation in India. In fact, India is the second-largest producer of coal in the world, after only China, and the third-largest consumer. About 70 percent of power generation in India currently comes from coal-fired power plants. Although authorities have pushed for sustainable, green alternatives, it's hard to make the move since coal is so plentiful and cheap, while the appetite for electricity consumption among 1.3 billion Indians is immense and growing quickly. Coal-fired power plants accounted for 44 percent of new energy production in India in 2019, an immense increase in dirty energy in the midst of a worldwide climate crisis. There are close to a dozen operating coal-fired power plants around Delhi alone, most of which are routinely flagged for violating or ignoring environmental regulations. According to India's Central Electricity Authority, only one of them is complying with a law requiring the installation of equipment to cut emissions of sulphur oxides linked to lung disease.

Just great, I think to myself while sucking in another mouthful of Delhi's exhaust-pipe air.

Strolling through Delhi's neighbourhoods, it's hard to believe that the energy system works at all. Alongside crumbling concrete buildings and mud-filled, crowded, dusty streets, one thing stands out: seemingly endless coils of electrical wires and fibre optic cables, bunched together like tangled spaghetti. Cables of all shapes and sizes droop over balconies, are bound together with string alongside makeshift telephone poles, are strung over the middle of streets, or in some places just hang low and splayed out over the sidewalk or droop through puddles of mud and filth. Dotting the top of nearly every one of those concrete buildings are cell arrays, satellite dishes, and other antennae, packed around one another, some pointing in this direction and others that. Nearly everyone is frantically swiping or texting as they shout and bump into each other in a street dance of congestion and mobile connectivity. The combination of poverty, packs of stray dogs, cows roaming the streets, and litter everywhere, alongside spools of electrical wire, cables, and DIY cell towers, makes for something out of a William Gibson novel.

I pick my way through a semi-complete but abandoned construction site that serves as a shortcut to my hotel, carefully avoiding potentially dangerous exposed cables and wires, and then stop frozen in my tracks at a railway overpass, in awe of the sight below me: the longest possible train I could have imagined, with open wagons full to the brim . . . of *coal*. It seems as if several minutes go by as the train passes underneath me, one coal-filled wagon after another, heading directly into the orange mist of the late-afternoon horizon — an orange mist that seems to coat all of Delhi like toxic candy floss.

Virtual, ethereal, weightless, clean, futuristic: these and other terms like them are what first come to mind for most people when they think of digital technologies. But the reality is far different. As long as I've studied information and communications technologies, I've been fascinated by its often overlooked but vast and inescapable physical infrastructure. No doubt my fascination is thanks to the influence of media ecologists like Harold Innis and Marshall McLuhan, whose contributions to the field were distinguished by their appreciation of communications technologies' material qualities. I've studied undersea fibre optic cables, toured landing stations off the east coast of Africa, and descended into the depths of a mountain-encased data centre that once served as a nuclear fallout shelter in Stockholm, Sweden. Friends and family poke fun at my obsession with cell towers, which I photograph and share on social media, usually accompanied with a nerdy explanation of how they comprise part of the "overlooked underbelly of cyberspace." Most users either ignore or take for granted this vast physical ecosystem. The electrical wires, power lines, cell towers, and satellite dishes are now just part of the taken-for-granted surroundings — so common and pervasive that they simply fade into the background.

But even if some elements are hard to ignore (as with Delhi's endless mesh of cables, dishes, and towers), they only tell part of the picture. Much of the materiality of social media is either hidden from view or difficult for the average person to experience first-hand, at least not without some effort. For much of our day-to-day lives we are presented instead with a kind of technological mirage. Our consumption of social media (and the communications ecosystem as a whole that supports them) generates a kind of hidden tax on the natural environment that we don't feel, see, smell, or touch as we blithely swipe away at a text or tweet. But it's there, and growing. It generates a full spectrum of strains on the natural world, from the mining and manufacturing through to the energy consumption and waste. As we grow further and further dependent on social media and its seemingly never-ending universe of consumer electronics, we devour ever larger quantities of energy and strain the planet's finite pool of natural resources. Although for a long time the topic was poorly studied, a small but growing number of scholars are beginning to recognize the fourth painful truth about social media and our communications ecosystem as a whole: that they are contributing to massive environmental degradation.

LET'S GO BACK TO THAT DEVICE you hold in your hand and take another close look. Have you ever stopped to contemplate how it's manufactured? Have you paused to consider all the various elements that make it up? Most of us simply take it for granted, that slender, solid piece of electronics we carry around with us at all times. Until it stops functioning, that is. We then discard it for an upgrade, our junk drawers becoming littered with electronic relics and their assorted unpackaged peripherals.

It's not just that we take it for granted. We are also actively discouraged from peering inside that device. Opening up and fiddling with your Apple product (tellingly known as "jailbreaking") is strongly discouraged by the company. Warns Apple, "Unauthorized modification of iOS can cause security vulnerabilities, instability, shortened battery life, and other issues," and "is a violation of the iOS end-user software license agreement and because of this, Apple may deny service." Apple's not alone. Manufacturers of consumer electronics of all kinds take extraordinary steps to discourage users from getting too curious about what goes on "beneath the hood," including placing "warranty void if removed" stickers on the underside, using proprietary screws and other components that require special tools, or applying glue and solder to bind components together, making it virtually impossible to open the device without causing irreparable damage. That smartphone you hold in your hand is what's known in engineering as a "black box"—you can observe its inputs and outputs, but its inner workings are largely a mystery to all but a select few.

Part of the reason has to do with planned obsolescence, a syndrome inherent to consumer culture. Our gadgets are built, by design, not to last. The sooner they stop working, the more likely you'll want an upgrade to a more recent version. And when you do, you'll need some accessories and peripherals too, or you won't be able to enjoy all of the new features. (Raise your hand if you have a Tupperware bin full of discarded cables, attachments, dongles, and adaptors.)

But part of it is also cultural. The less users know what goes on beneath the surface of the social media environment, the better for the industry that serves it up. Generally speaking, tech companies want us to focus on the virtual and ethereal layers — the compelling content that keeps us all hooked. They do not want us to observe the messy subterranean realm that keeps it all functioning. Perversely, at the same time that we are surrounded by technology as never before, we are actively discouraged, by laws and other regulations, from knowing what goes on inside the very devices and other appliances on which we depend. The more we are made to feel like it's all a special kind of magic that just works, the better for the industry.

What if you were encouraged to look inside? What would you find? It's astonishing to reflect on how something so small can perform such complex calculations. As we pull it apart and examine it, there is the LED display, the touch screen, the camera lens, the modem, the SIM card, the microprocessing chips, the circuits, and the lithium-ion battery. Even if we were to strip it down to its bare essentials and lay them out on the desk, we would still not be able to fully appreciate the material shadow that is cast by such a small thing. The production of each and every device involves hundreds of kilograms of fossil fuels, dozens of kilograms of chemicals, and thousands of kilograms of water. The data centres that process all those videos, documents, and emails consume hundreds of thousands of gallons of fresh water a day to operate. Semiconductor plants that fabricate the tiny components consume millions. Then there's the energy required to make it all run — something we think of only occasionally, when the battery icon goes red and we anxiously search for an electrical outlet to get a charge.

Sending an email, or even a simple smiley face over SMS, implicates a vast but largely overlooked planet-wide system of non-renewable resources, manufacturing, shipping, energy, labour, and non-recyclable waste. These are all part of the hidden externalities of our growing communications ecosystem. They are "sunk costs" not factored into the real costs of that email or smiley face. These costs do not show up in our monthly cell phone bills, no matter how outrageously expensive those may seem. But they are costs that we will reckon with down the road eventually, previews of which can be seen and felt now in a city like Delhi.

THERE'S NOTHING THAT QUITE embodies such internal contradictions as much as the virtuality, ephemerality, and endless novelty of our social media experiences, on the one hand, and the raw materiality, astronomical origins, and ancient roots of the components that go into the devices that make it all run, on the other. It's hard to believe that something so new and polished as a consumer-level mobile device contains elements whose genesis reaches back billions of years. To understand the ecological footprint of our communications ecosystem requires us to go back to the most basic raw materials: the so-called "rare earth elements" and other minerals without which our appliances would not function.

I've often thought how wonderful it would be if our devices had a list of ingredients in the way that packaged food items do. That might remind everyone of social media's intimate connection to the natural world. Much as canned ravioli has a combination of the familiar (tomatoes, water, carrots) and obscure chemicals and other ingredients (sodium phosphate, xanthan gum, carotenal, lactic acid), so too do our handheld devices. There's silica and sand, which are the main ingredients of our display glass; there's tin, which is used as solder in the electrical circuitry. There are tiny traces of gold, silver, and copper distributed through the motherboard and wiring. A device's processor is made up mostly of silicon but also includes phosphorus, antimony, arsenic, boron, indium, and gallium. And then there's a long list of so-called rare earth elements that are much more obscure: tantalum, terbium, yttrium, and more. In fact, around seventy of the eighty-three stable and non-radioactive elements in the entire periodic table can be found in a typical smartphone, including about sixty-two different types of metal. Our device's ingredient list would be a long one. And while some of them are employed in extremely tiny quantities, they all have to be dug up from the earth somewhere, and then processed, shipped, and manufactured.

Of these, rare earth elements are the most interesting for our purposes. Rare earth elements are not called "rare" because they are in short supply. In fact, they are plentiful. They are rare because they are hard to extract from the earth and separate from the other constitutive minerals with which they are found, at least without causing major ecological stresses. There are seventeen rare earth elements, of which sixteen are included in our handheld devices. These elements have extraordinary magnetic and conductive properties, which give life to many of the features we associate with our smartphones and tablets. For example, terbium, yttrium, gadolinium, and europium are essential to the vivid colours we see on our display screens. Neodymium and praseodymium are used to help our devices vibrate. And these elements are not limited to just our handheld devices; they are essential ingredients of a wide range of other consumer and military-grade electronic appliances, from electric cars and other transportation technologies to LED displays on modern weapons systems.

Most of the rare earth elements come from China, which occasionally makes for some interesting geopolitical dynamics. As president Deng Xiaoping declared in 1997, "the Middle East has oil, we have rare earth." China holds the world's largest reserves of rare earth elements, around 37 percent of the global total. (Vietnam and Brazil each have around 18 percent, while the United States has around one percent.) More importantly, Chinese firms control more than 85 percent of the existing rare earth element supply chain (down from about 97 percent in 2009), thanks to low labour costs and (until recently) lax environmental regulations around mining operations.

China's dominance of the rare earth metals market has led to some hand-wringing in D.C.-based think tanks. If China were to cut off the supply of elements, it could conceivably affect a broad range of electronic equipment critical to digital infrastructure across governments, business, research, health care, and other vital sectors. In 2010 China did just that, shutting off exports of the elements to Japan for two months following a dispute over a string of contested islands. In 2012, the United States, Japan, and other countries filed a complaint against China's export controls with the World Trade Organization, and the WTO ruled against China in 2015. The episode prompted countries to begin to diversify their supplies away from China, but its dominance in the market is still very strong.

However rare earth elements end up being used as a piece in the chess game of international security politics, and no matter where they end up being mined from and processed, a more salient factor is their impact on the natural world. Mining for rare earth elements can be highly toxic, both for surrounding and impacted ecosystems and for the labour force that works on the operations. The mining and refining activities consume vast amounts of water while generating a large quantity of CO_2 emissions. Rare earth elements have to be separated from the minerals of which they are a part, and it's these processes that involve a number of potential contaminants and waste. Generally speaking, rare earth elements are mined either by stripping away layers of topsoil or by drilling holes into the ground into which PVC pipes are inserted and then flushing out the earth with a mixture of chemicals and water. In both cases, the materials are transported to immense surface tailing ponds, where the separation takes place. The entire operation produces large volumes of potentially hazardous waste. According to David Abraham, author of *The Elements of Power*, "Only 0.2 percent of the mined clay contains the valuable rare earth elements" — the rest is "dumped back into the hills and streams."

All of these processes can introduce large volumes of ammonia and nitrogen compounds into ground and surface water, or leach out elements that cause major health risks, such as cadmium or lead. Sometimes radioactive materials cling to the rare earth elements, since they are mined near uranium deposits. Some rare earth elements involve unique processes that are toxic in different ways.

For example, the element cerium (which is used to polish the glass on our device screens) is extracted by crushing deposits of earth in which the element is found, and then dissolving the resulting mix in sulphuric and nitric acid. The entire process is undertaken at a huge industrial scale, generating very large quantities of noxious waste by-products. According to the Chinese Society of Rare Earths, for every one tonne of rare earth elements mined and processed, about seventy-five thousand litres of acidic water and one tonne of radioactive residues are left behind.

Wherever there are mines in China, one finds high levels of contaminants in the region's ground and surface water. Long-term exposure to these chemicals causes major health risks, for humans as well as wildlife. Nearby villagers report grotesque deformities in local livestock, including sheep that have developed two rows of teeth. Villagers who drank from local wells, where the water looked fine "but smelled really bad," later reported blackened gums and teeth falling out. A *Washington Post* investigation of villages located near graphite mining facilities describes "sparkling night air, damaged crops, homes and belongings covered in soot, polluted drinking water — and government officials inclined to look the other way to benefit a major employer."

While improvements are being made across China to address the ecological consequences of rare earth and other mining, the damage for local communities has already been done and will take billions of dollars to repair (if repairs can be done at all). Surface tailing ponds where the rare earth element leaching takes place are dispersed across several regions in China, usually near river systems and other ground and surface water systems. A slight breach of these tailing ponds (caused by a landslide, for example) can affect the safe drinking water sources for tens of millions of people living in major population centres downstream.

One of China's largest and longest-running rare earth mines is Bayan Obo, near the Inner Mongolian city of Baotou. As one BBC science journalist described it, Bayan Obo is the closest thing to "hell on earth." One of the site's unmistakable features is an eleven-square-kilometre sludge waste pond about three times as large as Vancouver's Stanley Park. The journalist described it as "a truly alien environment, dystopian and horrifying," that made him both depressed and terrified, realizing "this was the byproduct not just of the consumer electronics in my pocket, but also green technologies like wind turbines and electric cars that we get so smugly excited about in the West." Unsure of how to react, he did what most of us now do when we come across something that stuns us: he took photos and shot videos on his "cerium polished iPhone." According to the environmental NGO China Water Risk, the mine "has put a death-curse on nearby villages," and the giant waste pond (some say) "is a time bomb that could spell disaster for the Yellow River, which lies only 10 kilometres away."

A second major mining centre for medium and heavy rare earth elements is in China's south, near Ganzhou, known as the "Rare Earth Kingdom." Concrete leaching ponds and plastic-lined wastewater pools are a common sight in the area, some uncovered and open to the elements. Satellite images show dozens of them spread throughout the region's hills and mountains, precariously close enough to the region's water systems that contaminant spills are an ever-present risk. Rivers flowing through the area, like the Dongjiang, provide much of the drinking water to heavily populated cities and regions such as Hong Kong (7.3 million), Shenzhen (12 million), and Guangzhou (13 million).

There is also a black market for rare earth element mining, although measuring it is difficult by definition since the activities are not formally accounted for. Occasionally we get glimpses through seizures, such as the one tonne of rare earth elements found in a shipping container destined for South Korea and seized by Weihai Customs officials. In 2015, estimates suggested about forty thousand tonnes of rare earth metals were smuggled out of China each year, dwarfing the official export volume of twenty-eight thousand tonnes. Black market mining operations produce even more pollution, since illegal mines do not follow environmental guidelines and other standards. They also tend to use unregulated and primitive smelting and separation processes, which create more hazardous waste and environmental effluents than more modern separation techniques. Without oversight and compliance with regulations, toxic waste can be discharged without proper treatment, storage, and supervision, leaching into the surrounding water systems.

Although China dominates the world's production of rare earth elements, the market is slowly diversifying. But that doesn't mean the ecological impacts are necessarily lessening. To give one example, a substantial amount of rare earth element mining takes place in Australia, but companies involved in the mining typically outsource the most toxic processing activities abroad. Australia's Lynas Corporation exports its rare earth metal processing to Malaysia, where the poisonous by-products are left as waste. The company built the largest refining facility in the world in Malaysia, but it was plagued with "environmentally hazardous construction and design problems" from the beginning. One study estimates that around 580,000 tonnes of low-level radioactive waste is currently stockpiled at the refining facility.

RARE EARTH ELEMENTS, THOUGH critical, are not the only mineral components that go into our modern electronic appliances. Mining operations the world over are integral to the devices we take for granted, and they are also linked to pollutants, labour troubles, kidnappings, smuggling, and even violent conflict.

Take lithium, also known as "grey gold," which is used to power an increasing number of electronics, from the batteries in mobile phones to those that power electric vehicles. Lithium production is booming and expected to grow even more in years to come — somewhat ironically as pressures mount for more sustainable forms of battery-powered transportation and other sources of energy. For example, a single Tesla car requires about seven kilograms of lithium for each of its battery packs. Like rare earth elements, lithium is not in short supply. However, like rare earth elements, the lithium extraction process can involve techniques that cause environmental damage. As one author sardonically put it, lithium is "what links the battery in your smartphone with a dead yak floating down a Tibetan river."

Like the extraction of rare earth elements, mining for lithium involves energy-intensive and environmentally taxing processes. Lithium is found in the brine of salt flats. Holes are drilled into the salt flats and the brine is pumped to the surface, where it is left to evaporate in large ponds. The lithium carbonate is then extracted through a chemical process that, through spills, leaching, or air emissions, can harm nearby communities, water systems, wildlife, livestock, and farmland. Since lithium salt flats are usually located in arid territories, the mining process also diverts and puts a major strain on already thinly stretched water supplies. In Chile's Atacama and Argentina's Salar de Hombre Muerto regions, where lithium mining operations are located, local communities complain about water-related shortages and conflicts related to them, as well as contaminated water supplies.

By far the most concerning mining operations are

those in and around zones of conflict. Thanks to films like *Blood Diamond* and campaigns to regulate and eradicate trade in so-called "conflict minerals," most people have a general appreciation that mining operations in places like Central Africa are bound up with warfare, organized crime, poor labour practices, smuggling, and kidnapping. But what may be overlooked is how the elements that are mined in these regions, such as cobalt, copper, tantalum, tin, and gold, are integral to the components that make up our electronic devices.

More than half of the world's cobalt supply is sourced from the Democratic Republic of Congo (DRC), a country that for decades was ravaged by civil war, its countryside littered with hundreds of armed groups that routinely terrorize about 4.5 million internally displaced people. Investigations undertaken by Amnesty International and others have shown that cobalt mining operations in the DRC routinely use child labour in mines that involve hand-dug tunnels, where work is extremely hazardous and accidents common. Says the Amnesty International report, "Artisanal miners include children as young as seven who scavenge for rocks containing cobalt in the discarded by-products of industrial mines, and who wash and sort the ore before it is sold." The study found that workers were not outfitted with even the most basic health and safety equipment and worked in deep tunnels without proper ventilation; respiratory and other health problems from exposure to toxic elements are common. Health officials have linked breathing problems and birth defects in local communities to exposure to toxic metals associated with the mining activities. A University of Lubumbashi study found that "residents who live near mines or smelters in southern Congo had urinary concentrations of cobalt that were 43 times as high as that of a control group, lead levels five times as high, and cadmium and uranium levels four times as high." Injury and death are also common, as are exploitative labour conditions. A 2007 United States Agency for International Development study found that around four thousand children worked at mining sites in the southern DRC city of Kolwezi alone. Children were paid on average about one dollar per day. One author put this wage in perspective: "A child working in a mine in the Congo would need more than 700,000 years of non-stop work to earn the same amount as a single day of [Amazon CEO Jeff] Bezos' income."

All this for the mere five to ten grams of cobalt in the smartphone you hold in your hand.

The same dynamic plays out around the globe, wherever the mining operations for the elements integral to our devices are located. For example, tin is an essential component of the soldering necessary for electronic circuitry, and about one-third of the world's tin supply comes from mostly artisanal mining operations in Indonesia. According to computing historian Nathan Ensmenger (one of the few researchers who has studied in detail the full scope of environmental consequences related to computing technologies), Indonesia's tin mining operations are "an orgy of unregulated mining" that has reduced "a rich and complex system of rainforests and gardens to a post-holocaust landscape of sand and acid subsoil." Says Ensmenger, "The process of tin mining is low-tech, labor intensive, and extraordinarily dangerous to the workers who often sit for hours in a slurry of toxic mud. Among other ailments, exposure to tin can cause skin and tissue irritation, and ingestion nausea, vomiting, diarrhea, abdominal pain, fatigue, and tremors. Long-term exposure can damage the liver and kidneys, and can have long-term neurological effects." Most of the tin is sourced by Indonesia's national tin corporation, PT Timah, which supplies solder manufacturers like Chernan and Shenmao, which in turn supply consumer electronics companies like Sony, LG, and Foxconn. A special *Guardian* investigation titled "Death Metal: Tin Mining in Indonesia" notes, "If you own a mobile, it's probably held together by tin from the Indonesian island of Bangka." Some estimates put the annual death toll related to tin mining operations in Bangka at around several hundred.

Next time you casually swipe through your Facebook feed, try to pause for a moment and think about where the minuscule drops of solder that bind the electric circuitry inside your device are ultimately sourced, and at what human and environmental cost.

THE BASIC RARE EARTH ELEMENTS that are the essential ingredients of our digital devices are at the far end of the supply chain. After they are dug up from the earth and extracted from surrounding waste, they must then be packed up and shipped off to other processing and manufacturing centres, many thousands of miles away. For example, once cobalt is extracted (using child labour in toxic, dangerous mines), it is then routed through a labyrinth of corrupt small-time traders and middle companies (mostly dominated by Chinese firms and entrepreneurs) to coastal ports in Tanzania or South Africa. From there, it is typically shipped off to China, where most of the world's lithium-ion battery manufacturing takes place. Corruption, crime, and violence are endemic across every step of this supply chain, from the DRC village to the coastal ports and all points in between. What happens in one supply chain can be pretty much duplicated numerous times over, from the salt flats of Chile to the tin mines of Indonesia: hundreds of suppliers across dozens of countries undertake routine commercial exchanges with numerous transportation workers and other intermediaries.

Regulating such a vast and complex supply chain is challenging, to say the least. Supply chains of companies like Apple, Samsung, and Intel are difficult to unravel and layered on top of one another, "a complex structure of supply chains within supply chains, a zooming fractal of tens of thousands of suppliers, millions of kilometers of shipped materials and hundreds of thousands of workers included within the process even before the product is assembled on the line." A typical smartphone could have tens of thousands of individual components, sourced from hundreds of different companies, that snake their way through a sprawling network of miners, smelters, traders, shippers, and manufacturers in dozens of different jurisdictions. For example, the Apple A12 chip, designed in Cupertino, California, may be sourced from chip fabrication facilities in Taiwan, operated by a company like TSMC. From there, the chip may be packaged and tested by a company called Amkor, in the Philippines, and from there shipped to the Foxconn assembly plants in China before then being shipped around the world after assembly to wherever the consumers are located. Tracking the individual components of such a supply chain to ensure compliance with labour and environmental safeguards is extremely challenging for even the most well-intentioned company. For example, it reportedly took Intel four years to research its own supply chain well enough to ensure that no tantalum from Congo mines was included in its microprocessors. Between 2009 and 2013, the company undertook site visits to eighty-five smelters and refiners in twenty-one countries. No doubt, not every electronic components manufacturer is or can be as diligent.

Each step of the global electronics supply chain involves various forms of transportation and shipping, which are major contributors to CO_2 emissions worldwide. The container ships that chug across the planet's oceans, lakes, and rivers, circulating the elements, components, and final consumer products that comprise our communications ecosystem, are among the worst environmental offenders. It is estimated that one container ship can produce the same amount of pollution as about fifty million cars, especially sulphur and carbon dioxide. Container ships also pollute the marine environment through release of ballast water, diesel fuel, human waste, and other garbage. Often overlooked are the ways they contribute to sound pollution. Container ships are very loud, and the noise can have deleterious impacts on local and in many cases endangered marine populations, such as whales. Of course, container shipping is not solely used for trade in consumer electronics and other social media–related technology, but it is an inescapable and growing part of it.

Before they hit the market, our gadgets have to be assembled somewhere, usually immense assembly plants where repetitive stress injuries, labour violations, and voluminous toxic effluents are common. Taiwan-based Foxconn, which manufactures the vast majority of the world's iPhones, mostly within large assembly plants in China, has been dogged by persistent labour and environmental issues. In 2011, a massive explosion rocked a Foxconn plant outside of Shanghai; investigators attributed it to built-up noxious dust and other contaminants in the facility. In 2013, investigators discovered that Foxconn and another manufacturer, Unimicron, were dumping heavy metals into the Huangcangjing and Hanputang Rivers. Those two rivers flow into the Yangtze and Huangpu Rivers, which in turn supply

Shanghai (a city of twenty-four million residents) with its drinking water. In some cities where such electronics manufacturing takes place, city officials have suspended manufacturing altogether because of high levels of pollutants in nearby water systems. Although the companies and their clients (like Apple) make promises (and in many instances real efforts) to "green" their manufacturing processes, it's hard to avoid toxic by-products when so many chemicals are involved in the manufacturing. Electronic manufacturing plants use high volumes of chemicals and other substances like cadmium, chromium, copper, zinc, benzene, and others, and draw on enormous volumes of water in the manufacturing process that needs to be cleaned before and after it is used in production.

Alongside environmental stresses are the stresses manufacturing plants impose on workers. Perhaps not surprisingly, given China's chequered labour history, workers at Foxconn and other plants complain of long hours, low pay, few benefits, and repetitive stress and other health-related injuries. A Bloomberg investigation into working conditions at the Catcher Technology Company's factory in China, which makes iPhone casings, found that "some workers had to stand for ten hours a day in a noxious, potentially toxic, environment without proper safety equipment." Another investigation was undertaken by the NGO China Labor Watch, which managed to secretly place several investigators as employees in the Zhengzhou Foxconn factory — the largest iPhone factory in the world. The investigation found that factory employees reported they were "exposed to toxic chemicals every day, but do not receive sufficient personal protective equipment; when they are sick they are still forced to work overtime; managers verbally abuse workers on a regular basis and sometimes punish workers by asking them to stand." The investigation also found that female staff experienced sexual harassment from management while on production lines. Foxconn's Longhua factory is notorious for its suicide nets — installed in response to suicides linked to the reprehensible working conditions. In 2010, in response to reports of worker suicides, Steve Jobs promised to take action. Yet China Labor Watch's investigation eight years later showed working conditions had not improved. Both Foxconn and Apple disputed the majority of these allegations but admitted that they did need to correct some labour violations the investigators observed.

While electronic manufacturing is mostly outsourced to Asia, remnants of the wasteful processing practices survive in areas where the manufacturing has long since shut down. Nathan Ensmenger describes a ten-by-forty-mile strip of land around Santa Clara County, California, containing twenty-three "Superfund" sites — designated as such by the U.S. Environmental Protection Agency (EPA) because of hazardous pollutants requiring a long-term strategy to clean up — contaminated by shuttered semiconductor manufacturing, "including such highly toxic chemicals as trichloroethylene, Freon, and PCBs."

In fact, the manufacturing of digital devices produces far more waste and pollution than consumer-disposed e-waste, which usually garners more attention since it touches most consumers directly. For example, five times more waste (around 16.2 million tonnes) was produced from electronics manufacturing than the volume of e-waste collected from households (3.1 million tonnes) in the European Union in 2014. As much as four times the amount of chemicals that actually end up in our devices is generated as waste in the manufacturing process. The manufacture of flat-panel television and computer displays releases fluorinated greenhouse gases (F-GHGS) into the atmosphere, gases that the EPA says have "extremely high global warming potentials . . . with some persisting in the atmosphere for thousands of years, effectively causing irreversible impacts on the earth's climate system." Geographer Josh Lepawsky, another researcher who has closely studied the topic, says that together with mining, manufacturing processes account for about 95 percent of waste associated with digital technologies. That's 95 percent of waste before we even buy a phone. Says Lepawsky, "No amount of post-consumer recycling can recoup the waste generated before consumers purchase their devices."

WORK-FROM-HOME AND social isolation rules surrounding the COVID crisis prompted a huge increase in demands on the communications ecosystem. Uses of

Zoom, FaceTime, Google Hangouts, Skype, Microsoft Teams, and other means of teleconferencing ballooned as friends and family checked in virtually and office routines migrated into makeshift bedroom and living room offices. In the evenings, citizens around the world flocked to already popular streaming video services like Netflix, or to online games like *Doom* and *World of Warcraft*. Remarkably, the internet appeared to be holding up, in spite of usage surging to as much as 70 percent beyond normal loads. Meanwhile, air traffic, automobile, and other forms of fossil-fuelled transportation plummeted, lessening carbon emissions substantially (though temporarily). But don't be mistaken: the sudden and massive shift to remote networking was not without its own environmental costs.

Nowhere are the contradictions surrounding social media more pronounced than in the difference between how most of us perceive those media and the vast amounts of energy they actually consume. Streaming videos, FaceTime, and other video meet-ups seem almost like magic — insubstantial, weightless, *virtual*. Our digital experiences feel "clean." We don't smell or taste what we consume online (unless we fry our overheated electronics from excessive use).

But they are far from that. The devices, appliances, cell towers, networks, and platforms that make up our communications ecosystem together draw enormous amounts of energy. Just look around your own house and count the number of electronic appliances you plug in. How many of them are always on? Some estimates say Americans waste up to $19 billion annually in electricity costs through "vampire appliances," digital devices that draw power even when they are turned off. Those numbers are set to rise substantially as the Internet of Things rolls out worldwide: fridges, microwaves, home security systems, baby monitors, and more, all pulsating with continuous data streams, networked through our handheld devices. And that is just the beginning. Over half of the world's population is not yet connected to the internet, but that is changing fast.

It's difficult to measure with precision the carbon emissions and overall energy consumption related to our communications ecosystem, but it's fair to say they're large and growing. Prior to the global pandemic, I had seen references to estimates that placed the internet's energy and carbon footprints on a par with, or even exceeding, the airline industry's. One study suggests that the world's communications ecosystem currently consumes approximately 7 percent of global electricity, a number that could increase to as much as 21 percent by 2030. A study by the American Coal Association (strange, I know) estimated that a smartphone streaming an hour of video on a weekly basis uses more power annually than a new refrigerator. Some have tried to break down the energy consumption and carbon emissions by individual digital routines, to make it easier to comprehend. For example, looking at a web page or an image online emits an estimated 0.2 gram of CO_2

per second. One Google search accounts for 0.2 to 7 grams of CO_2 emissions — the latter roughly equivalent to boiling a cup of water with an electric kettle or driving a car fifty-five feet. That's one search. An email has an estimated carbon footprint of about four grams of CO_2 emissions, an email with a large attachment as much as fifty. Sending sixty-five emails is roughly equivalent to driving one kilometre in a car. Overall, the world's email usage generates roughly as much CO_2 as having an extra seven million cars on the roads. (I routinely send and receive dozens of emails a day.) A major study by a team of researchers at Canada's McMaster University found that the biggest contributions to carbon emissions are likely going to come from the explosion in smartphone usage, although the largest culprits right now are still data centres (45 percent of the total information and communications technology carbon footprint), followed by communications networks (24 percent).

Probably the most perverse example of energy consumption and waste related to digital technologies comes from the digital currency market: Bitcoin. A Bitcoin is a virtual commodity that exists only as binary digits in a distributed digital ledger called a blockchain. Unlike paper bills or coins, Bitcoins have no physical quality. And unlike the credit card issued by your bank, the currency is entirely decentralized, without any intermediaries. New Bitcoin currency is generated by a "mining" process that entails solving complex mathematical problems, which in turn require the use of vast and energy-intensive computing resources to solve. As Ensmenger puts it, "From Bitcoin 'mines' to server 'farms' to data 'warehouses,' the places and processes that are used to produce virtual commodities look surprisingly similar to those found in more traditional forms of industrial manufacturing." Ensmenger estimates that the Bitcoin network entails more computing power—"by several orders of magnitude"—than "all of the top 500 supercomputers in the world combined." For this reason, major Bitcoin mining operations tend to be located at the nexus between cloud computing facilities, nuclear power plants, and electrical grids. Many of them are located in countries where energy comes from coal-fired sources, like China. Central Asian countries like Uzbekistan and Kazakhstan have even gone so far as to advertise for Bitcoin mining operations to be hosted in their jurisdictions because of cheap and plentiful coal and other fossil-fuelled energy sources. Some estimates put electric energy consumption associated with Bitcoin mining at around 83.67 terawatt-hours per year, more than that of the entire country of Finland, with carbon emissions estimated at 33.82 megatons, roughly equivalent to those of Denmark. To put it another way, the Cambridge Centre for Alternative Finance says that the electricity consumed by the Bitcoin network in one year could power all the teakettles used to boil water in the entire United Kingdom for nineteen years.

A similar energy-sucking dynamic underlies other cutting-edge technologies, like "deep learning."

The latter refers to the complex artificial intelligence systems used to undertake the fine-grained, real-time calculations associated with the range of social media experiences, such as computer vision, speech recognition, natural language processing, audio recognition, social network filtering, and so on. Research undertaken at the University of Massachusetts, Amherst, in which the researchers performed a life-cycle assessment for training several common large AI models, found that training a single AI model can emit more than 626,000 pounds of carbon dioxide equivalent — or nearly five times the lifetime emissions of the average American car (including its manufacturing). It's become common to hear that "data is the new oil," usually meaning that it is a valuable resource. Studies like these give the analogy an entirely different and disturbing connotation.

While we are on the topic of analogies and metaphors, there is none more misleading than the omnipresent "cloud." While "the cloud" brings to mind something intangible and unsubstantial, it is precisely the opposite when it comes to the data infrastructure that underpins our communications ecosystem. "Black boxes" of their own sort, cloud computing facilities are typically housed in large buildings or repurposed warehouses, fenced off with security perimeters, guarded by private security, CCTVs, and other access controls similar to what one would find in a restricted government building. In the words of the University of Calgary's Mél Hogan, data centres are "hidden monuments" to our excessive data consumption. Having visited quite a few over the years, I've always thought the description "server farm" is a more apt metaphor than "the cloud" for what goes on inside those computing facilities. Server farms are characterized by rows upon rows of stacks of servers connected by fibre optic, ethernet and other cables and continuously drawing power and water in order to run and keep the facilities from overheating, like a technological doppelgänger of industrial livestock production. As with the latter, server farms pose health risks and contribute to environmental degradation. And as with industrial farming, their operations are largely concealed from consumers, who might not otherwise stomach what they see taking place in what one author appropriately called "energy hogs." Some experts believe that energy consumption by data centres will treble in the next decade and become unsustainable at current levels. Social media, streaming video services, cloud-based computer processing, and even email are all now inextricably linked to server farms. Prior to the COVID emergency, streaming media, and in particularly video, consumed massive amounts of bandwidth. Netflix and YouTube made up as much as 50 percent of internet traffic on a typical day in North America, and likely vastly more when individuals retreated into home isolation.

Server farms, co-location centres, cloud computing facilities — whatever language we use to describe them — are important chokepoints in the communications ecosystem, and are essential to the functioning of social media. While the internet may be spread around the world, many server farms are concentrated in industrial parks close to high-volume urban customers in order to reduce latency. For example, as much as 70 percent of the entire world's internet traffic passes through data centres housed in a single county in Virginia known by the nickname "data centre alley" (located there so as to be proximate to data-hungry U.S. defence, intelligence, and military agencies, and their various contractors). The electricity demand of data center alley is estimated to be about 4.5 gigawatts, "or roughly the same power output as nine large (500-megawatt) coal power plants." The local energy utility that serves the region, Dominion Energy, not only has one of the lowest percentages of renewable electricity in the United States, it is actually investing in more fossil fuel–based infrastructure projects, such as the $7 billion Atlantic Coast Pipeline.

Server farms not only consume enormous energy, they require huge volumes of water to keep their processes cool. Ensmenger estimates that a medium-sized high-density server farm can require as much as 360,000 gallons of clean, chilled water a day. According to a 2015 *Wall Street Journal* study, a mid-sized data centre uses roughly as much water as about one hundred acres of almond trees, three average hospitals, or more than two eighteen-hole golf courses. The U.S. Department of Energy's Lawrence Berkeley National Laboratory estimates that U.S. server farms will have used 174 billion gallons of water by 2020. Sometimes server farms are located in regions where access to clean water is challenging at the best of times, straining resources for local communities. Desperate for the employment that construction and labour might bring, these communities make deals with the platforms that guarantee access to scarce local water supplies. For example, in 2019 Mesa, Arizona, made a deal with Google to permit construction of a massive server farm that would guarantee up to four million gallons for cooling purposes. While Google has made significant public strides to "green" its server farms and other processes, the company considers its water use a proprietary trade secret and typically forbids public officials from disclosing its water consumption.

Greenpeace has closely studied the environmental consequences of cloud computing, and in 2017 they published an extensive ranking of social media platforms on the basis of their environmental sustainability efforts. Many companies, including Google (notwithstanding its water consumption), Facebook, and Microsoft have made significant improvements in recent years, either offsetting or directly powering their operations with 100 percent clean energy, and investing in server farms in areas like Iceland, where there is plentiful access to cool water and low temperatures.

However, many technology companies are doing very poorly, and they seem reluctant to take measures to reduce their energy consumption and other environmentally impacting practices, or to become more transparent in that regard. Among the worst is Amazon, whose cloud-based business, Amazon Web Services (AWS), makes up a sizable and growing proportion of its revenue. (AWS alone brings in more revenue than McDonald's.) Amazon also runs one of the largest warehouse, transportation, distribution, and logistical operations in the world, including dozens of its own cargo aircraft. Worldwide, Amazon owns 850 facilities in twenty-two countries, occupying 220 million square feet, making it the embodiment of globalization in a single corporation. However, it is also almost completely non-transparent about its energy footprint. Among cloud providers, only AWS refuses to disclose full details on its energy and environmental impacts. "Despite Amazon's public commitment to renewable energy, the world's largest cloud computing company is hoping no one will notice that it's still powering its corner of the internet with dirty energy," said Greenpeace USA senior corporate campaigner Elizabeth Jardim. Another poor performer is Netflix, to whom Greenpeace's 2017 study gave a grade of D, mostly because Netflix's services are so dependent on Amazon's. "Unlike other major video streaming platforms such as Apple, Facebook, or Google, Netflix does not regularly provide energy consumption data, greenhouse gas emissions, or the actual energy mix of its global operations," explained Greenpeace. "The reality is that Netflix's rapid growth is increasing demand for coal and other dirty sources of energy that are a threat to human health and the climate."

Disturbingly, the companies located in countries and

regions in which internet and social media growth is the fastest are also among the worst environmental offenders. Greenpeace gave China's tech giant Alibaba a D and Tencent a miserable F. Sixty-seven percent of Tencent's energy comes from coal power. It is also ranked as one of the least transparent companies when it comes to energy and sustainability. No information is available about its electricity use or CO_2 targets. It's a good bet that both Alibaba and Tencent make use of the world's largest server farm, which is the 6.3-million-square-foot Range International Information Hub, located outside Tianjin in northeast China. The Hub is estimated to emit more than one thousand grams of CO_2 for every kilowatt-hour of energy consumed.

Even more concerning from an environmental perspective is that many cloud computing companies are actually seeking out revenues from fossil fuel industries. Oil and gas giants like Chevron, ExxonMobil, Total, and Equinor have signed billion-dollar contracts with Google, Microsoft, and others for their cloud computing and artificial intelligence services. Environmental advocates speculate that one of the reasons Amazon may be backing away from its commitments to renewables is the market opportunities it sees in the oil and gas sectors. It has reportedly "aggressively courted" the fossil fuel industry, signing contracts with BP, Shell, and Halliburton to provide machine learning services to enhance exploration and oilfield automation and help create what its marketing arms call the "oil fields of the future"—proposing to archive the data, without apparent irony, on its "Amazon Glacier" file storage system.

WHILE IN DELHI, I SPEND several days following what I think of as the long, hidden tail at the far end of the supply chain: what happens to electronic equipment after it is no longer working. I meet up with Nilanjan Chowdhury, a senior producer in India's Al Jazeera office and someone who has covered the topic locally. Our first stop is a shopping area near his offices in Delhi's Nehru Place neighbourhood, which I can only describe as a kind of *Blade Runner*–style street bazaar. Crowds filter through a seemingly endless number of small shops and electronics stalls. There are people selling only pirated printer cartridges or motherboards. Others, nothing but replacement glass screens for damaged smartphones. Here and there are makeshift stands selling discounted SIM cards. There are dozens of repair shops lined up next to each other—each seemingly with its own specialty. It's loud and just a notch below chaotic: shop owners barter with customers, mobile phones cradled between the shoulder and the ear, another two or three splayed out on the counter. In between are stalls hawking knock-off jewellery, jeans, T-shirts, and cheap plastic toys and other consumer products, all imported from China. In the back alleys of the strip mall are vans being loaded with stacks of hard drives, desktop computer casings, printers and printer cartridges, motherboards, monitors, and just about every possible electronic component imaginable. India is currently the world's second-largest smartphone market, and what I see in Nehru Place certainly testifies to that statistic. I don't think I've ever seen as many variations of mobile devices and their various plastic components and accessories in one place as I do here. This district is a way station of sorts, a kind of technological halfway house interposed between consumers and India's semi-regulated reuse, repair, and remanufacturing sector. From here, we make our way by car to Seelampur in northeast Delhi, the next and final step in the long tail at the end of the supply chain.

According to the 2018 Global E-waste Monitor report, India generates about two million tonnes of e-waste annually and ranks fifth among e-waste producing countries, after the U.S., China, Japan, and Germany. It recycles less than 2 percent of the total e-waste it produces annually. But that doesn't mean it doesn't try. In recent years, Indian authorities have introduced laws and measures to try to standardize the industry around officially licensed recycling operations. However, most of India's recycling and processing — as much as 95 percent of it — is still managed by the informal sector and the so-called "unskilled" labour force. An estimated one million people are involved in and depend for their livelihood on these manual recycling operations, which have been in place and part of extended families' line of work for years. The district of Old Seelampur in Delhi is the capital city of it all.

To describe what I see in Old Seelampur as something "informal" and "unskilled" would give the wrong impression. What I witness is in fact highly organized, segmented, and specialized — albeit in what amount to septic conditions. It is here that the trucks from markets like Nehru Place reach their final destination. Anything that can't be repaired in a reuse and remanufacturing centre like Nehru Place is shipped here to be cannibalized down to its most basic elements. Seemingly endless alleys are divided into nearly identical-sized stalls, one after the other, each containing labourers specializing in their respective niche. I feel like I'm in one big open-air morgue, but for electronic instead of human corpses.

There are many misconceptions about recycling and waste that I confront while in Delhi, including my own. Media coverage of e-waste brings to mind vast dumps of discarded computer monitors and motherboards being shipped from the affluent North to the impoverished global South. The reality is much more nuanced. While some e-waste is traded and shipped internationally between North and South, a sizable proportion of e-waste trade is actually highly regionalized, and more e-waste is actually sent from developing countries to developed countries, rather than vice versa. As Josh Lepawsky says, "There is definitely a topography to the e-waste trade, it's just that the hills and valleys don't match up to the overly blunt imaginaries of world geography that divide the planet up into North and South, developed and developing, or corollaries like OECD and non-OECD." Within a country like India, which like most countries is characterized by massive and growing income inequality, the e-waste flows mostly inside the country and down the hills of wealth, from the rising middle class and a small number of elites, through the repair shops and recycling bazaars of Nehru Place, and finally, as a last resort, to the digital morgues of Old Seelampur.

Then there is the issue of e-waste itself. What I see first-hand in Delhi is an extraordinary supply chain of a different sort. "Not a single screw goes to waste," says Chowdhury as we pass by the Old Seelampur stalls. Every single stall has a different specialty in this predominantly Muslim district. (A few months after my visit, this district would become the epicentre of the aforementioned Delhi Riots, in which Hindu mobs indiscriminately attacked Muslims, some of whom then retaliated with violence of their own. Chowdhury would describe these to me as "the worst communal riots that the city has ever seen.") I pass by a man squatting in front of his stall on a mat, a large pile of small circuit boards spread out in front of him. Behind him are piles of what look to be the insides of discarded cellphones. He sits patiently with a screwdriver, carefully removing tiny components and then placing each component in neatly separated piles to his right. Buyers and sellers roam the mud-filled streets; giant plastic bags are flung over the shoulders of transporters moving parts from one stall to another, where a different stripping process is performed by another family, as meticulous in its own way as the last.

While India's reuse economy is truly remarkable, that doesn't mean that there are no waste or other issues. The open sewers I tread gingerly around are the first clue. It's disconcerting to see that among the stalls are many small children and young adolescents pulling apart end-of-life electronic equipment, putting the left-over materials through acid washes, and burning circuit boards in the hopes of extracting precious metals like gold and silver, all with bare hands and without any protective equipment. Toxic waste is routinely dumped into open drains, which in turn leaches into the water table. Adding to the squalor, Old Seelampur is on a low-lying plain that is highly susceptible to annual flooding. Raw sewage combined with acid wash from the e-waste dismantling processes flows directly into the Yamuna River, its shores clogged with the largest accumulation of discarded plastic water bottles I've ever seen in my life.

Putting aside the squalor and demoralizing child labour, there are many things to be learned from the Seelampur recycling district. For far too long, we have lived in a culture of disposable wealth and planned obsolescence. We have become accustomed to a regular turnover of our consumer electronics, and we don't give much thought to them once they no longer work. To be sure, some great strides have been made in recycling. Instead of simply discarding things, many of us now neatly separate our plastics, glass, paper products, and batteries and place them in blue bins. Companies have pledged to do better, thanks to pressure campaigns by environmental NGOs. For example, Apple has set a goal for itself to use 100 percent recycled components in the manufacturing of its iPhone and other consumer-level electronics. It has developed robots that can strip discarded iPhones for their material elements. The company now uses 100 percent recycled tin in the logic boards of its new iPhones.

But as stated before, Apple also strictly forbids and actively works against home repairs, and has come under fire for artificially slowing down and degrading battery management features on older devices, presumably to encourage upgrades. Put simply, it is more profitable for companies like Apple to make products that are designed to die than it is to make products that last. Apple churns out a bewildering variety of new components and accessories, typically made of and packaged in plastic (itself manufactured from petrochemicals) and impossible to either recycle or repair. Take AirPods—Apple's Bluetooth-enabled headphones. AirPods are powered by tiny lithium-ion batteries that work for about eighteen months but gradually start losing effectiveness after about a year. Because they are glued together, they can't easily be repaired either. They just get discarded.

Apple's contradictions are, in fact, our own. We live in a world of endless hyper-consumption and give little thought to the externalities produced by it all, from the energy-intensive and highly polluting mining and manufacturing to the energy that is required to power it all, and finally to all the waste that is squeezed out the other end. It's also good to remind ourselves that even highly efficient recycling is an energy-intensive industrial process. Stripping down discarded electronics to the valuable bits of copper, gold, cobalt, and other elements can entail a lot of machinery and labour, draw enormous energy, and produce huge volumes of waste. Jim Lynch, a recycling expert at the U.S.-based non-profit TechSoup Global, says adding extra life to computers saves between five and twenty times more energy than recycling them outright. To be sure, the philosophy of "not a screw going wasted" is one that could be helpfully duplicated the world over, and used as a way to claw back some control over the platforms and companies that actively lobby against the right to repair, reuse, and remanufacture. But that's still just treating one symptom of a much bigger underlying disease.

THE COVID-19 PANDEMIC reminded us in a brutal way that we are intimately and inescapably tied to nature. Most of us are now familiar with the term "Anthropocene," which refers to the human impacts on the natural environment — now reaching the point of existential risk because of the climate crisis. Some scientists have studied how climate change may impact the internet and social media. One study warns that rising sea levels risk flooding critical infrastructure located in coastal areas. Says the author of the study, Alejandra Borunda, "We find that 4,067 miles of fiber conduit will be under water and 1,101 nodes (e.g., points of presence and colocation centers) will be surrounded by water in the next 15 years." Meanwhile, a different article points to the risk of high temperatures overheating data centres, leading to the type of "meltdowns" some ISPs experienced in Australia, where 112-degree-Fahrenheit temperatures caused system blackouts. So, depending on your source, the internet is at risk of either flooding or burning up, or both.

At the same time, "virtual work," telecommuting, and remote networking have all been touted as ways to help resolve sustainability issues and lessen the impacts on the environment of fossil-fuelled power modes of transportation, like airplanes, buses, and automobiles. The COVID-19 pandemic accelerated moves in this direction, possibly demonstrating their effectiveness and convenience. But as it stands now, a huge uptake on "virtual" resources, without compensating factors to improve sustainability and reduce fossil-fuelled power consumption and electronic waste, will simply shove the problems into the background while increasing the burdens on the planet's support systems.

Unfortunately, the culture of social media largely obscures these problems and masks its own, very serious contributions to the climate crisis. We have for too long lived in a virtual hallucination. The early promotion of the "wired society" trumpeted a lot that we now know was naive, such as the assumption that the internet and other technologies would democratize societies and eliminate power hierarchies. That turned out to be flat wrong. But there have also been long-standing myths about how digital technologies are "weightless" and "atoms would be replaced by bits." The grimy, exhaust-filled industrial era would be overtaken by digital technologies that are clean, infinitely reusable, and virtual. We don't *see* the exhaust when we send that email, because it's out of sight and out of mind. As Ensmenger puts it, "For the most part, we experience only the positive benefits of information technology, in large part because the labor and geography associated with the construction, maintenance, and dismantling of our digital devices has been rendered largely invisible."

That device you hold in your hand is but a tiny manifestation of a vast and extended global supply chain, and the culmination of numerous labour-intensive, highly industrialized, energy-intensive, and environmentally damaging processes spread around the world. Each time you swipe, text, or search, in your own small way you are contributing to a planet-wide syndrome that risks our very survival as a species.

FIVE

RETREAT, REFORM, RESTRAINT

DECEMBER 2018. BAHR ABDUL RAZZAK, a Syrian immigrant who works as a Citizen Lab security researcher, received a LinkedIn message from a man who called himself Gary Bowman and described himself as a South African financial technology executive based in Madrid. The man explained he was interested in meeting Abdul Razzak to discuss an initiative to assist refugees in Europe. Abdul Razzak agreed, and Bowman arranged a meeting at Toronto's swank Shangri-La Hotel.

Fortunately, Abdul Razzak sensed something was awry as soon as they met and began to chat. Bowman's questions shifted at once from financial support for refugees to the Citizen Lab and our research on Israel-based spyware firm NSO Group. *Why do you write only about NSO? Do you write about it because it's an Israeli company? Do you hate Israel?* As Bowman spoke, he discreetly steered a mobile device he had placed on the table in

Abdul Razzak's direction. *Well, this is certainly suspicious,* Abdul Razzak thought to himself.

As soon as the meeting was over, Abdul Razzak returned to the Citizen Lab and notified us about the strange encounter. A preliminary investigation of Bowman's business card and email address made it clear to us that the representations being made to Abdul Razzak were false. The Madrid-based company that Bowman supposedly worked for, called FlameTech, had no web presence beyond a LinkedIn page and a few thinly populated social media profiles. Reverse image searches of the personnel's profile pictures showed they were stock photographs. A physical check of the building address listed for the company's office showed no such business there. It became quickly apparent that Bowman's identity had been manufactured for the specific purpose of targeting Abdul Razzak directly and deceiving him. We concluded that this was part of a malicious effort intended to gather information about the Citizen Lab and our staff, and we started thoroughly investigating Bowman's fraudulent credentials.

As we conducted our investigation, a second, separate outreach using a different cover identity (this time "Michel Lambert," presenting himself as a director of the fictitious Paris-based agricultural technology firm CPW-Consulting) targeted another Citizen Lab senior researcher, John Scott-Railton. This time we allowed the deceptive approach to play out. Scott-Railton flew to New York in order to be in a jurisdiction in which it is legally permissible to record one end of a telephone call without the consent of the other party. He recorded hours of telephone conversations in which Lambert feigned interest in a high-altitude, kite-based photography system that Scott-Railton had devised as part of his doctoral field research on land management and climate change issues in West Africa. Inevitably, Lambert proposed an in-person meeting, which took place on January 24, 2019, in Manhattan, over lunch at a five-star restaurant.

The lunch was a spy-vs.-spy affair. "It was like we were both playing Columbo to each other," said Scott-Railton. We assumed Lambert would attempt to clandestinely record the conversation, and sure enough he brought a large pen with him that he placed awkwardly in the middle of the table; Scott-Railton spotted a tiny camera lens peeking out from an opening in the top. "Is there a big competition between the people inside Citizen Lab?" Lambert asked Scott-Railton, positioning the pen closer. "Work drama? Tell me, I like drama!" Meanwhile, Scott-Railton had equipped himself with his own recording equipment — several devices hidden in his suit pockets. We had also invited Associated Press's Raphael Satter and his colleagues to observe the meeting from afar, and they intervened at Scott-Railton's signal (just after the crème brûlée arrived) to question Lambert about his fictitious company and true employer. Lambert was stunned. He fumbled for his papers and bag, tried to shield his face from the cameras, and knocked over a chair while beating a hasty retreat.

The ensuing AP story was a bombshell, with the face of the operative splashed all over the world, his cover now blown. Thanks to our sting operation, "Michel Lambert" was outed as former Israeli intelligence officer Aharon Almog-Assouline, now working for the Israel-based private intelligence firm Black Cube. Black Cube — which is staffed primarily by veterans of Israel's elite spy agency, Mossad — specializes in intelligence gathering for a range of dubious clients, and it is known for surreptitiously recording targets to construct incriminating evidence for use in legal proceedings or even blackmail. (At the same time we were organizing our sting, journalist Ronan Farrow was also tracking Black Cube operatives hired by convicted rapist and former Hollywood mogul Harvey Weinstein. Farrow heard from a source that they were on our tail too, as detailed in his book *Catch and Kill*.) Although NSO denied hiring Black Cube, the timing (NSO was facing multiple lawsuits because of our research) and the questions Black Cube operatives raised about our motivations for doing the research made it seem obvious they were involved in some manner.

Although we came out of the episode safely, the experience was frightening. We assumed it wouldn't be the last such incident, either. Months later, several credible sources warned us that Black Cube operatives had resumed their malfeasance against us, but we had no specific details. While we were accustomed to being proactive about digital security measures, this type of *physical* threat was unnerving. It created a new and more disturbing type of risk. Travelling now meant more than proactively securing our laptops and devices; it meant looking over our shoulders, not disclosing our hotels or other locations when abroad, and generally feeling very paranoid of strangers passing by or getting into the same elevators as us. We were forced to ramp up physical access controls to the Citizen Lab's space, and we became leery of any unannounced visit. It was as if we were becoming one of the very targets we had been studying.

The entire episode seemed like a microcosm of the disturbing worldwide descent into unhinged despotism we had been tracking. That a public interest research group at Canada's top university could be targeted by a private intelligence agency made up of veterans of one of the world's most elite espionage forces, looking to dig up dirt and undermine our credibility (and who knows what else), is sinister and dastardly. And yet the Black Cube operation passed without so much as a mention by Canadian authorities, let alone what we thought would have been appropriate: a strong public condemnation and a criminal investigation. We felt hung out to dry by our own government.

If an organization such as ours — whose mission is to undertake evidence-based research on threats to human rights and to the security and openness of global communications — can be targeted with such impunity, then is nothing out of bounds? Is this really the type of world in which we now live? One in which groups, like the Citizen Lab, that seek to hold powerful actors to account are harassed into submission? One in which journalists, lawyers, and human rights defenders routinely have their phones hacked by elite spy agencies? One in which autocrats like Mohammed bin Salman murder critics and journalists with impunity?

Or will it become one where we effectively marshal our will and resources to push back against the unaccountable exercise of power? Will it be one in which the very devices we hold in our hands help enrich, rather than belittle and even endanger our lives? Will the communications technologies that surround us support, rather than diminish, human liberty, security, and sustainability?

The choice is ours to make.

THERE IS AN UNDENIABLE GESTALT in the air, a dawning recognition that something of our own making is contributing to a serious kind of social and political sickness. "Our very tools and techniques threaten to wipe us out," says Siva Vaidhyanathan in *Antisocial Media*. "We display unlimited talents but no mastery. We process infinite data but display no wisdom." It's remarkable to think that it was only a few short decades ago that the internet was heralded as a wonderful new tool that would enlighten and liberate us, dissolve the boundaries of time and space, and tie us together more closely into a single global village. But in the span of a single generation, it has transmogrified into something far more complex and disturbing, its effects suddenly very ominous. What started out as something so simple as desktop PCs networked together via a common protocol has morphed into an always-on, omnipresent data vacuum-cleaning operation undertaken by gigantic corporate platforms with unparalleled abilities to peer inside our minds and habits and subtly shape our choices. Their operations implicate a planet-wide network of gigantic, energy-sucking data farms. The companies trumpet their powerful machine learning and artificial intelligence systems, but their enterprises are "actually held together by tens of millions of anonymous workers tucked away in warehouses, data centres, content-moderation mills, electronic sweatshops, [and] lithium mines . . . where they are left unprotected from disease and hyper-exploitation," as author Naomi Klein so aptly summarized.

The ecosystem has spawned a bewildering variety of invasive species that thrive by feeding on the continuously expanding pools of data that spew forth each millisecond of every day: app developers, data brokers, location trackers, data fusion companies, artificial intelligence start-ups, and private intelligence firms. Accountability is weak and insecurity is endemic throughout the entire system, creating seemingly endless opportunities for malevolent exploitation by spies, kleptocrats, dark PR firms, and other bad actors. It's as if we have sleepwalked into a new machine-based civilization of our own making, and we are just now waking up to its unforeseen consequences and existential risks. Listen to just about any tech podcast these days and these themes are unavoidable (notwithstanding the irony).

Like our podcast on how social media spells the end of civilization as we know it? Spread the word, hit "like" and "subscribe"!

I can't count how many times I have given a public lecture and someone has come up to me afterwards and said they were going to throw their phone in the ocean and never use social media again. Later I'll see the same person swiping or texting as they walk out of the auditorium, slightly sheepish but no less attached to their device.

Let's face it, I'm not immune either. Almost every morning, my wife and I have our first coffee in bed. And although we acknowledge that we should not reach for our devices, that we should enjoy each other's company and just "chit-chat," an awkward silence eventually descends. The unmistakable trance of individuals together yet apart, engrossed in their respective digital silos. Two people in the early morning not talking to each other, glued to our screens, swiping through an avalanche of news, humour, crises, and tragedies, all before we get out of our bed. "We shouldn't be doing this," we say to each other, tossing the devices on our bedside tables in frustration. Then, gradually, inevitably, without fail, we reach for them again, our precious phones.

IT IS CLEAR THERE IS A GROWING consensus that many things are wrong with our social media habits. Symptoms of this malaise are seemingly everywhere, fairly easy to identify, and increasingly enumerated by scientific studies. But what to do about them is less obvious; there is nowhere near a consensus when it comes to a cure.

This lack of a clarity around solutions is certainly understandable. The challenges thrown up by social media, surveillance capitalism, and near-total state surveillance have arisen so swiftly that we have barely had time to understand how they work, let alone fix them. So much of the important stuff happens in the background, behind the scenes, making it challenging to know what's going on. Adding to the mix is the daily flood of information, which leaves little space and time to step back from the swarm of current events and reflect on their larger significance. Social media are biased against the very type of reasoned contemplation we need to perform in order to repair them. Moreover, the challenges are not only novel but also constantly changing. We are not now nor have we ever been in a fully formed kind of "stasis" long enough to be able to properly evaluate the media landscape and take concerted action. How can you pin down a continuously evolving target? As soon as we figure out what to do about one problem, a new one seemingly arises. Exhaustion and paralysis set in. Like all of the existential crises that surround us, it may be part of human nature that, when faced with an emergency, we freeze, or at least get overwhelmed by the apparent futility of trying to figure out how to change it all. Like the climate crisis, it may seem so overwhelming that we throw up our hands in frustration and resign.

But of course it's not all just ennui and fatalistic acquiescence in the face of social media's harms. Proposals for mitigation or alternatives to social media as currently constituted are frequently raised and plentiful. Some are quite interesting and worth considering. Others may be flawed in various ways, or self-serving. Many that are worthwhile are incomplete. Many of them feel like fragments of a missing whole of which they might be a part.

Take the family of recommendations to mitigate social media harm that I call "retreat." These are the solutions that advocate for some variation of going "off the grid," either by throwing out our devices and applications completely and going back to a time before social media, or (in slightly more reasonable form) simply taking a break from them once in a while. Proposals such as these can be found in pleas to "unplug," "disconnect," or perform periodic cleanses — "digital detoxification," as it's widely described. Probably the most well-known variation of retreat is the #DeleteFacebook campaign, which started as a viral protest against that particular company's data surveillance practices but has become a rallying cry for rejection of surveillance capitalism as a whole. The hashtag trends every time Zuckerberg says something outrageous or some new Facebook-related privacy scandal is uncovered (trending, ironically, on social media themselves).

As they have throughout modern history, communes have sprouted up where social media are either banned or strongly discouraged. There are even literal "retreats"— New Age resorts that prohibit devices on their premises and offer clients expensive blends of yoga, mindfulness, and deep meditation in their place. At London's Floatworks, for example, visitors are immersed in sensory deprivation tanks as a way to reduce stress and anxiety (it helps that electronic devices and saltwater tanks don't mix well). At the luxurious Grand Velas Riviera Nayarit in Mexico, guests who opt in to the digital detox program are met by a concierge who "cleanses" their suite "by removing the flat screen television from the room, replacing it with classic board games and then whisking away their personal electronic devices . . . to a safe."

A growing number of self-help books advocate for some variation of digital retreat. Cal Newport's book *Digital Minimalism* suggests users follow his guidelines for a thirty-day "digital declutter" process, followed by a conservative approach to the use of social media that includes regular, lengthy periods of solitude. Recognizing the growing demand arising out of the retreat movement, social media platforms have even begun to build in tools and techniques to assist in the digital cleanse. Apple's Screen Time feature gives warnings to those who use an application beyond an allotted period of time, as does an Android app called Digital Wellbeing. These don't go far enough for virtual reality pioneer Jaron Lanier, whose book *Ten Arguments for Deleting your Social Media Accounts Right Now* refers to all social media by the acronym "BUMMER," which stands for "Behaviors of Users Modified, and Made into an Empire for Rent." His recommendation is to just dump them all.

At the heart of these recommendations to retreat is a familiar kind of romanticism, a plea for going "back to nature" that has a long pedigree, stretching back at least to the eighteenth-century philosopher Jean-Jacques Rousseau, and echoed in criticism of popular entertainment and mass consumer culture going back decades, as in Bill McKibben's *The Age of Missing Information,* written largely in response to television, or Lewis Mumford's *The Pentagon of Power,* which advocates for a return to a Da Vinci–inspired arts and crafts communitarianism. The concept of a digital retreat is appealing on many levels. There is a simplicity to it that makes it alluring. It is true that one thing we need to recover is our connection to the natural world. Slowing down is a good idea too.

But there's a major problem so obvious that it may be easy to overlook. Sure, it's fine if a few isolated communities completely detach, unplug, and retreat. And there's no doubt we could all use a little digital detox once in a while. Meditation is great too (and best done without an app). But can it scale? What if everyone quite literally *unplugged*? How would we then manage ourselves, our social relationships, our problems, and our politics? How would we address, to borrow a phrase from John Dewey, "the public and its problems" if the "public" had no means to exchange information and communicate? And if the global pandemic showed us anything, it is that the "public" is now truly planetary in scope and scale. Thanks to hundreds of years of modern industrial technological development, we now live in a "global village" (to borrow McLuhan's phrasing). There's no turning back. Complex interdependence binds us together in a single habitat that systems theorist and futurist Buckminster Fuller once aptly called "Spaceship Earth." We're in this together, for better or for worse.

Detachment and retreat also ignore or at least slight the many positive uses of digital technologies, social media included. In spite of disinformation and overreaching surveillance, social media have proven highly useful for many problems. They have helped families, communities, and co-workers connect during the COVID crisis. Data on population movements (properly anonymized and secured to prevent abuse, that is) have no doubt been essential to documenting the pandemic's spread and will assist us in our decisions about where to concentrate precious resources. It now seems quite clear that had China not taken steps to systematically suppress information about the virus outbreak, mitigation could have happened far more rapidly and effectively. Dr. Li and his colleagues were right to use WeChat to raise alarms; the Chinese government was wrong to suppress them.

Our networked devices can function like a collective nerve system, which could allow us to share information about hotspots, large gatherings of people violating quarantines, or sudden mass migrations that will require emergency measures in response, all the while informing ourselves and keeping us connected (and, yes, even suitably distracted).

Even prior to the COVID-19 pandemic, digital technologies were used extensively to monitor the environment; to share information in ways that the original designers intended (think of Wikipedia); to mobilize social movements and hold bad actors to account; to lift the lid on corrupt and despotic leaders in the way the Citizen Lab, the Electronic Frontier Foundation, Amnesty International, R3D, Derechos Digitales, AccessNow, Bellingcat, Privacy International, and other civic watchdogs do. If we all unplugged completely, we would be left without these benign uses of information and communications technologies. Throwing away the technology is not a viable solution for humanity as a whole; we need to find alternative ways to organize our communications environment instead. That's not to say that a break is not useful — it's essential, in fact. It's just that we can't all go back to another time and still hope to build a sustainable future together on this single planet.

Furthermore, it is frankly impossible to live in complete detachment from social media today. Even the self-isolation and social distancing in response to the COVID emergency did not dissolve digital connections among people — in fact, it deepened our reliance on them. Even if you were to try and completely escape from social media, unplug your router, throw away all your devices, and never look at social media again, you'd still be subject to surveillance. Facebook and other social media have "shadow profiles" of people who do not even use their services. CCTV cameras are everywhere. Go ahead, live the dream and move to rural Montana; you'd still be watched by drones, planes, and satellites. No matter where you go, you will be counted.

Digital technologies have so deeply embedded themselves into everything we do, it is unrealistic to expect that we can turn the clock back entirely. Nor should we. We need an open and secure means of communicating globally in order to manage our planet and our collective affairs. It is just that the current design for it, based around personal data surveillance, is counterproductive to those aims. Outright rejection of social media is thus both undesirable and futile. Harkening back to Buckminster Fuller, we do indeed live in Spaceship Earth, but we are stuck with a poorly designed operating manual.

THEN THERE ARE THE PROPOSALS that advocate for some variation of "reform" — that is, adjustments to one or another element of social media's business practices. Reform proposals range along a spectrum from minor to major adjustments and lesser to greater degrees of formal government intervention. The intent is not to dismantle social media, but to fine-tune them instead.

For example, corporate social responsibility, ethical design, and other such initiatives typically involve the least intrusive measures and entail only minor fixes to superficial elements of social media. These initiatives typically advocate for norms rather than laws, persuasion rather than coercion. The goal is to have business executives acknowledge certain principles and govern their business practices accordingly, but without any kind of specific enforcement mechanism to hold them to their promises.

It's easy to be cynical and dismiss corporate social responsibility principles as futile, especially when companies so often and flagrantly abuse them. Facebook's Mark Zuckerberg has repeatedly made promises to be more responsible and protect users' privacy (usually in response to some scandal). *We hear you, and understand we need to do better.* He's even advocated for certain types of regulation, which he says the company would welcome. You'd be naive to think these statements are not calculated to ward off what Facebook considers to be undesirable laws, and to channel regulation in directions that benefit Facebook. Facebook has even gone so far as to set up what it calls a "Supreme Court" — a panel of forty independent experts to adjudicate a small selection of controversial content-removal cases. Although strictly speaking the panel is neither "supreme" nor a "court" (Facebook refers cases to the board, whose decisions are binding but not enforced by law), it is a modest step in the direction of greater public accountability. Regardless of any particular CEO's sincerity, however, there is a hard limit to reforms associated with this type of corporate self-governance. However much the promises made by the companies to better protect privacy or police their networks may be genuine, the effects will be questionable as long as the core business imperative to collect it all, all the time, remains unchanged. As long as social media are propelled forward under the regime of surveillance capitalism, pledges to "do better" to protect privacy will remain little more than window dressing — a coat of paint to make their platforms more appealing, and ultimately draw more consumers into their fold.

Many have proposed fact-checking as a way to ameliorate the excesses of social media and a corrective to the spread of online disinformation. According to some estimates, there are as many as 188 fact-checking entities in more than sixty countries — some that are quite complex and elaborate. However, the efficacy of fact-checking is decidedly mixed. In order for someone to be persuaded that something they encountered online was misinformed, they need to actually see the correction. Fact-checking competes with (and can easily be drowned out by) the flood of real-time news and the continuous surfacing of extreme, sensationalist, and emotion-based content. Advocates of fact-checking also assume that everyone reasons the same way, and that differences in opinion are due to deficits of verified information, when in fact people approach information with "directionally motivated reasoning," "confirmation bias," and other cognitive traits that make them less inclined to change their minds when presented with corrections. Even more concerning, studies show that fact-checking can actually reinforce the spread of false information; information that is not flagged may be assumed to be legitimate even when it's not. Other studies have shown that general warnings about the veracity of news can actually reduce confidence in all news sources. Fact-checking is kind of like ideational pest control. As lies spread like cockroaches, we call in the exterminators. But if the kitchen is always dirty, the cockroaches will just keep coming back, which keeps the pest control operation in business. (Just ask journalist Daniel Dale, who graduated from the *Toronto Star* to CNN on the basis of his fact-checking of Donald Trump.)

Others advocate for reform of social media through "media literacy," which aims to give people the tools to critically interpret and engage with the communications environment around them. Media literacy goes back decades, first becoming popular within school curricula in the 1970s as a result, in part, of the influence of Marshall McLuhan. As our reliance on social media has grown, so too have calls for and programs about media literacy. On first glance, this seems like a no-brainer. Upon deeper introspection, media literacy is incomplete and may even be enabling social media's pathologies when it encourages fluency with the very tools and techniques that are helping to produce the negative externalities in the first place. By training people to navigate social media, media literacy can help fetishize those media. It's worth remembering that some of the most innovative and "media literate" uses of social media have come from those who aim to sow confusion and undermine accountability. Donald Trump tweets a steady stream of lies, insults, and encouragement of hatred to his nearly one hundred million followers. Russian trolls, murderous Islamic extremists like ISIS, and far-right conspiracy theorists, like followers of QAnon, are all among the most "media literate" entities of our age.

Among the partial or fragmented solutions are the technological fixes: *We just need a new app to help us correct the errors and false information circulating on all the other apps!* Among these are the proposals to use machine learning and artificial intelligence to sweep through social media, keeping humans with all their cognitive biases and other shortcomings on the sidelines. If algorithms are responsible for surfacing extreme, sensational, and misinformed content (so the theory goes), maybe algorithms can be designed to make it all go away? We got a glimpse of just how this might play out when the COVID emergency hit and Facebook sent its team of thousands of manual fact-checkers into self-isolation. Their AI systems swept through all right, removing all sorts of innocuous content for millions of its users. Oops! It was a "bug," said Guy Rosen, Facebook's vice-president of integrity.

In fact, there is no shortage of proposals to reform and regulate social media in some manner or form. Some advocate for giving users a legal right "not to be tracked" by advertisers in exchange for using social media. Many believe that governments need to enact strong data protection regimes with independent regulators who have the power and authority to punish social media platforms that violate the rules of those regimes. It is common to hear calls for more scrutiny of the machine-based algorithms companies use to sort their users — what's known as "algorithmic accountability." Proposals have been made to legislate greater transparency in the social media advertising space — particularly around political advertising. Many advocate for social media platforms to be forced (or otherwise encouraged) to incorporate human rights due diligence into their operations, and follow international human rights laws when making decisions about content moderation. Movements to ban the use of emerging technologies are growing in frequency and volume, including in reference to drones, AI, genetic engineering, digitally implanted systems, and facial recognition systems. Some believe that alternatives to social media that are not based on surveillance capitalism need to be promoted — encouraging the development of "civic media" as a "social" or "public" (instead of commercial) "good." Indeed, there are several privacy-protecting search engines and social media platforms that do not organize their systems on the basis of personal data surveillance, such as

DuckDuckGo and Mastodon. Some believe we should treat social media as "publishers," or regulate them in the same way we regulate large utilities like electricity and water. Others believe that they should be broken up by using antitrust tools instead.

Evaluating all these ideas can be difficult and confusing. How do they fit together? Which ones make sense relative to others? Do any of them contradict each other? Which might be outliers? Or counterproductive? Is there an underlying link between antitrust on the one hand and digital detoxification on the other? Is there a deeper framework that might pull them all together in a coherent way, and help guide us in our decisions moving forward?

ONE POTENTIALLY HELPFUL WAY to think of these various proposals is as if they are ingredients of a long-lost recipe. We know the basics from memories passed down through the generations, but without the original formula, we hesitate and second-guess ourselves. *Do I finish the pasta in the sauce or pour the sauce over the cooked pasta? Do I roast the garlic or mince it?*

Much like a folk recipe passed down by word of mouth, the various proposals to reform social media can be seen, in greater or lesser terms, as incomplete fragments or partial elements of a more comprehensive formula, but lacking an underlying philosophical framework that would tie it all together and to which we could continuously refer. Because we lack a conceptual apparatus — a formula or recipe — for how to approach the challenges of our social media age, we rely instead on policy reflexes. While many of the proposals may have merits, on their own and without an explicit acknowledgement of this foundation, they remain a series of ad hoc insights — fragments of a larger whole.

The term "reset" is most often associated with computers; it refers to the process of shutting down processes or systems that are "hanging." It can also refer to starting over completely fresh with factory settings. We have extensive digital security / travel protocols at the Citizen Lab that require me to wipe a Chromebook and restore it to its default settings before crossing a border, so I do resets fairly often. While inconvenient, a reset also feels like a fresh start — another widely used connotation of the term. In sports, coaches call a time out when the team is on their heels, the purpose of which is to reset the players and get the team back on track. A reset provides an opportunity to take stock of the big picture. It gives us breathing room to evaluate what's working and what isn't, and to make adjustments accordingly when moving forward. Most importantly, it provides us with space and time to start over from first principles and a solid foundation, and to dispense with those practices that have become a hindrance to larger aims.

There are several compelling reasons to have a solid framework to guide us after a reset. Having an underlying bedrock of principles to which we can continuously refer helps steer our strategies and inform our decisions, especially as novel problems arise. For at least a decade now, technological innovation has been undertaken mostly in the absence of any such foundation, other than a simple imperative to collect more data. A well-articulated set of principles, particularly one that links technologies to wider political ideals, can help remind us that political principles should take priority over technology, and technologies should be designed and developed to further our political aims, rather than work against or be insulated from them. It can also help us understand the relationship between reform proposals that otherwise may seem disparate or unrelated. It can help us evaluate and prioritize—see the larger whole of which the various fragments are a part.

Second, having a principled foundation can anchor our approach in a rich historical tradition, and help us feel connected to well-tested and long-established wisdom and practical experiments on analogous challenges that societies have faced in the past. Our social media universe feels uniquely novel in so many ways that it may blind us to the fact that societies have experienced technological upheavals and large-scale societal challenges before. Human societies have had to adjust and adapt throughout their history in the face of new material circumstances much like those we are experiencing today. We can learn from what's come before, and from the collected wisdom of those who have experienced and reflected on it.

Third, such a foundation helps combat fatigue, pessimism, and defeatism among critics of social media and surveillance capitalism by showing there are viable and robust alternatives. If we demonstrate the common roots of numerous disparate efforts to detach, reform, and regulate social media, we show that everyone's efforts are weaving something larger than their own separate struggles. This suggests that the whole is larger than the sum of its parts, and that there are alliances to be forged among like-minded advocates, policymakers, and researchers — particularly among civil society in different jurisdictions worldwide. It can help chart a path towards an alternative agenda on which groups can work together more confidently.

Here we can take a lesson from responses to the climate crisis. We are at a point in the social media / surveillance capitalism trajectory similar to the time when alarm bells were first rung about the environment. The first stage was very much about pointing out the negative implications of our reliance on fossil fuels, toxic industrial processes, and unbridled consumption. It wasn't long before those raising the alarms were asked, "So what do you propose instead?" The growing critical commentary on social media and surveillance capitalism is at a stage similar to the environmentalism of the 1960s and 1970s. The works of Shoshana Zuboff, Siva Vaidhyanathan, Bruce Schneier, and others are, in this respect, the social media equivalent of Rachel Carson's *Silent Spring*, Barry Commoner's *The Closing Circle*, and

Paul Ehrlich's *The Population Bomb*. They have dissected what's wrong and have helped wake us up to a serious pathology, but they have yet to carve out a confident alternative way to organize ourselves.

TO GET US STARTED, I PROPOSE a single, simple, but hopefully potent principle: *restraint*. Restraint is primarily defined as "a measure or condition that keeps someone or something under control or within limits." Secondarily, it also means "self-control," as in "unemotional, dispassionate, or moderate behaviour." Both senses of the term point to general qualities that will be essential to preserving rights and freedoms in our supercharged, hyper-networked world of data. We need to restrain what governments and corporations do with all the extraordinarily powerful tools of surveillance that are now in their hands. We need to restrain what they do with all the data about us and our behaviours. Restraints will be essential to ensure the security of the broader information and communications space in which we live, particularly restraints on bad actors exploiting us for despotic, corrupt, or criminal ends, or governments exploiting it for their narrow national security aims. We'll need personal restraints too: restraints on our endless appetite for data, restraints on our emotions and anger as we engage online in the absence of the physical cues that normally help contain them. We will need restraints on each other: mutual restraints that apply to individuals, organizations, and even sovereign states. If there is one single mantra, one simple concept that should become our slogan and guide us as we chart our path forward, I believe it should be... *restraint*.

While most everyone is familiar with the concept of restraint, what may be less familiar to many is that this seemingly simple term is derived from and is essential to a long tradition of theorizing about political liberty and security, going back centuries. It is most intimately connected to that broad family of political thought that for most of us is so entrenched in our habits and dispositions, it is more like an instinct than a self-conscious philosophy. I'm talking of course about *liberalism*.

Broadly defined, liberalism is a tradition that supports individual rights, civil liberties, and political reform that pushes societies in the direction of individual freedom, democracy, and social equality. Political theorists will be quick to point out that liberalism is not a single "theory" but a large family of ideas and prescriptions for how to manage societies that goes back hundreds of years. Most of us can rhyme off the key features of liberalism, so ingrained are they into our collective approach to politics: free and fair elections, constitutions, limited government, the rule of law, separation of powers, pluralism, social justice, and protection for human rights. There are many tangled threads that weave their way through liberalism. There are also competing schools of thought within its large and diverse tent. Those who consider themselves adherents range from libertarians and free-market fundamentalists on one end of the spectrum to democratic socialists on the other.

In spite of competing schools, however, liberalism of all stripes shares a fundamental principle. At its core is the belief that in order to preserve and maximize freedom while countering insecurity and fear, we must build legally binding restraints on those we entrust to discharge authority: restraints on the exercise of political power, to prevent abuse. Within the liberal tent, the specific school of thought that is most associated with this principle of restraint is known as "republicanism." Republican political theory enjoys a "ghostly afterlife" (to use the phrase of one of its most eloquent proponents, Johns Hopkins University professor Daniel Deudney)—ubiquitous to some degree, in that we can find references to it, and proposals inspired by it, everywhere. But there is a strange kind of amnesia about its history, its rich theoretical tradition, and the various real-world adaptations proposed and experiments performed to apply restraint measures in the face of changing circumstances or complex challenges.

Now, right off the bat it's important to clarify that by "republicanism" we are not talking about the morally bankrupt and graft-ridden political party of today's United States that goes by the name. As confusing as it may be, it is essential to clearly distinguish between these two associations of the term. What the Republican political party stands for and represents today is, to a large degree, the antithesis of republican political theory and practice. Indeed, one shorthand way to think about republican political theory is to take virtually anything that Republican Senate majority leader Mitch McConnell advocates and think of the exact opposite of that position. That would likely be a pretty good indication of what republican political theory embodies. (Oddly, the same goes for the colloquial use of the term "liberal" in the United States, which is usually employed derisively to refer to someone who has "left leanings." It is strange, I realize, that the meanings of both concepts have become so twisted in the country that applied them so extensively in its founding.)

In fact, the idea of applying restraint as a design principle for political systems is one of the most venerable in political theorizing, with roots reaching all the way back to ancient Greece. It began to develop more comprehensively in the late Renaissance and early modern period in Europe. Historians of republics have linked the Venetian, Dutch, and British maritime polities with important constitutive features of restraint principles, such as the separation of powers. Most agree that republican-inspired restraint experiments reached their apex and had their fullest articulation around the founding of the United States of America. (Sadly, those founding principles have been gradually eroded by the steady concentration of power and authority in the executive branch, and the massive military-industrial complex president Dwight Eisenhower warned about at the height of the Cold War.) Republican principles of restraint also inspired such innovations in international relations as the League of Nations, the United Nations, and later the European Union, which were explicitly conceptualized as systems of mutual restraint accomplished through co-binding arrangements entered into by sovereign states. Republics (and republican theorists) seek to tie down and restrain the exercise of power not only domestically but also across borders, through "leagues," "confederations," and formal "alliances" with other like-minded republics.

Each of these historical moments has featured important thinkers who were inspired by and themselves helped define the key restraint principles at the heart of republicanism, such as Polybius in Greece; Machiavelli, particularly in *Discourses on Livy*, written in the Italian city-states period; Baron de Montesquieu and the Scottish Enlightenment thinkers; through to the various drafters of the U.S Constitution and the authors of the Federalist Papers, who wrote collectively under the pen name "Publius." Republican principles were revived and proposed as solutions to the challenges of the late nineteenth- and early twentieth-century global industrial age, finding expression in the world federalist proposals put forth by H. G. Wells and the ethical internationalism and transnational pluralism associated with John Dewey, and then again in proposals for nuclear and other arms control regimes as propounded by Bernard Baruch, Jonathan Schell, and others (and subsequently updated and reformulated by Daniel Deudney).

While many of these thinkers would be dumbfounded by the awesome technological advances that define our age, they'd be familiar with the general challenges these throw up for how to organize political structures. Republican theorists understood well that principles of restraint require adaptation to local and changing circumstances. The changes wrought by technology and other material factors were explicitly addressed by many of them. Republican theorists recognized unambiguously that material factors play a major role in shaping political outcomes, and political practices should account for and sometimes adapt to these factors with institutional innovations of various sorts.

For example, it has long been recognized that republican polities tend to be rare and relatively fragile, and that specific geographic features, like oceans and mountains, provide support for their viability. Republicans saw "nature," in other words, as itself a mechanism of restraint. Size was thought to be an important component of the viability of republican polities, but also one of their inherent weaknesses. Self-government requires citizens to be engaged, which in turn limits the size of any viable self-governing regime. But their small size made republican polities inherently fragile, and open to predation from outsiders. The exceptions were in those circumstances where material factors provided a degree of protection, as in the city-states of ancient Greece, where the broken geography and rocky outcrops helped compensate for the vulnerabilities inherent in small size.

Likewise, many republican commentators (the most famous of whom was Montesquieu) attributed material factors to the unique political makeup of early modern Europe, which was considered by him and others to be a "republic by nature," given the varied topographical elements that favoured division and self-rule and acted as a retardant against continent-sized empires emerging (until the Industrial Revolution altered the equation, that is). Changing material circumstances, particularly related to technological innovation, can throw up challenges to or even make obsolete the natural restraints of prior eras. Reading about how these thinkers understood material factors and configured restraint in their own respective situations can help inspire innovative applications of restraint measures in our own times.

ALTHOUGH REPUBLICANISM HAS something to say about many principles, at its heart it is about preventing the centralization and thus abuse of power. As Deudney has put it, "Republicanism is an institutionalized system of decentralized power constraint" manifested in "a cross-checking architecture of binded and bound authorities." For republicans, unchecked concentrations of power threaten liberty and security because they are apt to be abused, and so "checks and balances" (a widely known phrase that comes from republican thought) must be institutionalized to distribute power pluralistically and keep it that way. Related concepts include "mixed government" (which Aristotle analyzed in his treatise *Politics*) and "separation of powers" (advocated in different ways by Kant, Montesquieu, and, of course, the framers of the U.S. Constitution, where it was formalized in the cross-cutting authorities provided to the executive, judicial, and legislative branches of government).

The republican opposition to concentration of power rests on assumptions of human frailty: humans tend to be both self-interested and prone to lapses in judgement. When opportunities present themselves, they are tempted by power, which can in turn bring about corruption and other abuses. As Montesquieu famously observed, "Every man invested with power is apt to abuse it." The republican political program seeks to create a political architecture that restrains the potential for the abuse of power, typically enshrined in a constitution or other framing document. In the words of James Madison, "You must first enable the government to control the governed; and next oblige it to control itself." Republican theorists were acutely aware of the accumulation of unchecked and oppressive power in the hands of government as a threat to individual liberty and security, and so they devised an elaborate system of power-restraint devices to thwart it.

These devices are a form of "friction" introduced into political processes to make the exercise of authority less efficient. Strange as it may sound, at a time of near-total surveillance potential in the hands of government agencies, we need to challenge ourselves to think of ways to artificially reduce the efficiency of our governments' security agencies. The republican attention to material factors tells us why. Oceans, mountains, and other rugged terrain, as well as inhospitable climates and even endemic diseases, created obstacles for invading armies, slowing them down, impeding conquest, and protecting long-term control of populations — a kind of accidental friction by circumstance. All things being equal, the farther away people are from the centre of control, or the more natural barriers shelter them, the less efficient the exercise of that control tends to be. Hence, in times prior to social media and the internet, activists could flee their home countries out of fear of persecution and feel safe thousands of miles away from the reach of the power elites they left behind.

In a similar fashion, the same might be said with respect to the way that the walls of homes (for those who could afford them, anyway) helped preserve individual liberty, since an outside observer (e.g., a police officer) would not be able to see what's going on inside a person's "four-square walls." To be sure, the lack of a properly authorized warrant may have prevented a police officer from "eavesdropping" on targets' conversations, but so did the fence that bordered their property, the walls of their home or apartment, and even the relative "anonymity" of a large urban crowd.

As we discussed in chapter 3, with social media and other digital technologies, these natural barriers have been almost entirely dissolved. We now live in something approximating a "friction-free" environment in which outside forces, be they companies or governments, can pry into our most intimate details, even when we're behind closed doors. Thanks to new technologies, all of us can be tracked to a degree and in a fashion that is both unprecedented in human history and nearly comprehensive in its potential totality. When our fridges, baby monitors, video conferencing facilities, smart TVs, and even brains are all networked with the outside world, "natural" restraints that we once took for granted no longer serve the same function. We now face an entirely new challenge from the material context, thanks to the changing nature of technology. Implanted technologies have the potential to pinpoint details even down to a biological level with a precision that borders on precognition. This great leap forward in remote control raises the prospect of severe abuse of power and near-totalitarian control. The application of restraint measures to the design and functioning of both private and public sectors will thus be critical to preserving liberty and security.

THE FIRST PLACE TO START is by reviewing the type and effectiveness of existing restraint mechanisms around governments. While companies can abuse power too, and collect a lot of sensitive, fine-grained, and highly revealing data about us (which they can, in turn, share with governments), only a government can take away a person's liberty — by force. The security arms of the state — the police, armed forces, and other security agencies — have a "monopoly on violence" (one of the definitions of sovereign statehood). They have lethal means at their disposal, can arrest people and lock them up, and in some jurisdictions can even end their lives through capital punishment. In response to emergencies, governments can also take all sorts of exceptional measures that infringe on liberties, including declaring martial law or simply suspending constitutionally protected rights that we take for granted — as we discovered with the COVID pandemic.

Liberal mechanisms to restrain governments have evolved to become more elaborate and complex, but not necessarily more effective. Hundreds of years ago, republics were defined by elemental restraints: separation of powers, checks and balances, term limits, free and fair elections, judicial warrants, and so on. Over time, and largely in response to the growing size and reach of governments, these restraints have been supplemented by additional measures with which most people are familiar: parliamentary oversight committees, special prosecutors, ombuds offices, privacy commissioners, intelligence and surveillance courts, inspectors general, and so on. Major scandals sometimes precipitate the formation of new restraint measures. For example, after the 1970s Church Committee investigations into abuses of domestic surveillance associated with the Nixon administration, Congress passed the Foreign Intelligence Surveillance Act, which established the Foreign Intelligence Surveillance Court (FISC) — an eleven-member judicial panel that oversees government requests for surveillance warrants. In Canada, thanks largely to the Snowden disclosures, a new omnibus national security legislation (C-59), passed into law in 2019, updated Canada's national security oversight regime, including establishing a completely new watchdog agency, the National Security and Intelligence Review Agency.

But more or different oversight does not always bring more effective restraint. The FISC proceedings are undertaken in secrecy and without any adversarial input, since the court only hears from the government. It has been criticized as a "rubber stamp" agency because it rarely turns down a request for a warrant. Many state security agencies have benefited from rising budgets, more resources and capabilities, and access to sophisticated equipment. The long "war on terror," which began with the events of 9/11 and has continued ever since, has provided them with enormous latitude to conduct their operations under the cover of secrecy and shielded from public accountability. The disturbing worldwide descent into authoritarianism has helped further normalize these practices. Meanwhile, oversight mechanisms have been subject to systematic erosion or outright evasion by those who are intent on bolstering executive authority or merely have corrupt aims, or both. Oversight agencies already lacking capacity have had their personnel and budgets slashed. For example, at the time of writing, the

Trump administration has still not filled the positions in at least five inspector general offices, which remain vacant and thus rudderless, while four other inspectors general were unceremoniously fired by Trump over a period of six weeks in early 2020. Some oversight bodies have simply been eliminated altogether, along with the restraints on power that go with them, as have numerous regulations that provide legal restraints. The mantra of "deregulation," colloquially referred to by its supporters as "cutting red tape" (or "draining the swamp") can function like a lawnmower on power restraint mechanisms. During his first term in office, President Trump used a range of levers, including executive actions, cabinet-level decisions, and new legislation to shave back a large number of rules and regulations, and the power and capacity of regulatory agencies like the Food and Drug Administration (FDA) and the Environmental Protection Agency (EPA).

It's important to remember that restraints can just as easily be eliminated or weakened as they can be imposed or strengthened. Laws and regulations that prevent the concentration or abuse of power are human inventions. Though written down in constitutions and law books, they are ultimately social constructs—part of what Levitsky and Ziblatt call "the soft guardrails of democracy," resting only on the collective agreement of the people they are meant to protect. What can be "constructed" can also be subverted, dismantled, or simply ignored.

Although it still remains to be seen how the COVID emergency will play out, it is worth noting that numerous states of emergency have been declared across the world, giving wide discretion and new powers and authority to security agencies. Military, intelligence, and police forces have all been employed in the fight against COVID, given their technologically enhanced capabilities to undertake surveillance and track populations. And as shown in chapter 3, this comes at a time when there has already been a profound great leap forward in these capabilities, thanks to surveillance capitalism and the private security and intelligence services that circulate as part of the marketplace. The combination of deregulation, securitization of health, and the introduction of supercharged surveillance tools will pose an existential risk to those remaining (and already fragile) restraints on the abuse of power. The "new normal" that emerges after COVID could be an ominous one for the sanctity of liberal democratic institutions.

The first task of our reset should be to evaluate the effectiveness of the restraint mechanisms we have inherited. Do we need to supplement them with new resources, capabilities, and authorities? After the Watergate hearings and the Church Committee investigations in the United States, entirely new restraint mechanisms were created. Do we need to do something similar in response to the great leap forward in technologies of remote control? Will we need new or strengthened oversight and accountability measures to compensate for the "new normal" that emerges after COVID-19?

One simple rule of thumb that may help guide us is as follows: *restraint should increase proportionately to the intrusiveness of the practices in question.* The more invasive a technology is, the more likely it lends itself to abuse of power, and so the stronger and more elaborate the restraints should be. Consider location tracking via cellular and telecommunications data. As we saw in chapter 3, most everyone carries around a networked device all the time that pings cell towers and local telco networks on a continuous basis and is standardly outfitted with GPS and Bluetooth beacons. Most all of us have dozens of apps that routinely grab location history and data too, and use them primarily for advertising purposes. Prior to COVID-19, these data could be accessed by law enforcement, military, and intelligence agencies, but under widely different conditions; in some countries, certain of those agencies might require a warrant or a production order, while in others they might simply walk into the headquarters of telecommunications companies and demand them.

As I write, there are numerous proposals worldwide to employ digital location data to assist in the effort to combat the spread of COVID-19, although their efficacy is unclear. In a world where we reflexively look to big tech for solutions, it's not surprising that Google and Apple have teamed up to develop a protocol for "anonymized" contact tracing through smartphone apps. But as Cambridge computer security expert Ross Anderson warns, such apps will be wide open to malfeasance that could distort the utility of the data collected: "The performance art people will tie a phone to a dog and let it run around the park; the Russians will use the app to run service-denial attacks and spread panic; and little Johnny will self-report symptoms to get the whole school sent home." Like others who have already weighed in on the issue, I believe that however much these prove to be useful in public health emergencies, the safeguards around them must be exceptionally strong too. Some basic restraint mechanisms should include strict limits on data retention, clear limitations on use, and restrictions on access to ensure that the data are not illegitimately redeployed for other reasons (like catching chicken wing thieves and jaywalkers . . . or monitoring human rights defenders). Other restraints could include mandatory transparency on how the data are obtained, used, deleted, and so forth. All of it would need to be overseen by independent regulators armed with real-time oversight capabilities and meaningful authority to mandate penalties and correct abusive behaviour.

Similarly, strong restraints should be applied to the use of commercial spyware and hacking tools by government security agencies, which are among the most intrusive and (as we have demonstrated in our research) highly prone to abuse. The commercial spyware market is a "Wild West," which is another way of saying it is characterized by an almost complete absence of restraint.

As the UN special rapporteur for freedom of expression, David Kaye, said, "It is insufficient to say that a comprehensive system for control and use of targeted surveillance technologies is broken. It hardly exists." States purchasing spyware are at liberty to abuse it with limited or no transparency or regulation. Companies that manufacture and sell it have unbridled freedom to rake in revenues by the tens of millions, largely without fear of criminal liability or concern for how their technology impacts human rights. The net result: harassment, blackmail, and even murder of countless innocent civilians worldwide.

The introduction of strong legal restraints, both domestically and internationally, could turn this abysmal situation on its head. Governments that purchase spyware could be mandated to be both transparent and more accountable about when and how they deploy it, to ensure that its use is necessary, limited, and proportionate. Regulations could ensure that the purchase of spyware is restricted to an "allow list" of companies that undertake thorough due diligence to prevent abuse, and thus marginalize serial abusers like Hacking Team or NSO Group. Governments in whose jurisdictions surveillance companies are located have benefited from the kind of rubber-stamp approval that Israel's ministry of defence provides for NSO Group's sales. Instead, host governments could deploy strong measures that only provide export licenses in exchange for companies taking meaningful steps, written into their sales agreements, to prevent abuse of their products. Governments all over the world could build robust legal regimes that hold both companies and states accountable for hacking the devices of individuals within their borders without proper legal permission; spyware vendors who enable such hacking could be held legally liable as well.

What goes for spyware is equally applicable to the broad range of insecurities introduced by governments into our communications ecosystem in the name of national security. For years, government military, intelligence, and law enforcement agencies have not only stockpiled knowledge of software bugs ("zero days") as tools that could facilitate their investigations and other operations, they've also deliberately introduced such flaws into critical systems as "back doors" — a kind of insecurity by design. Very little is known about these practices, how extensive they are, and what criteria guide the decision making around them, because they are shrouded in secrecy. At best, a few governments have sketched out some high-level principles that amount to a general admission, but little else in terms of either transparency or accountability. These practices have led to widespread abuses of their own kind, which have in turn jeopardized public safety. For example, thanks to the Snowden disclosures, we now know that a flawed encryption protocol was foisted clandestinely on much of the world by the U.S., Canadian, and U.K. signals intelligence agencies, which enabled them to crack the code of their adversaries' communications. Critical infrastructure throughout the world depended on the integrity of this protocol. It's unclear how many other governments or criminals knew of and exploited it, or whether any people were harmed in the process — but it is conceivable some malfeasance took place because of it. The so-called "vulnerabilities equities process," as it's referred to by governments, is a national security practice around which greater restraints are urgently needed. These could include mandated transparency and reporting, greater accountability to legislators, and independent oversight bodies (which could contain citizens and businesses representatives), all designed to ensure that governments report to software vendors the vast majority of vulnerabilities they discover. When they do withhold them as assets, such oversight could guarantee that they do so infrequently, proportionally, and for reasons clearly justified by the public interest. Absent these restraint mechanisms, governments have drilled holes into our communications ecosystem like the digital equivalent of Swiss cheese, all narrowly justified in the name of "national security." A more robust oversight regime would ensure that governments instead treat our communications ecosystem as a shared commons, to be secured for all users.

We will almost certainly need to create entirely new measures of restraint as new technologies throw up unexpected challenges and unforeseen problems. Among the areas that pose the greatest risks for abuse of power, and even existential risks (when projected forward in time), are artificial intelligence, artificial superintelligence (a computer vastly more intelligent than any human), machine learning, quantum mechanics, and facial recognition — either separately or, more likely, in combination. Abuses and built-in discrimination around the use of some of these technologies today, in policing, immigration, and criminal justice practices, are already well documented. The prospects for even greater harms down the road are incalculably large and daunting to contemplate. Should computing systems develop to the point of acquiring far superior intelligence, and even autonomy from humans, they may decide to turn on their masters altogether and either enslave or outright eliminate us (a recurring theme in science fiction but one that seems increasingly less far-fetched with each passing day). Some observers have advocated a wholesale ban on the use of AI and facial recognition until proper accountability mechanisms are in place, which would be a major mandatory restraint of its own kind (and indeed, some jurisdictions have already gone so far as to impose such a ban).

But going forward, we have to assume that security agencies will be under enormous pressure to develop and deploy these technologies for law enforcement and intelligence gathering. Outright bans on technologies are extremely difficult to verify and enforce, especially when development is undertaken secretly by military agencies, involves weaponization, and is spread across multiple state jurisdictions. Restraints through close regulation and enforced accountability, on the other hand, are more practical and can begin in one or several jurisdictions and then develop more broadly. As an example, Erik Learned-Miller, one of the pioneers of facial recognition, now feels that the negative aspects of these technologies are growing and simply too dangerous to leave unregulated, and he proposes that there be an equivalent to the FDA for facial recognition. Just as the original FDA regulates medical devices for safety before they are approved for use by the public, so should this FDA2 do the same with respect to facial recognition technology.

To be clear, the point of imposing restraints is to prevent abuse of power, not disable public security agencies from doing their jobs altogether. Restraints should limit and contain what the state can do, not neuter it entirely. Acts of wickedness, crime, and organized violence are inherent to human societies. We need well-equipped and trained law enforcement to ensure that criminal offences are investigated and prosecuted, as much to protect liberty and other rights as anything else. As long as we live in a world divided into sovereign states, many of them in the clutches of despots, we will also need well-outfitted armed forces and intelligence agencies to defend our republics from outside threats. But we should not let those agencies' priorities threaten the populations they are ostensibly designed to protect in the first place. Unfortunately, since 9/11 that is precisely what has happened: the most secretive and martial wings of the state have ballooned in size, their missions have swollen out of proportion to their prior limits, and much of our society has been transformed by militarization, superpower policing, and the securitization of civilian life. Applying new restraints, while reinvigorating existing ones, will be essential to preserving rights and freedoms.

APPLYING RESTRAINTS TO what governments can do is only part of the solution. We live in an age in which gigantic corporations, and especially technology giants, dominate the social and political landscape. This type of outsized corporate power is not unique to our era. The late nineteenth-century "gilded age" was another. Back then, titanic industrialists and "robber barons" had near-unbridled power that allowed them to rig markets in their favour and corrupt the machinery of government with bribes and threats. What makes today different is the degree to which corporate power rests on the unprecedented and extraordinary visibility of everyone's personal lives, right down to the genetic and possibly even subconscious levels (thanks to the platforms' legal appropriation of users' data as property). To know everything about a person down to the atomic level (and commercialize it) provides unprecedented ability to control that person — as if B. F. Skinner's behaviourism has burst out of laboratories and is undertaking experiments on the entire social world. As Tim Wu describes it, "We may not be there yet, but there is a theoretical point — call it the Skinnerlarity — where enough data will be gathered about humanity to predict, with some reasonable reliability, what everyone on earth will do at any moment." The powers of unbridled surveillance capitalism are truly awesome, and when combined with state authority are potentially totalitarian. Shaping our desires to persuade us to consume this or that product is disturbing enough, but the prospect of corporations and states colluding in broader population control is downright dystopian. Just ask a Tibetan or a Uyghur.

In addition to the risks of abuse of power related to fine-grained remote control technologies, there is another reason to impose restraints on surveillance capitalism. The engine at the heart of the business model — which prejudices sensational, extreme, and emotional content — amplifies our baser instincts, creates irresistible opportunities for malfeasance, and helps pollute the public sphere. It also continuously accelerates our consumption of data. More is better. Faster too. But endlessly accelerating consumption of data, on the part of both consumers and firms mining our behaviour, taxes the planet's finite resources, draws volumes of fossil-fuelled power energy, and contributes to (rather than helps solve) one of humanity's most pressing existential risks. Introducing friction and other restraints on surveillance capitalism can help improve the quality of our public discourse while tempering the insatiable hunger for more data, faster networks, and disposable gadgets.

New privacy laws that have been enacted in recent years give us a partial glimpse of such restraints. The EU's General Data Protection Regulation (GDPR) and California's Consumer Privacy Act are by far the most well known and far reaching. These regulations are ambitious in many ways, bolstering the rights of those subject to data collection and outlining duties of those entities that control or process those data. They limit transfer of data to third parties, create supervisory authorities to monitor companies and follow up on complaints, and set out remedies for breaches that include financial penalties. They both certainly caught the attention of the industry's executives; at the very least, they created a whole new swathe of employment for compliance lawyers and industry lobbyists. But there are fair questions as to their long-term effectiveness. For most users, the visible effect of the GDPR is a sudden cornucopia of janky consent banners of all sorts, shapes, colours, and sizes—yet more irritants to be swatted away unthinkingly in the rush to get access to content. However promising, these statutes on their own are not so much prompting a fundamental behavioural shift as they are further trivializing informed consent. The privacy laws have also done little to decelerate the jet engine of surveillance capitalism. Companies deal with fines in the same way users deal with consent banners: as minor irritants (or, for them, mere "rounding errors").

Deeper and more effective restraint measures would involve something like what Tim Wu has called a true "codified antisurveillance regime"—one that would limit the gratuitous mining and relentless accumulation of personal data. Bringing about these deeper and more effective restraints would amount to what law professor Julie Cohen, drawing from the political economist Karl Polanyi, calls a "protective counter movement" to surveillance capitalism—a serious and concerted multipronged legal and regulatory effort to rein in surveillance capitalism, including the appropriation of our personal data as the platform's private property. More ambitious restraints of this sort would restrict data collection to clearly defined purposes—"an app designed to help you mix cocktails would not, for example, be allowed to collect location data," says Wu. Laws pertaining specifically to the freewheeling data broker industry are sorely needed and would be part of the equation too. All firms would be required to delete data they collect, anonymize and fully encrypt what they keep, and share data with third parties, especially governments, only under strictly controlled circumstances that are both transparent and accountable to independent oversight bodies with the power to levy meaningful punishments. GDPR times ten, in other words.

Also included in such a regime could be measures to introduce friction into the circulation of information. To slow things down is a hallmark of republican practice. Hasty decisions are usually bad, so one of the justifications for checks and balances has been to slow the tempo of decision making and cool inflamed passions that otherwise incite the type of factionalism and mob rule thought to be responsible for republican decline in the ancient world. For example, in justifying a bicameral legislature, which was viewed by the framers in precisely this manner, George Washington is said to have explained to Thomas Jefferson that the purpose of the Senate was to cool the passions of the House, just as a saucer is used to cool hot tea.

In contrast, today we are faced with a rising tempo of information consumption, and huge time constraints on deliberation brought about by the speed of information delivery and the pace of news cycles pushed to us in real time via our vibrating devices. Some days it feels like one major crisis after another. Yesterday's scandal quickly fades into distant memory as viral stories rain down on us continuously. It may seem laughable to think we could "slow down" this hypermedia environment, but there's no practical reason why not. Consider WhatsApp, whose platform's "group chat" function was widely associated with inflaming ethnic animosity, inciting violence, and spreading disinformation around the world. Since its messages are end-to-end encrypted, which limits the platform's ability to screen actual content, WhatsApp took steps to limit the size of groups and the number of times content could be forwarded to others — a technical tweak a group of Brazilian researchers explicitly described as introducing friction into the application. Although the measures were taken by the company itself, there is no reason such technical tweaks could not be mandated by law.

Proposing such mandatory measures might have seemed unrealistic only a few years ago, but times are changing fast. The COVID crisis could help underscore why these restraint measures are necessary, with a sense of urgency. While social media companies initially dithered about what to do with dangerously misleading health information on their platforms, they all eventually decided to carry highly visible pointers to credible scientific content about the crisis at the top of their feeds, and actively removed disinformation when discovered (they even issued a rare joint statement in March 2020 saying they would elevate "authoritative content"). But as you might expect when platforms are writing their own rules, the measures were fragmented, inconsistent, and lacking transparency. Coming out of the crisis, we can expect there to be a greater social appetite for making measures such as these mandatory, their worth having been demonstrated to wide segments of users.

One thing is for sure: business as usual can no longer be tolerated. Decisions that have major effects on the public's sharing and consumption of information should not happen in the shadows, or behind a proprietary algorithm. Harvard researcher Evelyn Douek, who has studied social media regulation extensively, argues that "platforms should be forced to earn the kudos they are getting for their handling of the pandemic by preserving data about what they are doing and opening it up for research instead of selective disclosure." (Instructively, "force" indicates a legal requirement, not a choice.) Says

Douek, in terms that fit squarely within the philosophy of restraint, "Right now the public is asking tech platforms to step up, but we also need to keep thinking about how to rein them in."

To be sure, there are balances to be struck around free expression, content moderation, and abuse prevention. There are very real risks that mandatory or poorly constructed measures could be perverted as an instrument of authoritarian control, abused by despots and autocrats to enforce their rule, much like the way Malaysia has used "fake news" laws to stifle criticism of the regime, or the way China requires its social media companies to censor posts that poke fun at Xi Jinping by comparing him to Winnie the Pooh (they do look an awful lot alike). While many citizens may want Facebook to prioritize peer-reviewed scientific content about public health issues, there will be plenty of despots who want them to do the opposite.

One cannot speak about regulating social media without considering section 230 of the U.S. Communications Decency Act. This legislation protects online intermediaries that host or republish speech from being held liable for what users say and do over their platforms, in the way that more traditional publishers are. Section 230 was not only critical to the early development of the internet, it has helped maximize innovation and online free expression. With the exception of certain criminal and intellectual property claims, section 230 ensures that the platforms are not subject to endless and potentially chilling lawsuits. Now that the platforms have matured and routinely manipulate their content, some commentators have called for additional exceptions to section 230's immunity clauses. To be sure, the prospect of revising section 230 is daunting; it would be extraordinarily complex legislatively and would entail huge potential pitfalls. (To wit: in May 2020, Donald Trump publicly advocated abolishing section 230 entirely as part of a personal vendetta against Twitter for flagging his tweets.) Not only are liability protections critical to ensuring free speech online, they reduce barriers for new entrants to the online space, which is essential for competition. Should additional exceptions to immunity be added or other laws introduced, the key will be to make sure that social media platforms manage content in ways that are transparent, limited, proportional, and in compliance with internationally recognized human rights. These standards may not be possible in all jurisdictions right now, but they should be an imperative for those that consider themselves liberal democracies.

ONE OF THE INTERESTING ASPECTS of how republican theory materialized in late eighteenth-century America was the understanding of the utility of division as a restraint measure. The artificial character of the Union's states, "shaped by geometry rather than natural morphology and [containing] a range of topographies, economic activities, and political orientations," as Deudney puts it, was perceived as a bulwark against the rivalry and factionalism that might come from consolidations of political rule if collectives were left to their own devices. Creating eccentric states with unnatural borders was a deliberate strategy meant to avoid the region-wide anarchy that the framers of the U.S. Constitution saw plaguing the "Westphalian" European states system of the day.

While redrawing political boundaries may be a stretch today (and largely irrelevant to the challenges of social media), the republican principle of division is certainly not, and it can be used to breathe life into and give deeper meaning to the exercise of antitrust regulations. Antitrust laws are a straightforward extension of the republican animus against concentration of power, whether in the hands of a state or a large corporation. Generally speaking, for republican thinkers "big is bad." The more power is concentrated in fewer hands, the more likely that power will be abused. Restraint measures are used to ensure that power is distributed (the opposite of concentration) or to break it up when it gets to the point of becoming overbearing, as with large corporations.

One of the chief articulators of the republican concept of division as it applies to big corporations was Louis Brandeis, who would go on to become one of the most important Supreme Court justices in U.S. history. As Tim Wu (author of *The Curse of Bigness*) explains, Brandeis "believed that great economic power results in immense political power, which, when combined with lax campaign finance laws, pollutes democratic governance." Powerful corporations exert disproportionate influence over the machinery of the government in their self-interest, and thus distort public needs for private gain.

Consider Amazon, what anticompetition jurist Lina Khan calls "the titan of twenty-first century commerce." Amazon started out as a mere online retailer but is now also a marketing firm; a global transportation, delivery and logistics supplier; a payment vendor; a credit lender; an auction network service; a book publisher; a producer of television programs and films; a streaming media service; a hardware manufacturer; a neighbourhood security service provider; a facial recognition service provider; one of the world's leading cloud hosting providers; and a grocery retailer (thanks to its acquisition of Whole Foods), among others. Amazon employed a predatory pricing policy to undercut competitors and then expand to the point of becoming essential infrastructure for a large number of other businesses. It did so while craftily evading antitrust measures, which themselves had been watered down over time, thanks to neo-liberal capitalism. As Khan says, "It is as if Bezos charted the company's growth by first drawing a map of antitrust laws, and then devising routes to smoothly bypass them." And this has paid off in spades: Jeff Bezos was named by *Forbes* magazine the "richest man in modern history" after his net worth increased to $150 billion in July 2018 — though it's declined somewhat since that time, thanks to some risky investments and a costly divorce settlement in 2019. (It's worth underlining here that Amazon, Facebook, and Google spent nearly half a billion dollars on lobbying efforts in Washington, D.C., over the past ten years, no doubt in response to the creeping prospect of greater government regulation and to ward off antitrust initiatives.)

Let's face it, there may be an element of vengeance at play in the "let's break them up" rallying cry. Who doesn't want to see billionaires get the equivalent of a regulatory spanking? And, absent other measures, antitrust alone may be only a partial and perhaps even ineffective solution. Forcing Google, Facebook, and Amazon to break up without addressing the underlying pathologies of surveillance capitalism may perversely leave us with dozens of swarming little Googles, Facebooks, and Amazons — like breaking open a spider's nest (which is why a codified antisurveillance regime, as described earlier, would be an essential complement).

However, antitrust regulation is a well-established restraint tool, the benefits of which have been demonstrated throughout modern industrial history. It was particularly effective during the early twentieth century, when enormous oil, banking, and other companies gathered up vast concentrations of wealth and used it to exert influence over politics and the market. Big corporations like Rockefeller's Standard Oil were a relatively new phenomenon at the time, but the conceptual and theoretical language that lawmakers and analysts used to address these challenges was old, and fundamentally republican in nature. In his dissenting opinion in *United States v. Columbia Steel Co.*, for example, Justice Brandeis lamented the "curse of bigness," and said that "industrial power should be decentralized. It should be scattered into many hands so that the fortunes of the people will not be dependent on the whim or caprice, the political prejudices, the emotional stability of a few self-appointed men... It is founded on a theory of hostility to the concentration in private hands of power so great that only a government of the people should have it." Although many tend to think of antitrust as just an economic tool, Brandeis's remarks remind us of its inherently political rationale. As Wu says, "We have forgotten that antitrust law... was meant fundamentally as a kind of constitutional safeguard, a check against the political dangers of unaccountable private power."

Antitrust is only one measure to deal with large monopolies. Entities that have grown too large can be broken up into parts, or designated as a natural monopoly and then regulated as a "public utility," much the way many highways and electricity and water systems are. In exchange for being designated as a monopoly (which can be organized as either a private or public venture), entities are subject to specific legal restraints: requirements to limit pricing, spend money on research, or contribute to the public good in other ways (all examples, by the way, of restraints on their unhindered operation). Some commentators have proposed that the large tech platforms be designated as public utilities, particularly in the wake of the COVID emergency, during which our dependence on them has been highlighted. (One by-product — for better or worse — might be resurrection of the old 1990s term "information superhighway" to describe the internet.) According to Mark Scott, the chief technology correspondent at *Politico*, "By becoming monopolies in each of their digital arenas, these firms have done things that, say, a litany of mini-Googles could not have done: provide a one-stop-shop for people in dire need of information, communication and other basic online services." Designating them as public utilities could allow regulators to mandate that platforms adopt green manufacturing and environmentally sustainable products and services; enforce audits of their software and algorithms according to public interest standards; treat workers more equitably, including allowing them to form unions; and eliminate the gross inequalities in compensation among owners, managers, and labour that are a hallmark of the gig economy. The downside is that doing so could effectively "lock in" the existing big tech giants as quasi-permanent features of the communications ecosystem, slow down the development of new features, and potentially stifle competition (something to be left for further debate among economists and public policy experts).

To be clear, either of these restraint measures — anti-trust regulation or public utility designation — would dramatically impact the character of our social media experiences. Many users will find it inconvenient or strange, especially at first. There would be a major push-back too. Firms would complain about the "nanny state" and the shackles around their ability to innovate (as if "innovation" for its own sake should be the only priority in life). They would pour billions into lobbying efforts aimed at stymieing the restraint measure. Unlike many other industrial sectors, the tech platforms have emerged from the pandemic stronger, as opposed to weaker, and are already positioning themselves as indispensable to public health and even national security. But coming out of the COVID crisis, which may demonstrate the value of regulation in the social and political interest, there will be an opportunity for substantial change if the requisite political will can be mobilized.

SOME REPUBLICAN-INFLUENCED restraint mechanisms are very much context-dependent, and really make sense only in a particular time and within specific material circumstances. Such is the case with the citizens' militia, enshrined in the notorious Second Amendment of the U.S. Constitution. The framers of the Constitution perceived a citizens' militia as the ultimate check on the risk of excessively centralized authority. "A well-regulated Militia, being necessary to the security of a free State, the right of the people to keep and bear Arms, shall not be infringed." Should the federal government begin to encroach too far on the liberties of local populations, the recessed threat of rebellion, guaranteed by law in the right to bear arms, was conceptualized by the framers as a constraint. Armed militias were also thought to restrain the central government from undertaking foreign adventures and unpopular wars, since doing so would require the mobilization of these well-armed members of civil society.

Political practices can persist long after the material context changes, producing a situation where they are in contradiction or live on like anachronistic relics. No better illustration exists than the Second Amendment, which has been fetishized by a rabid and extremely dangerous "gun rights" movement nurtured by the National Rifle Association and its enormous lobbying efforts. However, the "arms" of the eighteenth century were primitive — not even in the same universe — compared to those that are available to purchase in the United States today. U.S. citizens now have access to modern automatic assault weapons whose power, accuracy, and lethality would no doubt have been shocking to the framers and have become a major source of domestic insecurity wherever they are sold.

While the Second Amendment may be an anachronistic relic, it's worthwhile to ask whether the "right to bear arms" restraint principle could be reimagined in our own age, not as a recessed lethal force per se, but as a recessed capacity of citizens to take control of their personal data and equipment. Consider the enormous leap forward in personal computing capacities, which in some ways parallels the awesome leap forward in the power and lethality of modern firearms, but with different results. As recently as 1976, the fastest supercomputer in the world was the Cray-1, which cost around $8 million and was considered so powerful it was classified by the U.S. government as a munition and placed on an export control list. Computer performance is measured by floating point operations per second (FLOPS), and the Cray-1 was capable of a whopping 160 megaFLOPS. In contrast, the computing performance of the Apple iPhone 7, released in 2016 and costing around $700, is measured at an astonishing 368 *giga*-FLOPS — about 2,300 times more powerful. And yet this enormous computer processing power in the pockets of individuals has not translated into greater personal autonomy and empowerment (relative to large organizations) in ways that one might have imagined (and that had been promised). That's because each person's device is networked back to massive data farms operated by the technology platforms. Those platforms then exploit their several orders of magnitude more powerful computing capabilities to monitor, shape, extract, and analyze data from users at scale. While the device in your pocket has extraordinary computing power, that power is primarily directed at more efficiently monitoring you. You may pay for that device, but it (and even more so the data that is derived from it) is not something you really own. Under the existing legal regime of surveillance capitalism, it is the platforms that are the principal beneficiaries, thanks to the ways in which they have appropriated everyone's data as their property. What we have in place now is in fact a kind of digital feudalism. Recessed restraints would aim to better restore that imbalance and place those awesome computing capabilities and associated data more directly under the control (and ownership) of users.

Some examples of these types of recessed restraints might include laws that require governments and companies to retain records on how they handle our data: what they collect, how long they retain it, and with whom and under what conditions they share it with other companies and governments. Companies could be compelled to provide citizens with data access rights and disclose such practices to them upon request. As part of what we might call "the right to review," laws could be developed that compel entities like platforms to open up their algorithms to outside independent scrutiny. Another recessed power might be "data portability" and "interoperability" requirements, which would require companies to allow their users to pack up their data and take it to a different platform, and open up their platforms to competitors (i.e., "the right to relocate").

The so-called "right-to-repair" movement, which would free users from the proprietary clutches of large vendors like Apple, could be conceived as another recessed power. Right-to-repair legislation would "force companies to support independent repairs by making manuals, parts, and diagnostic codes available, and by ending the illegal practice of voiding warranties for customers who use independent repair services," in the words of one its most eloquent advocates, author Cory Doctorow. The COVID emergency may have helped kick the right-to-repair movement into high gear, or at least demonstrated its utility. With ventilators and other medical equipment in short supply, the right to repair became in some cases a matter of life and death. Technicians scrambled to circumvent the software and other controls medical device manufacturers use to prevent users from doing repairs, and widely shared repair manuals and other proprietary instructions. To be sure, the "right to repair" is a long way from the "right to bear arms." There's a big difference between having the right to take a screwdriver to your iPhone and carrying around a concealed Colt AR-15. But the Second Amendment was not fundamentally about carrying this or that weapon so much as it was designed as a restraint mechanism to check and constrain centralized authority. The "right to review," "right to relocate," and "right to repair" are all fundamentally types of recessed power, and thus a way to preserve and enhance the autonomy of individuals in relation to governments and companies in the context of our massively expanding datasphere.

And what if companies and governments are resistant to having their power restrained? Where does that leave us? No doubt there will be many such situations in countries all over the world, to greater and lesser degrees. In these circumstances, active forms of resistance, including civil disobedience, whistleblower alarms, and ethically minded hacktivism, may be appropriate for those who choose to take the risks.

It's important to remind ourselves that civil disobedience has a long provenance in political struggles the world over, and was instrumental in the civil rights movement and resistance to South African apartheid, communist dictatorships, and other forms of unjust political rule. Whistleblowing also has a long pedigree, with the first whistleblower protections enacted in the United States in the late eighteenth century. Cultivating and even nurturing among citizens a healthy distrust of authority is itself an important restraint on abuse, and a critical element of recessed power in the hands of citizens.

Today, most liberal democracies have various statutory protections for whistleblowers as a recognition of their restraint potential, but whistleblowers have run up against aggressive government investigations and prosecutions. Curiously, the Barack Obama administration, which campaigned on a promise to open government, led what most observers saw as a "war on whistleblowing," undertaking more Espionage Act prosecutions than all prior administrations combined, while harassing and even indicting as co-conspirators the journalists whose reporting was based on whistleblowers' revelations. In light of how much data on our personal lives is entrusted to governments and corporations, whistleblower protections should be an essential restraint on the abuse of power.

AS WE SAW IN CHAPTER 2, toleration of difference, respect for one another, and many of the other qualities that define a healthy public sphere are noticeably absent in social media spaces. While there are no doubt many reasons for this decline in civility, the engine of surveillance capitalism, with its bias towards extreme, emotionally charged content at the expense of reasoned discourse, is at least partially to blame. While a codified antisurveillance regime may help temper the pace and thus some of the anger and chaos associated with social media, deeper and more fundamental measures will be required. Here again, the concept of restraint can help guide us.

An often overlooked component of republicanism is its emphasis on civic virtue. In classical antiquity, the concept of virtue was debated endlessly and featured prominently in the works of Plato and Aristotle, and later, in Rome, of Seneca. Although it has a positive connotation, virtue doesn't simply equate to doing "good." Depending on the era and thinker, it is more broadly about the appropriate type of personal conduct that makes a good citizen. Virtue focuses on the type of personal character that is integral to a healthy republic, and it thus emphasizes the importance of thinking and acting in terms of one's duty to the collective. Virtue thus touches on the second meaning of "restraint," defined as dispassionate and moderate behaviour, self-control, prudence, and judiciousness.

Although they're now largely an afterthought, the restraints associated with civic virtue were considered as important to the American founding as was the separation of powers. The framers believed that liberty was sustained by virtue, which they perceived as a mixture of self-restraint, compromise, and a skilled knowledge of and deference to civic institutions. Most importantly, civic virtue was an object of extensive mass education. According to Deudney, "This republican civic identity was reinforced and reproduced through mass public education, ceremonies and rituals, and public architecture and iconography. President Washington, the exemplar of republican virtue, was a founder representing self-restraint and was immortalized as a Cincinnatus rather than a Caesar."

Much of today's discussion around tempering the extremes of social media focuses on the roles and responsibilities of the platforms, which to be sure are important. But we should not expect private companies to flawlessly regulate social norms; well-intentioned moderation could very easily slide into heavy-handed suppression of contrary and unpopular views. We want the platforms' interventions to be restrained here too (and that may mean tolerating a lot of disagreeable, misinformed, and otherwise malicious speech as a by-product of individual expression). Cultivation of civic virtue has to come from somewhere else, the most obvious source being public education. Unfortunately, training in "civics" and "virtue" has become barely an afterthought in most curricula, dwarfed by the priority given to developing skills necessary to feed the mega-machine: science, technology, engineering, and math (known by the acronym STEM). Parents and educators alike now increasingly see public education as a pathway to employment rather than as a mechanism to build the character required for good citizenship. That needs to change.

To turn this around would require a major rethink of the purpose, value, and content of public education. Any public education curriculum should include a deep dive into the history and purposes of civic rights and responsibilities themselves, and encourage familiarity with the perennial struggle to restrain abuses of power throughout history. Given how much our lives is mediated by complex technological systems, part of the curriculum should motivate young people to critically interrogate technologies that surround them and not take for granted the "black boxes" of our communications ecosystem within which power is exercised and hidden from public scrutiny. This approach is far broader and more critically minded than the narrow functional notion of "media literacy"; it is more closely aligned with the concept of ethically minded hacking that seeks to nurture a curiosity about how technological systems work "beneath the surface."

Public education should also foster a society-wide attitude about the information and communications environment equivalent to the attitude we hope citizens will one day have towards the natural environment: as something over which we exercise stewardship and restraint. Through public education, citizens could be encouraged to see ethics, civility, social tolerance, and respect for difference as part of what creates a healthy public sphere. Simultaneously, public education could encourage a more robust sense of personal data ownership, and a less frivolous attitude towards data consumption. Seen this way, efforts to "unplug" and "disconnect" can be linked to a deeper sentiment around conservation: aversion to over-consumption of both energy and data, and a strong distaste for planned obsolescence and other forms of waste.

It is worth underscoring how efforts to tame unbridled surveillance capitalism and encourage civic virtue and self-restraint mutually reinforce each other in ways that also support environmental rescue. Environmentalism's ideals — getting "back to nature," conserving resources, slowing down, recognizing the value of difference, and replacing instant gratification and endless consumption with an acknowledgement of the impact of our current practices on future generations — are the sorts of qualities we will need to embrace to mitigate the harms around social media. Conceptualizing "transgenerational publics" in the way that environmentalists do can help us think differently about the shadow cast on future generations not only by our excessive consumption and waste, but also by the data mining to which we consent that affects other individuals down the road (such as when we relentlessly photograph and then share over social media images of children who have not yet reached the age of consent). As runaway climate change begins to take its toll, and presents in unavoidable ways the ecological consequences of unbridled industrialization, it's quite likely that users will cast a critical eye upon their digital consumption habits as well. *Do we really need to have a weather app monitor all our social contacts?* Restraints on surveillance capitalism will work hand-in-glove with the restraints we need to undertake environmental rescue. As presently constituted under surveillance capitalism, social media are clearly dysfunctional to that imperative, and are indeed contributing to the problems. As the climate crisis becomes more acute, these deficiencies will become more glaring, underscoring the importance of a clear program that helps define and frame our collective approach to governing ourselves and our communications systems.

Universities will have a special role to play in reclaiming social media for civil society, and in serving as important institutions of political restraint in their own right. In order to carry out this role, however, the mission of the university has to be reclaimed as well. Most universities' mission statements are similar to my own at the University of Toronto, and as such it's worth quoting at length:

> The University of Toronto is dedicated to fostering an academic community in which the learning and scholarship of every member may flourish, with vigilant protection for individual human rights, and a resolute commitment to the principles of equal opportunity, equity and justice...
>
> Within the unique university context, the most crucial of all human rights are the rights of freedom of speech, academic freedom, and freedom of research. And we affirm that these rights are meaningless unless they entail the right to raise deeply disturbing questions and provocative challenges to the cherished beliefs of society at large and of the university itself...
>
> It is this human right to radical, critical teaching and research with which the University has a duty above all to be concerned; for there is no one else, no other institution and no other office, in our modern liberal democracy, which is the custodian of this most precious and vulnerable right of the liberated human spirit.

I could think of no better articulation of a mission statement for the university. However, the reality is different than the sentiment may lead one to believe. For example, it has become increasingly commonplace for universities to justify their programs in terms of an investment in or contribution to the economy. Research programs sell themselves in terms of employment training, which can skew research priorities in directions aligned with dominant industries. For their part, industries are increasingly major sources of research funds, many of which come with strings attached. Pressure from corporations and even governments can dissuade researchers from looking into certain areas of inquiry because doing so may jeopardize funding or employment opportunities for students, or risk some kind of legal or other penalty. Who wants to interrogate a hidden social media algorithm if it will invoke the wrath of a company's powerful legal department or blacklist graduates from prospective jobs?

To recover the original mission of the university will require several steps. First, the hollowing out of the social sciences, humanities, and arts will need to be radically reversed, not only to enrich society's emphasis on civic education, ethics, and virtue, but also to help broaden the techno-functionalist disciplines of engineering and computer sciences out of their narrow lanes of inquiry. Interdisciplinary collaboration should be incentivized so we can better understand the wider social and political implications of our machine-based civilization.

Second, and relatedly, projects and methods that peer into corporate and state secrets will need extra protection. At a time when power is increasingly hard-coded into the algorithms that surround us, academics need the ability to lift the lid on proprietary systems and systematically peer inside what large organizations do with data behind the scenes. Reverse engineering — a general term that covers a wide variety of tools, techniques, and methods — should be strongly entrenched as a core principle of academic freedom and an essential element of civic rights. Such protection may require adjustments to existing laws and regulations that ensure fair use for academics and shield them from frivolous lawsuits that aim to chill dissent. As Esha Bhandari, staff attorney with the ACLU's Speech, Privacy, and Technology Project, put it (following a federal court ruling on the topic in the ACLU's favor), "Researchers who test online platforms for discriminatory and rights-violating data practices perform a public service. They should not fear federal prosecution for conducting the 21st-century equivalent of anti-discrimination audit testing."

Third, to guard against the encroachment of outside influences that encourage secrecy and non-disclosure, universities should strongly advocate for openness as a core principle of academic freedom: open access, open data sets, and open source code. Universities should, as a matter of core policy, reject research funding that places unreasonable limits on free speech and openness or induces other types of secrecy.

As our own research at the Citizen Lab has shown, careful peer-reviewed and evidence-based research can be a powerful means to expose abuses of power and hidden privacy and security risks for citizens. But as our experiences have also demonstrated, powerful actors will not just stand aside and let it happen. They'll fight back, using any means at their disposal. A concerted and sustained effort will be required to protect adversarial research of the sort in which we have engaged. In a world of "truth decay" and general mistrust of all public institutions, universities have a special role to play not only as a credible source of authentic information and a safe space for principled debate, but also as a base from which to speak truth to unaccountable power.

RESTRAINTS PUT POLITICAL PRINCIPLES before technology, which reverses decades-long trends in internet and social media innovation, in which we saw unbridled technological development for its own sake treated mostly as an inherent good. The fascination with each new astounding digital or networked invention helped mythologize dot-com entrepreneurialism as an answer to every social and political problem. Technical fixes are still widely proposed as first-order solutions in just about every walk of life (as we witnessed with the bonanza of contact tracing apps rolled out as solutions to the COVID pandemic). While technology alone is no cure for the problems that ail social media, that doesn't mean technological innovation has no role to play in restructuring our communications ecosystem. In fact, certain types of technologies hold out the promise of greatly enhancing principles of restraint. Perhaps the most obvious but easy to overlook is encryption. By turning private communications into gibberish for all but those who hold the key, robust and peer-reviewed encryption provides a major check on the ability of outside forces to monitor what we do. That not only keeps us safe, it also protects against the abuse of power. End-to-end encryption messaging applications, such as those now standard on Signal and WhatsApp, will be essential to protecting privacy and human rights. Encryption of data at rest can help protect users against cybercrime, and provide another form of recessed restraint to prevent unauthorized access and use.

Other technologies also provide recessed power and restraint on the abuse of power: circumvention technologies allow us to bypass internet censorship, while tools like Tor give users the means to anonymously browse the web. More broadly, we will need to purposefully encourage innovation around alternative means of distributed communication that preserve the great strides we have made to connect individuals to each other and to vast stores of information on a planetary scale, without at the same time manipulating them towards their basest instincts. Prioritizing security of the global communications ecosystem as a whole — one that is distributed, secure, and open — would help pivot away from how it has been increasingly treated: as a "domain" to be fought over (and often seen as collateral damage) in the zero-sum game of interstate competition. An alternative "human-centric" approach to cybersecurity strives for indivisible network security on a planetary scale for the widest possible scope of human experience, and seeks to ensure that such principles are vigorously monitored and defended by multiple and overlapping forms of independent oversight and review.

IF THERE IS ANYTHING the COVID emergency makes clear, it is that we are living in a shared habitat, a true "global village," diseases and all. Thanks to machine civilization, globalization, and our lightspeed networks, our lives are now inextricably bound together in a web of our own making. The practical context for all politics has become a very particular and finite place we share: planet Earth.

Unfortunately, the architecture for global governance is only partially developed, flawed in fundamental ways, and mostly insufficient to manage the planet's challenges with anything approaching true cooperation and coordination. One hallmark of republican theorizing has been advocacy for the extension of restraint mechanisms to the international sphere through various techniques, like co-binding, federation, leagues, and supranational alliances. The legacy of this advocacy remains with us in the spectrum of global governance regimes with which most of us are familiar: the United Nations, the European Union, the World Trade Organization, the International Monetary Fund, the World Bank, the Organisation for Economic Cooperation and Development, and many others.

However, some of these regimes have been usurped by dominant class interests, while others have been hollowed out and are wobbling in the face of rising populist, nationalist, and isolationist sentiments. This degeneration is predictable as a direct consequence of the resurgence of authoritarianism and decline of democracy described in chapter 3. International institutions are but manifestations of the interests of the elites that make them up.

Where global governance in general goes, so too does governance of the internet and social media. As with global governance writ large, governance of information and communications technologies includes a wide spectrum of forums and institutions, from those that coordinate technical issues at the infrastructural level, like the Internet Engineering Task Force (IETF), to those that involve high-level discussions among states about "the rules of the road" in cyberspace, such as the U.N.'s Group of Governmental Experts on cybersecurity. There are also "multi-stakeholder" venues, like the Internet Governance Forum or the Freedom Online Coalition, where states, the private sector, and civil society meet on a regular basis and exchange ideas for norms and best practices.

Like global governance as a whole, however, this regime complex is flawed in important ways, mostly because of the enormous tide that has been moving in, in the form of militarization, securitization, and state control of information and communications. Discussions to develop norms of appropriate state behaviour in cyberspace, while laudable on one level, seem entirely theoretical at the current time in light of the practical reality of massive investments by states in offensive hacking, superpower policing, mass surveillance, and influence operations. Having spent well over a decade at many of these forums, I witnessed first-hand well-intentioned and hard-working government bureaucrats (usually associated with the poorly resourced human rights divisions of foreign affairs departments) push for an approach to cybersecurity based on human rights. Meanwhile, their governments' security agencies back home violated those principles in practice, hoarding software vulnerabilities, engaging in unwarranted mass and targeted surveillance, feeding a massive cybersecurity industrial complex, and fuelling a dangerous "arms race" in cyberspace.

We should not expect international institutions to be anything other than reflections of self-interested and power-seeking sovereign states, as long as restraints on the abuse of power are not deeply entrenched in domestic spheres. Only once restraints, divisions, and separations are established in individual republics can they then be extended internationally, first to like-minded states and then gradually to others. Liberal democratic systems of government can ensure that social media platforms and other technology giants are subjected to common standards of governance so that they cannot play jurisdictions against each other. Only with such a united front can they develop a truly robust response to the state-centric model of social media and internet governance being propagated by authoritarian countries like Russia and China.

Here again, the ubiquitous motto of environmental thinking, "think globally, act locally," can provide inspiration. While it may be daunting to think about governing the globe, or even a single sovereign state, it may be less daunting to think about governing at the municipal level. Firm restraints on the collection and use of municipal data are an obvious starting point for reclaiming our communications ecosystem for civil society, particularly when many so-called "smart" and "safe" cities are being rolled out with surveillance-by-design built in. As part of a recovery of their digital locales, citizens can militate against runaway surveillance capitalism, mandated "back doors," warrantless monitoring, and superpower policing in their own backyards. They can require companies located in their jurisdictions to follow best practices and undertake due diligence in conformity with internationally recognized human rights principles.

These "local" initiatives can be joined together through transnational civil society networks, which in turn can encourage pluralism across borders. Concerted efforts can be made to connect with and support those living in closed and oppressive societies, while simultaneously pushing back on the spread of authoritarian controls through privacy- and censorship-evasion tools and vigorous and relentless research in the public interest. International regimes that seek to securely govern our entire communications ecosystem, like the IETF, can be insulated from the machinations of power politics and populated by individuals drawn from civil society in many countries, united by an approach that perceives the internet and social media as "commons" over which they perform stewardship and act as guardians. Governing the global communications ecosystem is a worldwide challenge, but it can start from the bottom up.

THE PAINFUL TRUTHS OUTLINED in this book paint a very bleak picture. They also present a troubling forecast for the future of the human condition. It seems undeniable now that the disturbing worldwide descent into neo-fascism, tribal politics, and unbridled kleptocracy, along with the accompanying spread of ignorance and prejudice we have witnessed in recent years, is at least in part because the social media environment (presently constituted under the regime of surveillance capitalism) created conditions that allowed such practices to thrive and flourish. Personal data surveillance and authoritarian state controls present a "perfect fit": seemingly endless lucrative business opportunities that undermine public accountability and facilitate despotic rule. These negative externalities may have been amplified by the surge in demand for social media during the COVID pandemic, the enhanced power of the platforms that went along with it, and the unprecedented emergency measures that tapped into those platforms' surveillance potential.

On top of that, our insatiable lust for data and disposable devices is silently taxing resources, sucking up vast amounts of energy, and thus contributing to, rather than helping to mitigate, the climate crisis. While the COVID pandemic has given some reprieve in terms of CO_2 emissions, thanks to a short reduction in airline and other fossil fuel–powered transportation, that reprieve will eventually pass. However, the sudden embrace of digital networked technologies will not, and may in fact deepen. Combined, both real and virtual consumption could increasingly strain natural resources, draw from dirty energy sources, drive up emissions, and contribute to waste. As climate scientists warn, continuing down that path will lead to collective ruin. Our precious apps will mean little when humans are either wiped out altogether or consigned to a Hobbesian state of nature, dispersed in small tribes struggling against each other for the scarce resources needed for survival. It is not unrealistic to imagine a time when the internet and all of its associated infrastructure will be reduced to rusting artifacts submersed in rising oceans or covered over by tangled weeds, if consumption practices continue apace. That would be one way to mitigate social media's negative consequences, but obviously not worth the price.

Much of what has been outlined above and in earlier chapters is, sadly, not surprising. These are "truths" because they are widely recognized now by a growing community of experts. But the time has come to move beyond diagnosis and start the hard work on solutions. We must squarely and comprehensively address the intertwined pathologies of social media and surveillance capitalism, starting with that device you hold in your hand. Fortunately, we have a recipe — a set of principles—that can help guide us in this task. We do not even need to invent something new. Humans have faced enormous political challenges thrown up by new material situations before, and there is a long tradition of practical theorizing that can be adapted to our own unique circumstances. It is time to reset, to start over from first principles, and to work towards the construction and stewardship of a communications ecosystem that serves, rather than diminishes, human well-being.

To be sure, everything described above will take many years to accomplish. We need to realistically acknowledge that there are major hurdles to overcome, and deeply entrenched and powerful interests that will work in opposition (and not always by the rules). A comprehensive strategy of long-term reform is therefore required, extending from the personal to the political, from the local to the global. We must begin now, with practical and manageable small steps simultaneously undertaken by many of us spread across the planet. The COVID emergency reminds us of our shared fate.

We have a once-in-a-lifetime opportunity to "reset." We can reclaim the internet for civil society. The principle of restraint should be our guide.

NOTES

What follows is an abridged set of endnotes. For the unabridged version, please go to https://reset-bibliography.ca/.

INTRODUCTION

Right-wing, neo-fascist populism flourishes online and off, igniting hatred, murder, and even genocide: Venier, S. (2019). The role of Facebook in the persecution of the Rohingya minority in Myanmar: Issues of accountability under international law. *Italian Yearbook of International Law Online, 28*(1), 231–248; Vaidhyanathan, S. (2018). *Antisocial media: How Facebook has disconnected citizens and undermined democracy.* Oxford University Press.

Shady data analytics companies like Cambridge Analytica: Cadwalladr, C., & Graham-Harrison, E. (2018). The Cambridge Analytica files. Retrieved from https://www.theguardian.com/news/series/cambridge-analytica-files

I organize these problems as "painful truths": Deibert, R. J. (2019). The road to digital unfreedom: Three painful truths about social media. *Journal of Democracy, 30*(1), 25–39.

Desktop computers were eventually networked together: Abbate, J. (2000). *Inventing the internet.* MIT Press; Hafner, K., & Lyon, M.

(1998). *Where wizards stay up late: The origins of the internet.* Simon and Schuster.

Before long, the internet was in everything: Waltz, E. (2020, January 20). How do neural implants work? Retrieved from https://spectrum.ieee.org/the-human-os/biomedical/devices/what-is-neural-implant-neuromodulation-brain-implants-electroceuticals-neuralink-definition-examples; Strickland, E. (2017). Silicon Valley's latest craze: Brain tech. *IEEE Spectrum, 54*(7), 8–9; DeNardis, L. (2018). *The internet in everything: Freedom and security in a world with no off switch.* Yale University Press.

Security experts have routinely discovered: Jaret, P. (2018, November 12). Exposing vulnerabilities: How hackers could target your medical devices. Retrieved from https://www.aamc.org/news-insights/exposing-vulnerabilities-how-hackers-could-target-your-medical-devices

Engineers are experimenting on systems: Moore, S. K. (2019, May 14). Wireless network brings dust-sized brain implants a step closer. Retrieved from https://spectrum.ieee.org/the-human-os/biomedical/devices/wireless-network-brings-dustsized-brain-implants-a-step-closer

We are all now "cyborgs": Haraway, D. (1991). A cyborg manifesto: Science, technology, and socialist feminism in the late twentieth century. In *Simians, cyborgs and women: The reinvention of nature* (149–181). Routledge.

Much of it is rendered invisible through familiarity and habituation: Edwards, P. M. (2017). The mechanics of invisibility: On habit and routine as elements of infrastructure. In I. Ruby & A. Ruby (Eds.), *Infrastructure space* (327–336). Ruby Press.

Sometimes gaping vulnerabilities: Anderson, R. (2001, December). Why information security is hard—An economic perspective. *Seventeenth Annual Computer Security Applications Conference* (358–365). IEEE.

An "accidental megastructure": Bratton, B. H. (2016). *The stack—On software and sovereignty.* MIT Press.

A bewildering array of new applications: Lindsay, J. R. (2017). Restrained by design: The political economy of cybersecurity. *Digital Policy, Regulation and Governance, 19*(6), 493–514. https://doi.org/10.1108/DPRG-05-2017-0023

Merriam-Webster defines social media: Merriam-Webster. (n.d.). Social media. In Merriam-Webster.com dictionary. Retrieved April 21, 2020, from https://www.merriam-webster.com/dictionary/social%20media.

Designed secret "back doors": On the legal implications of "remote, surreptitious brain surveillance," see Kerr, I., Binnie, M., & Aoki, C. (2008); Tessling on my brain: The future of lie detection and brain privacy in the criminal justice system. *Canadian Journal of Criminology and Criminal Justice, 50*(3), 367–387.

Google's security team says: Huntley, S. (2020, May 27). Updates about government-backed hacking and disinformation. Retrieved from https://blog.google/threat-analysis-group/updates-about-government-backed-hacking-and-disinformation

North Korea depends on the internet for illicitly acquired revenues: Sanger, D. (2020, February 9). North Korea's internet use surges, thwarting sanctions and fueling theft. Retrieved from https://www.nytimes.com/2020/02/09/us/politics/north-korea-internet-sanctions.html; See also Deibert, R., & Pauly, L. (2019). Cyber Westphalia and beyond: Extraterritoriality and mutual entanglement in cyberspace. In D. Bigo, E. F. Isin, & E. Ruppert (Eds.), *Data politics: Worlds, subjects, rights*. Routledge.

Offensive action . . . takes place just below the threshold of armed conflict: But not always. For exceptions and discussion, see Zetter, K. (2014). *Countdown to zero day: Stuxnet and the launch of the world's first digital weapon*. Broadway Books; Greenberg, A. (2019). *Sandworm: A new era of cyberwar and the hunt for the Kremlin's most dangerous hackers*. Doubleday; For a contrary view, see Rid, T. (2013). *Cyber war will not take place*. Oxford University Press USA.

Spreading false information is as old as humanity itself: See Posetti, J., & Matthews, A. (2018, July 23). A short guide to the history of "fake news" and disinformation. Retrieved from https://www.icfj.org/

news/short-guide-history-fake-news-and-disinformation-new-icfj-learning-module

Nonetheless products of history: See Deibert, R. (1999). Harold Innis and the empire of speed. *Review of International Studies, 25*(2), 273–289; Ruggie, J. G. (1993). Territoriality and beyond: Problematizing modernity in international relations. *International Organization, 47*(1), 139–174.

In his seminal book... Innis explained: Innis, H. A., & Innis, M. Q. (1972). *Empire and communications.* University of Toronto Press.

The rise of individualism... and nationalism: Anderson, B. (1983). *Imagined communities: Reflections on the origin and spread of nationalism.* Verso; Deibert, R. (2000). *Parchment, printing, and hypermedia: Communication and world order transformation.* Columbia University Press; McLuhan, M. (1963). *The Gutenberg galaxy.* University of Toronto Press.

As... Naomi Klein has put it: Klein, N. (2019, August 21). Why the Democratic National Committee must change the rules and hold a climate debate. Retrieved from https://theintercept.com/2019/08/21/climate-debate-dnc/

CHAPTER ONE: THE MARKET FOR OUR MINDS

Initial coverage of the PRISM program: Greenwald, G., & MacAskill, E. (2013, June 7). NSA Prism program taps in to user data of Apple, Google and others. Retrieved from https://www.theguardian.com/world/2013/jun/06/us-tech-giants-nsa-data; Gellman, B. (2020). *Dark mirror: Edward Snowden and the American surveillance state.* Penguin.

A top secret program called Dishfire: Poltras, L. V., Rosenbach M., & Stark, H. (2013, September 15). NSA monitors financial world. Retrieved from https://www.spiegel.de/international/world/how-the-nsa-spies-on-international-bank-transactions-a-922430.html

A program code-named HAPPYFOOT: Soltani, A., Peterson, A., & Gellman, B. (2013, December 11). NSA uses Google cookies to pinpoint targets for hacking. Retrieved from https://www.washingtonpost.com/news/the-switch/wp/2013/12/10/nsa-uses-google-cookies-to-pinpoint-targets-for-hacking/

The NSA collected hundreds of thousands of contacts: Gellman, B., & Soltani, A. (2013, October 14). NSA collects millions of e-mail address books globally. Retrieved from https://www.washingtonpost.com/world/national-security/nsa-collects-millions-of-e-mail-address-books-globally/2013/10/14/8e58b5be-34f9-11e3-80c6-7e6dd8d22d8f_story.html

An NSA program to exploit unpatched vulnerabilities: Rosenbach, M., & Stark, H. (2013, September 9). How the NSA accesses smartphone data. Retrieved from https://www.spiegel.de/international/world/how-the-nsa-spies-on-smartphones-including-the-blackberry-a-921161.html

"Can the dot-com party go on forever? Not likely": Yang, C. (2000, April 3). Earth to dot com accountants. Retrieved from https://www.bloomberg.com/news/articles/2000-04-02/commentary-earth-to-dot-com-accountants

The stock value of the … top 280 internet companies: Kleinbard, D. (2000, November 9). Dot.coms lose $1.755 trillion in market value. Retrieved from https://money.cnn.com/2000/11/09/technology/overview/; Howcroft, D. (2001). After the goldrush: Deconstructing the myths of the dot.com market. *Journal of Information Technology, 16*(4), 195–204. http://doi.org/10.1080/02683960110100418

Principals at Google adjusted their strategy: Levy, S. (2011). *In the plex: How Google thinks, works, and shapes our lives.* Simon and Schuster.

"This new form of information capitalism": Zuboff, S. (2015). Big other: Surveillance capitalism and the prospects of an information civilization. *Journal of Information Technology, 30*(1), 75–89. https://doi.org/10.1057/jit.2015.5, 75.

The early modern bureaucratic state and its mass record keeping: Koopman, C. (2019). *How we became our data: A genealogy of the informational person.* University of Chicago Press; Bouk, D. (2015). *How our days became numbered: Risk and the rise of the statistical individual.* University of Chicago Press; Crosby, A. (1996). *Taking measure of reality: Quantification and Western society, 1250–1600*. Cambridge University Press; Porter, T. (1995). *Trust in numbers: The pursuit of objectivity in science and public life*. Princeton University Press; Beniger, J. (1989). *The control revolution: Technological and economic origins of the information society*. Harvard University Press; Lyon, D. (1994). *The electronic eye: The rise of surveillance society*. University of Minnesota Press; Standage, T. (1998). *The Victorian internet: The remarkable story of the telegraph and the nineteenth century's online pioneers*. Phoenix.

You need different sensors and inputs…And to the consumer, it needs to feel like one: Matyszczyk, C. (2019, July 23). A Google exec admits the ugly truth about the smart home. Retrieved from https://www.zdnet.com/article/a-google-exec-admits-the-ugly-truth-about-the-smart-home/

Our ignorance is their bliss: Zuboff, S. (2019, January 24). 'Surveillance capitalism' has gone rogue. We must curb its excesses. Retrieved from https://www.washingtonpost.com/opinions/surveillance-capitalism-has-gone-rogue-we-must-curb-its-excesses/2019/01/24/be463f48-1ffa-11e9-9145-3f74070bbdb9_story.html

Why not equip them with cameras to map the houses: Porter, J. (2019, June 21). Amazon patents 'surveillance as a service' tech for its delivery drones. Retrieved from https://www.theverge.com/2019/6/21/18700451/amason-delivery-drone-surveillance-home-security-system-patent-application

Why not vacuum up internet data: Kiss, J. (2010, May 15). Google admits collecting Wi-Fi data through Street View cars. Retrieved from https://www.theguardian.com/technology/2010/may/15/google-admits-storing-private-data

Patent applications that Facebook has made: Chinoy, S. (2018, June 21). What 7 Creepy Patents Reveal About Facebook. Retrieved from https://www.nytimes.com/interactive/2018/06/21/opinion/sunday/facebook-patents-privacy.html

What the academic Jan Padios calls "emotional extraction": Padios, J. M. (2017). Mining the mind: Emotional extraction, productivity, and predictability in the twenty-first century. *Cultural Studies, 31*(2–3), 205–231. http://doi.org/10.1080/09502386.2017.1303426

"This information does not pass through a cognitive filter as it is created and stored": Greene, A. K. (2019, August 12). Data sweat. Retrieved from https://reallifemag.com/data-sweat/

They say "the app can even predict how a person will feel next week": Sheridan, K. (2018, October 4). A startup's bold plan for a mood-predicting smartphone app is shadowed by questions over evidence. Retrieved from https://www.statnews.com/2018/10/04/mindstrong-questions-over-evidence/

Facebook has data-sharing partnerships with at least sixty device makers: Dance, G. J. X., Confessore, N., & LaForgia, M. (2018, June 3). Facebook gave device makers deep access to data on users and friends. Retrieved from https://www.nytimes.com/interactive/2018/06/03/technology/facebook-device-partners-users-friends-data.html

Privacy International (PI) published a report: Privacy International. (2018, December). *How apps on Android share data with Facebook (even if you don't have a Facebook account)*. Retrieved from https://privacyinternational.org/appdata

PI examined an app called Maya: Privacy International. (2019, September 9). No body's business but mine: How menstruation apps are sharing your data. Retrieved from https://privacyinternational.org/long-read/3196/no-bodys-business-mine-how-menstruation-apps-are-sharing-your-data

Browsers can tell a lot about a user: Price, D. (2018, October 12). 10 types of data your browser is collecting about you right now. Retrieved from https://www.makeuseof.com/tag/data-browser-collects-about-you/

Researcher Sam Jadali found that Nacho Analytics: Fowler, G.A. (2019, July 18). I found your data. It's for sale. Retrieved from https://www.washingtonpost.com/technology/2019/07/18/i-found-your-data-its-sale/

Jadali... could nonetheless access usernames, passwords: Jadali, S. (2019, July 18). DataSpii: The catastrophic data leak via browser extensions. Retrieved from https://securitywithsam.com/2019/07/dataspii-leak-via-browser-extensions/

As noted in Air Canada's privacy policy: Air Canada. (2019, October 8). Privacy policy. Retrieved January 2019 from https://www.aircanada.com/ca/en/aco/home/legal/privacy-policy.html

Tala's CEO said that "repayment of a loan...": Aglionby, B. (2016, July 5). "US fintech pioneer's start-up in Kenya." Retrieved from https://www.ft.com/content/05e65d04-3c7a-11e6-9f2c-36b487ebd80a

What... Keith Breckenridge calls "reputational collateral": Breckenridge, K. (2018). The failure of the 'single source of truth about Kenyans': The NDRS, collateral mysteries and the Safaricom monopoly. *African Studies, 78*(1), 91–111. http://doi.org/10.1080/00020184.2018.1540515; Johnson, K., Pasquale, F., & Chapman, J. (2019). Artificial intelligence, machine learning, and bias in finance: Toward responsible innovation. *Fordham Law Review, 88*(2), 499.

Zynga... gives its games permission to access...: Levine, S. (2019, May 10). The 5 worst apps for your privacy. Retrieved from https://nordvpn.com/blog/worst-privacy-apps/

The illuminating example of Pokémon Go: Zuboff, S. (2019). *The age of surveillance capitalism: The fight for a human future at the new frontier of power.* PublicAffairs.

Google Maps functions... in this manner: Investopedia. (2019, November 14). How does Google Maps make money? Retrieved from https://www.investopedia.com/articles/investing/061115/how-does-google-maps-makes-money.asp

The higher-level function is to use us as free labour: Crawford, K., & Joler, V. (2018, September 7). Anatomy of an AI system: The Amazon Echo as an anatomical map of human labor, data and planetary resources. Retrieved from https://anatomyof.ai/.

In 2014, Pew Internet undertook an analysis: Atkinson, M. (2015, November 10). Apps permissions in the Google Play store. Retrieved from https://www.pewresearch.org/internet/2015/11/10/apps-permissions-in-the-google-play-store/

Android apps harvested location data: Ng, A. (2019, July 8). More than 1,000 Android apps harvest data even after you deny permissions.

Retrieved from https://www.cnet.com/news/more-than-1000-android-apps-harvest-your-data-even-after-you-deny-permissions/

CVS...sent a user's GPS coordinates to over forty different third parties: Egelman, S. (2017, August 25). CVS discretely shares your location with 40+ other sites. Retrieved from https://blog.appcensus.io/2017/08/25/cvs-discretely-shares-your-location-with-40-other-sites/

Apps targeting children: Egelman, S. (2017, July 27). We tested apps for children. Half failed to protect their data. Retrieved from https://www.washingtonpost.com/news/the-switch/wp/2017/07/27/we-tested-apps-for-children-half-failed-to-protect-their-data/

Facebook used contact information...for targeted advertising: Gebhart, G. (2018, September 27). You gave Facebook your number for security. They used it for ads. Retrieved from https://www.eff.org/deeplinks/2018/09/you-gave-facebook-your-number-security-they-used-it-ads

The People You May Know functionality: Hill, K. (2018, August 8). "People You May Know:" A controversial Facebook feature's 10-year history. Retrieved from https://gizmodo.com/people-you-may-know-a-controversial-facebook-features-1827981959

As I described in a Globe and Mail *editorial*: Deibert, R. (2015, May 21). When it comes to cyberspace, should national security trump user security? Retrieved from https://www.theglobeandmail.com/opinion/when-it-comes-to-browsers-user-security-trumps-surveillance/article24547582/

Parents unwittingly splash their children's biometric data: See Eichhorn, K. (2019). *The end of forgetting: Growing up with social media*. Harvard University Press.

23andMe and Airbnb have partnered: Valle, G. D. (2019, May 22). Airbnb is partnering with 23andMe to send people on "heritage" vacations. Retrieved from https://www.vox.com/2019/5/22/18635829/airbnb-23andme-heritage-vacations-partnership

GlaxoSmithKline acquired: Brodwin, E. (2018, July 25). DNA-testing company 23andMe has signed a $300 million deal with a drug giant. Here's how to delete your data if that freaks you out. Retrieved from https://www.businessinsider.com/dna-testing-delete-your-data-23andme-ancestry-2018-7

Those who share their genetic fingerprints: Resnick, B. (2018, October 15). How your third cousin's Ancestry DNA test could jeopardize your privacy. Retrieved from https://www.vox.com/science-and-health/2018/10/12/17957268/science-ancestry-dna-privacy; There are also unique risks around the use of DNA data for African Americans because of the vulnerabilities they face around racialized surveillance. See Nelson, A. (2018). The social life of DNA: Racial reconciliation and institutional morality after the genome. *British Journal of Sociology, 69*(3), 522–537. https://doi.org/10.1111/1468-4446.12607; Khandaker, T. (2018, July 26). Canada is using Ancestry DNA websites to help it deport people. Retrieved from https://news.vice.com/en_ca/article/wjkxmy/canada-is-using-ancestry-dna-websites-to-help-it-deport-people; Molnar, P., & Gill, L. (2018, September). *Bots at the gate: A human rights analysis of automated decision-making in Canada's immigration and refugee system*. Citizen Lab Research Report No. 114. Retrieved from https://citizenlab.ca/wp-content/uploads/2018/09/IHRP-Automated-Systems-Report-Web-V2.pdf

A security researcher discovered that…Zoom: Doffman, Z. (2019, July 9). Confirmed: Zoom security flaw exposes webcam hijack risk, change settings now. Retrieved from https://www.forbes.com/sites/zakdoffman/2019/07/09/warning-as-millions-of-zoom-users-risk-webcam-hijack-change-your-settings-now/

Hundreds of millions of its users' phone numbers: Whittaker, Z. (2019, September 4). A huge database of Facebook users' phone numbers found online. Retrieved from https://techcrunch.com/2019/09/04/facebook-phone-numbers-exposed/

Millions of its users' passwords were stored: Krebs, B. (2019, March 21). Facebook stored hundreds of millions of user passwords in plain text for years. Retrieved from https://krebsonsecurity.com/2019/03/facebook-stored-hundreds-of-millions-of-user-passwords-in-plain-text-for-years/

More than twenty million Ecuadoreans: Meredith, S. (2019, September 17). Almost everyone in Ecuador has had their personal information leaked online. Retrieved from https://www.cnbc.com/2019/09/17/ecuador-data-breach-leaks-personal-information-for-millions-of-citizens.html

3,800 publicly disclosed breaches had exposed an astounding 4.1 billion individual records: Winder, D. (2019, August 20). Data breaches expose 4.1 billion records in first six months of 2019. Retrieved from https://www.forbes.com/sites/daveywinder/2019/08/20/data-breaches-expose-41-billion-records-in-first-six-months-of-2019/

"Our privacy crisis is a crisis of design": Warzel, C. (2019, July 9). Your inbox is spying on you. Retrieved from https://www.nytimes.com/2019/07/09/opinion/email-tracking.html

Facebook did not provide a simply explained "opt-out" for users for its facial recognition scanning technology: Germain, T. (2019, September 3). Facebook updates facial recognition settings after CR investigation. Retrieved from https://www.consumerreports.org/privacy/facebook-updates-facial-recognition-setting/

Shazam... was drawing audio from its surroundings: Leyden, J. (2016, November 15). Shhh! Shazam is always listening—even when it's been switched 'off.' Retrieved from https://www.theregister.co.uk/2016/11/15/shazam_listening/

Human contractors... listen in on audio recordings to transcribe what's being said: Oremus, W. (2019, July 27). Amazon is watching. Retrieved from https://onezero.medium.com/amazon-is-watching-d51b20f1668a

Google's audio recordings were activated without the trigger words being uttered: Hee, L. V., Baert, D., Verheyden, T., & Heuvel, R. V. D. (2019, July 10). Google employees are eavesdropping, even in your living room, VRT NWS has discovered. Retrieved from https://www.vrt.be/vrtnws/en/2019/07/10/google-employees-are-eavesdropping-even-in-flemish-living-rooms/

A group of California citizens launched a class-action lawsuit: *Kumandan et al. v. Google LLC et al.*, 5:19-cv-04286 (N.D. Cal. 2019).

What…Cory Doctorow has called "peak indifference": Doctorow, C. (2016, July 3). Peak indifference. Retrieved from https://locusmag.com/2016/07/cory-doctorow-peak-indifference/

A recent survey of American attitudes: Ladd, J. M., Tucker, J. A., & Kates, S. (2018, October 24). 2018 American Institutional Confidence Poll: The health of American democracy in an era of hyper polarization. Retrieved from http://aicpoll.com/

Devices have allowed tech platforms to appropriate our personal information: Cohen, J. E. (2019). *Between truth and power: The legal constructions of informational capitalism.* Oxford University Press USA.

What media scholar Tim Wu calls the "attention merchants": Wu, T. (2016). *The attention merchants: The epic scramble to get inside our heads.* Knopf.

CHAPTER TWO: TOXIC ADDICTION MACHINES

Commonplace around any major news event: For a discussion of the meanings of disinformation, misinformation, propaganda, etc., see Jack, C. (2017). *Lexicon of lies: Terms for problematic information.* Data & Society Research Institute. Retrieved from https://datasociety.net/library/lexicon-of-lies/

The WHO went so far as to label COVID-19 an "infodemic": World Health Organization. (2020, February 2). *Novel coronavirus (2019-nCoV): Situation report 13.* Retrieved from https://www.who.int/docs/default-source/coronaviruse/situation-reports/20200202-sitrep-13-ncov-v3.pdf

Russian propaganda outlets spread disinformation: Breland, A. (2020, February 3). Russian media outlets are blaming the coronavirus on the United States. Retrieved from https://www.motherjones.com/politics/2020/02/russian-disinformation-coronavirus/

Widely accepted throughout Chinese society: Gilbert, D. (2020, April 6). The Chinese government has convinced its citizens that the U.S. Army brought coronavirus to Wuhan. Retrieved from https://www.vice.com/en_us/article/wxe9yq/

the-chinese-government-has-convinced-its-citizens-that-the-us-army-brought-coronavirus-to-wuhan

One YouTube video... falsely claimed that Africa was immune: Shanapinda, S. (2020, April 7). No, 5G radiation doesn't spread the coronavirus. Here's how we know. Retrieved from https://theconversation.com/no-5g-radiation-doesnt-cause-or-spread-the-coronavirus-saying-it-does-is-destructive-135695

More than thirty incidents of arson and vandalism: Satariano, A., & Alba, D. (2020, April 10). Burning cell towers, out of baseless fear they spread the virus. Retrieved from https://www.nytimes.com/2020/04/10/technology/coronavirus-5g-uk.html

Mob violence and armed clashes with police in Ukraine: Miller, C. (2020, February 20). A viral email about coronavirus had people smashing buses and blocking hospitals. Retrieved from https://www.buzzfeednews.com/article/christopherm51/coronavirus-ukraine-china

In Canada, racist tropes: Do, E. M., & Quon, A. (2020, February 2). As coronavirus dominates headlines, xenophobic and insensitive social media posts go viral. Retrieved from https://globalnews.ca/news/6479939/coronavirus-racism-xenophobia-sinophobia-china/

IBM X-Force... warned that more was to come: Zorz, Z. (2020, February 3). Wuhan coronavirus exploited to deliver malware, phishing, hoaxes. Retrieved from https://www.helpnetsecurity.com/2020/02/03/wuhan-coronavirus-exploited-to-deliver-malware-phishing-hoaxes/

Ransomware, digital espionage attacks, and phishing schemes: Satter, R., Stubbs, J., & Bing, C. (2020, March 23). Exclusive: Elite hackers target WHO as coronavirus cyberattacks spike. Retrieved from https://www.reuters.com/article/us-health-coronavirus-who-hack-exclusive/exclusive-elite-hackers-target-who-as-coronavirus-cyberattacks-spike-idUSKBN21A3BN

Mistakenly removed links: Orr, C. (2020, March 17). Facebook is removing links to coronavirus information on government websites. Retrieved from https://www.nationalobserver.com/2020/03/17/news/facebook-removing-links-coronavirus-information-government-websites

Platforms introduced measures to point users: Gadde, V., & Derella, M. (2020, March 16). An update on our continuity strategy during COVID-19. Retrieved from https://blog.twitter.com/en_us/topics/company/2020/An-update-on-our-continuity-strategy-during-COVID-19.html

Arrested for messages sent to an online chat group: Shih, G., & Knowles, H. (2020, February 4). A Chinese doctor was one of the first to warn about coronavirus. He got detained—and infected. Retrieved from https://www.washingtonpost.com/world/2020/02/04/chinese-doctor-has-coronavirus/

Health workers told reporters they felt overwhelmed: Fisher, M., & Taub, A. (2019, April 11). How YouTube radicalized Brazil. Retrieved from https://www.nytimes.com/2019/08/11/world/americas/youtube-brazil.html

An opportunity for climate change denialists to propagate disinformation: Ryan, H., & Wilson, C. (2020, January 22). As Australia burned, climate change denialism got a boost on Facebook. Retrieved from https://www.buzzfeed.com/hannahryan/facebook-australia-bushfires-climate-change-deniers-facebook

Conspiracy theories circulated across social media: Knaus, C. (2020, January 11). Disinformation and lies are spreading faster than Australia's bushfires. Retrieved from https://www.theguardian.com/australia-news/2020/jan/12/disinformation-and-lies-are-spreading-faster-than-australias-bushfires

At least one prominent politician bought into it: Capstick, S., Dyke, J., Lewandowsky, S., Pancost, R., & Steinberger, J. (2020, January 14). Disinformation on Australian bushfires should not be spread by ministers. Retrieved from https://www.theguardian.com/environment/2020/jan/14/disinformation-on-australian-bushfires-should-not-be-spread-by-ministers

"What Australians... need is information and support": Ryan & Wilson. As Australia burned.

Oxford Bibliographies defines the "public sphere": Wessler, H., & Freudenthaler, R. (2018). Public sphere. Retrieved from https://www.

oxfordbibliographies.com/view/document/obo-9780199756841/obo-9780199756841-0030.xml

European coffee houses and salons: Habermas, J. (1991). *The structural transformation of the public sphere: An inquiry into a category of bourgeois society*. MIT Press; For critiques of Habermas's notion of the public sphere, see Fraser, N. (1990). Rethinking the public sphere: A contribution to the critique of actually existing democracy. Social text, (25–26), 56–80; and Squires, C. R. (2002). Rethinking the black public sphere: An alternative vocabulary for multiple public spheres. *Communication Theory, 12*(4), 446–468.

"The shares of America's five biggest technology firms have been on an astonishing bull run": *Economist*. (2020, February 21). So much for the techlash? Retrieved from https://www.economist.com/graphic-detail/2020/02/21/so-much-for-the-techlash

Facebook's stock jumped close to 2 percent: Jee, C. (2019, July 15). Facebook is actually worth more thanks to news of the FTC's $5 billion fine. Retrieved from https://www.technologyreview.com/2019/07/15/134196/facebook-is-actually-richer-thanks-to-news-of-the-ftcs-5-billion-fine/

Facebook's $5.7 billion investment in India's Jio: Pham, S. (2020, May 7). India's Jio Platforms lands $1.5 billion from Vista Equity, marking 3 big investments in 3 weeks. Retrieved from https://www.cnn.com/2020/05/07/tech/reliance-jio-vista-india-intl-hnk/index.html

"Digital colonialism,"as Global Voices' Ellery Biddle calls it: Solon, O. (2017, July 27). "It's digital colonialism": How Facebook's free internet service has failed its users. Retrieved from https://www.theguardian.com/technology/2017/jul/27/facebook-free-basics-developing-markets

"Infrastructural imperialism," in which companies like Google increasingly structure our choices: Vaidhyanathan, S. (2011). *The Googlization of everything: (And why we should worry)*. University of California Press.

An experiment to prove the point: Ben-Shahar, O., & Schneider, C. E. (2011). The failure of mandated disclosure. *University of Pennsylvania Law Review, 159*(3), 647–749. Retrieved from https://

www.law.upenn.edu/journals/lawreview/articles/volume159/issue3/BenShaharSchneider159U.Pa.L.Rev.647(2011).pdf

"The negative impact the electronic contracting environment has on our habits and dispositions": Frischmann, B. M., & Selinger, E. (2016). *Engineering humans with contracts.* Cardozo Legal Studies Research Paper No. 493. https://dx.doi.org/10.2139/ssrn.2834011

Enables them to appropriate users' data: Cohen. *Between truth and power.*

Creating a kind of "consent fatigue": Utz, C., Degeling, M., Fahl, S., Schaub, F., & Holz, T. (2019). (Un)informed consent: Studying GDPR consent notices in the field. *Proceedings of the 2019 ACM SIGSAC Conference on Computer and Communications Security.* Retrieved from https://arxiv.org/abs/1909.02638v2

A report published by the International Center for Media & the Public Agenda: University of Maryland. (2010). New study by Merrill prof finds students everywhere addicted to media. Retrieved from https://merrill.umd.edu/2011/04/new-merrill-study-finds-students-everywhere-addicted-to-media/

Social media affect brains like falling in love: Penenberg, A. L. (2010, July 1). Social networking affects brains like falling in love. Retrieved from https://www.fastcompany.com/1659062/social-networking-affects-brains-falling-love

Your level of oxytocin: Seiter, C. (2016, August 10). The psychology of social media: Why we like, comment, and share online. Retrieved from https://buffer.com/resources/psychology-of-social-media

People addicted to social media: Griffiths, M. D. (2013). Social networking addiction: Emerging themes and issues. *Journal of Addiction Research & Therapy, 4*(5). https://doi.org/10.4172/2155-6105.1000e118; Blackwell, D., Leaman, C., Tramposch, R., Osborne, C., & Liss, M. (2017). Extraversion, neuroticism, attachment style and fear of missing out as predictors of social media use and addiction. *Personality and Individual Differences, 116*, 69–72; Van Den Eijnden, R. J., Lemmens, J. S., & Valkenburg, P. M. (2016). The social media disorder scale. *Computers in Human Behavior, 61*, 478–487; Hawi, N. S., & Samaha, M. (2017). The relations among social media addiction, self-esteem, and life satisfaction in university students. *Social Science Computer Review, 35*(5), 576–586.

The mere presence of a switched-off smartphone: Berthon, P., Pitt, L., & Campbell, C. (2019). Addictive de-vices: A public policy analysis of sources and solutions to digital addiction. *Journal of Public Policy & Marketing, 38*(4), 451–468. https://doi.org/10.1177/0743915619859852

Why many of us habitually pull out our phones: Berthon et al. Addictive de-vices.

Through "loot boxes" containing unknown rewards: Wiltshire, A. (2017, September 28). Behind the addictive psychology and seductive art of loot boxes. Retrieved from https://www.pcgamer.com/behind-the-addictive-psychology-and-seductive-art-of-loot-boxes/

Effects on the release of dopamine: Dopamine. (n.d.). *Wikipedia*. Retrieved May 6, 2020, from https://en.wikipedia.org/wiki/Dopamine

Techniques and tools to draw you back in: Herrman, J. (2018, February 27). How tiny red dots took over your life. Retrieved from https://www.nytimes.com/2018/02/27/magazine/red-dots-badge-phones-notification.html

Typical behaviour extensively studied by neuroscience: Kuss, D. J., & Griffiths, M. D. (2012). Internet and gaming addiction: A systematic literature review of neuroimaging studies. *Brain sciences, 2*(3), 347–374. https://doi.org/10.3390/brainsci2030347

Designed to give users "a little dopamine hit": Solon, O. (2017, November 9). Ex-Facebook president Sean Parker: Site made to exploit human "vulnerability." Retrieved from https://www.theguardian.com/technology/2017/nov/09/facebook-sean-parker-vulnerability-brain-psychology

"We now know how to design cue, activity, and reward systems to more effectively leverage our brain chemistry": Davidow, B. (2013, June 10). Skinner marketing: We're the rats, and Facebook likes are the reward. Retrieved from https://www.theatlantic.com/technology/archive/2013/06/skinner-marketing-were-the-rats-and-facebook-

likes-are-the-reward/276613/; Davidow, W. (2012). *Overconnected: The promise and threat of the internet*. Delphinium Books.

One case…is Snapchat: Berthon et al. Addictive de-vices.

The app's promotion of "streaks": Sattelberg, W. (2020, March 14). Longest Snapchat streak. Retrieved from https://www.techjunkie.com/longest-snapchat-streak/

Referred to in social psychology as a Zeigarnik effect: Berthon et al. Addictive de-vices; Montag, C., Lachmann, B., Herrlich, M., & Zweig, K. (2019). Addictive features of social media/messenger platforms and freemium games against the background of psychological and economic theories. *International Journal of Environmental Research and Public Health, 16*(14), 2612.

Other products where addiction is a factor: Hanson, J., & Kysar, D. (1999). Taking behavioralism seriously: Some evidence of market manipulation. *Harvard Law Review, 112*(7), 1420–1572. https://doi.org/10.2307/1342413; Buettner, R. (2017). Predicting user behavior in electronic markets based on personality-mining in large online social networks. *Electronic Markets, 27*(3), 247–265; Matz, S. C., Kosinski, M., Nave, G., & Stillwell, D. J. (2017). Psychological targeting as an effective approach to digital mass persuasion. *Proceedings of the National Academy of Sciences, 114*(48), 12714–12719. Retrieved from https://www.pnas.org/content/114/48/12714

"The findings of social psychology and behavioural economics are being employed to determine the news we read": Shaw, T. (2017, April 20). Invisible manipulators of your mind. Retrieved from https://www.nybooks.com/articles/2017/04/20/kahneman-tversky-invisible-mind-manipulators/

Psychological experiments on consumers: Matz et al. Psychological targeting. Alter, A. (2017). *Irresistible: The rise of addictive technology and the business of keeping us hooked*. Penguin.

Large professional conferences (like the Traffic & Conversion Summit): Traffic & Conversion Summit. (n.d.). Traffic & Conversion Summit 2020. Retrieved June 16, 2020, from https://trafficandconversionsummit.com/

"Marketers use information about the customer to actively design more addictive offerings": Berthon et al. Addictive de-vices.

Game developers... employ psychological techniques to make their products as "unquittable" as possible: Jabr, F. (2019, October 22). Can you really be addicted to video games? Retrieved from https://www.nytimes.com/2019/10/22/magazine/can-you-really-be-addicted-to-video-games.html

Facebook's admission that it had successfully modified over seven hundred thousand users' emotions: Arthur, C. (2014, June 30). Facebook emotion study breached ethical guidelines, researchers say. Retrieved from https://www.theguardian.com/technology/2014/jun/30/facebook-emotion-study-breached-ethical-guidelines-researchers-say; Flick, C. (2016). Informed consent and the Facebook emotional manipulation study. *Research Ethics, 12*(1), 14–28.

An experiment Facebook undertook in 2010: Zhukova, A. (2017, April 27). Facebook's fascinating (and disturbing) history of secret experiments. Retrieved from https://www.makeuseof.com/tag/facebook-secret-experiments/

Facebook researchers then checked public voting records: Zhukova. Facebook's fascinating history.

Facebook announced a breakthrough in its research into machine learning algorithms: BBC News. (2019, July 31). Facebook funds AI mind-reading experiment. Retrieved from https://www.bbc.com/news/technology-49165713

Neuralink... is reportedly developing "a high bandwidth brain-machine interface": Wong, J. C. (2019, July 17). Elon Musk unveils plan to build mind-reading implants: 'The monkey is out of the bag'. Retrieved from https://www.theguardian.com/technology/2019/jul/17/elon-musk-neuralink-brain-implants-mind-reading-artificial-intelligence

Ryan Calo has ominously warned where these experiments might lead: Calo, R. (2014). Digital market manipulation. *George Washington Law Review 995*(82). http://dx.doi.org/10.2139/ssrn.2309703

Social media "instill trust by getting 2.2 billion users to forget about the platform": Selinger, E. (2018, June 4). Facebook fabricates trust through fake intimacy. Retrieved from https://onezero.medium.com/facebook-fabricates-trust-through-fake-intimacy-b381e60d32f9; Frischmann, B., & Selinger, E. (2018). *Re-engineering humanity*. Cambridge University Press.

It leverages the trust around information sharing among friends: Waldman, A. E. (2016). Privacy, sharing, and trust: The Facebook study. *Case Western Reserve Law Review, 67*(1). Retrieved from https://scholarlycommons.law.case.edu/caselrev/vol67/iss1/10

Adolescent girls tend to engage in forms of indirect aggression: Debevec, T. M. (2011). A psychoanalytic inquiry into social aggression as a form of bullying among female students. Electronic Theses and Dissertations, 560. Retrieved from https://digitalcommons.georgiasouthern.edu/etd/560

Used repeatedly to shame and belittle, leading to increased depression and other mental health risks: Howard, J. (2019, January 4). Link between social media and depression stronger in teen girls than boys, study says. Retrieved from https://www.cnn.com/2019/01/03/health/social-media-depression-girls-study/index.html

Higher prevalence of internet addiction among adolescent males: Fumero, A., Marrero, R. J., Voltes, D., & Peñate, W. (2018). Personal and social factors involved in internet addiction among adolescents: A meta-analysis. https://doi.org/10.1016/j.chb.2018.05.005

The World Health Organization and the American Psychiatric Association added "internet gaming disorder": Jabr. Can you really be addicted to video games?

Higher levels of screen time... are linked with increased symptoms of depression: Boers, E., Afzali, M. H., Newton, N., & Conrod, P. Association of screen time and depression in adolescence. *JAMA Pediatrics, 173*(9), 853–859. http://doi.org/10.1001/jamapediatrics.2019.1759

"Psychological, physical, societal, and economic harms": Berthon et al. Addictive de-vices. However, see also Coyne, S. M., Rogers, A. A.,

Zurcher, J. D., Stockdale, L., & Booth, M. (2020). Does time spent using social media impact mental health?: An eight year longitudinal study. *Computers in Human Behavior, 104*, 106160.

Dating back at least to the time of the printing press: Levine, N. (2017). The nature of the glut: Information overload in postwar America. *History of the Human Sciences, 30*(1), 32–49. https://doi.org/10.1177/0952695116686016; Schick, A. G., Gordon, L. A., & Haka, S. (1990). Information overload: A temporal approach. *Accounting, Organizations and Society, 15*(3), 199–220; Toffler, A. (1984). *Future shock*. Bantam.

James Grier Miller... proposed dealing with information overload: Heterick, R. C. J. (1998). Educom: A Retrospective. *Educom Review, 33*(5), 42–47. Retrieved from https://www.educause.edu/ir/library/html/erm/erm98/erm9853.html

"Every second, on average, around 6,000 tweets are tweeted": Twitter Usage Statistics. (n.d.). Retrieved June 16, 2020, from https://www.internetlivestats.com/twitter-statistics/

On average, 1.47 billion people log onto Facebook daily: Noyes, D. (May 2020). The top 20 valuable Facebook statistics. Retrieved from https://zephoria.com/top-15-valuable-facebook-statistics/

Facebook videos are viewed eight billion times per day: Constine, J. (2015, November 4). Facebook hits 8 billion daily video views, doubling from 4 billion in April. Retrieved from https://techcrunch.com/2015/11/04/facebook-video-views/

Every minute, more than 3.87 million Google searches are conducted: Domo. (June 18, 2018). Data never sleeps 6.0: How much data is generated every minute? Retrieved from https://web-assets.domo.com/blog/wp-content/uploads/2018/06/18_domo_data-never-sleeps-6verticals.pdf

"Human cognitive architecture": Lin, H. (2019). The existential threat from cyber-enabled information warfare. *Bulletin of the Atomic Scientists* (75), 187–196; See also Matthews, J. (2019, April). A cognitive scientist explains why humans are so susceptible to fake news and misinformation. Retrieved from https://www.niemanlab.

org/2019/04/a-cognitive-scientist-explains-why-humans-are-so-susceptible-to-fake-news-and-misinformation/

Combined controlled laboratory experiments with systematic analysis of hundreds of online ads: Akpinar, E., & Berger, J. (2017). Valuable virality. *Journal of Marketing Research, 54*(2), 318–330. https://doi.org/10.1509/jmr.13.0350; Bakir, V., & McStay, A. (2017). Fake news and the economy of emotions: Problems, causes, solutions. *Digital Journalism, 6*(2), 154–175. https://doi.org/10.1080/21670811.2017.1345645; Einstein, M. (2016). *Black ops advertising: Native ads, content marketing and the covert world of the digital sell*. OR Books; Matz et al. Psychological targeting.

Social media's flood of content also amplifies other cognitive biases: Beasley, B. (2019, December 26). How disinformation hacks your brain. Retrieved from https://blogs.scientificamerican.com/observations/how-disinformation-hacks-your-brain/

"The availability heuristic" and "the illusory truth effect": Kuran, T. (2007). Availability cascades and risk regulation. University of Chicago Public Law & Legal Theory Working Paper No. 181, 683–768. Retrieved from https://chicagounbound.uchicago.edu/cgi/viewcontent.cgi?article=1036&context=public_law_and_legal_theory; Pennycook, G., Cannon, T. D., & Rand, D. G. (2018). Prior exposure increases perceived accuracy of fake news. *Journal of Experimental Psychology: General, 147*(12), 1865. http://dx.doi.org/10.1037/xge0000465

Many people still receive the vast majority of their information from traditional news: Nyhan, B. (2016, September 7). Relatively few Americans live in partisan media bubble, but they're influential. Retrieved from https://www.nytimes.com/2016/09/08/upshot/relatively-few-people-are-partisan-news-consumers-but-theyre-influential.html

News organizations increasingly analyze the popularity of their stories over social media: Ferrucci, P. (2018). Networked: Social media's impact on news production in digital newsrooms. *Newspaper Research Journal, 39*(1), 6–17. https://doi.org/10.1177/0739532918761069

"Tweets were deemed equally newsworthy as headlines": McGregor, S. C., & Molyneux, L. (2020). Twitter's influence on news judgment: An experiment among journalists. *Journalism, 21*(5), 597–613. https://doi.org/10.1177/1464884918802975

What one group of researchers calls "online firestorms.": Pfeffer, J., Zorbach, T., & Carley, K. (2013). Understanding online firestorms: Negative word-of-mouth dynamics in social media networks. *Journal of Marketing Communications, 20*(1–2), 117–128. https://doi.org/10.1080/13527266.2013.797778

Women, minorities, and people of colour may be particularly prone to self-censorship: Amnesty International. (2018). "Toxic Twitter — The silencing effect." Retrieved from https://www.amnesty.org/en/latest/research/2018/03/online-violence-against-women-chapter-5/; Doxing. (2020, May 8). *Wikipedia*. Retrieved from https://en.wikipedia.org/w/index.php?title=Doxing&oldid=955625156

Which increased in the nineteenth century with advances in telecommunications: Scheuerman, W. (2001). Liberal democracy and the empire of speed. *Polity, 34*(1), 41–67. https://doi.org/10.2307/3235508

"Without abiding attachments associations are too shifting": Dewey, J. (1927). *The public and its problems*. Ohio University Press.

An explosion of social media–enabled PR: Nadler, A., Crain, M., & Donovan, J. (2018). *Weaponizing the digital influence machine: The political perils of online ad tech*. Data & Society Research Institute. Retrieved from https://datasociety.net/library/weaponizing-the-digital-influence-machine/

John Hill, founder of . . . Hill & Knowlton: Brandt, A. M. (2012). Inventing conflicts of interest: A history of tobacco industry tactics. *American Journal of Public Health, 102*(1), 63–71. https://doi.org/10.2105/AJPH.2011.300292; Critical Frequency (Producer). *Drilled* [Audio podcast]. (February 27, 2020). Season 3, episode 7. Retrieved from https://www.criticalfrequency.org/drilled

"Much of the classic, foundational research . . . was funded during the cold war": Shaw, T. (2018, March 21). The new military-industrial complex

of big data psy-ops. Retrieved from https://www.nybooks.com/daily/2018/03/21/the-digital-military-industrial-complex/

"Cyber-enabled capabilities that Hitler, Stalin, Goebbels, and McCarthy could have only imagined": Lin. The existential threat.

"Since 2011, at least 27 online information operations have been partially or wholly attributed to PR or marketing firms": Silverman, C., Lytvynenko, J., & Kung, W. (2020, January 6). Disinformation for hire: How a new breed of PR firms is selling lies online. Retrieved from https://www.buzzfeednews.com/article/craigsilverman/disinformation-for-hire-black-pr-firms; For more on "black PR" firms, see Nyst, C., & Monaco, N. (2018). State-sponsored trolling: How governments are deploying disinformation as part of broader digital harassment campaigns. Retrieved from http://www.iftf.org/statesponsoredtrolling

Actively taking advantage of the already propitious environment that social media present: Gunitsky, S. (2015). Corrupting the cyber-commons: Social media as a tool of autocratic stability. *Perspectives on Politics, 13*(1), 42–54. Retrieved from https://ssrn.com/abstract=2506038

"Censorship through noise": Bloomfield, S. (2019, August 10). *This Is Not Propaganda* by Peter Pomerantsev review – Quietly frightening. Retrieved from https://www.theguardian.com/books/2019/aug/10/this-is-not-propaganda-peter-pomerantsev-review; Pomerantsev, P. (2019). *This is not propaganda: Adventures in the war against reality.* Hachette UK.

"Professional, organized lying": Rid, T. (2020). *Active measures: The secret history of disinformation and political warfare.* Farrar, Straus and Giroux.

"Third-generation" techniques: Deibert, R., & Rohozinski, R. (2010). Control and subversion in Russian cyberspace. In R. Deibert, J. Palfrey, R. Rohozinski, & J. Zittrain (Eds.). *Access controlled: The shaping of power, rights, and rule in cyberspace* (15–34). MIT Press; Blank, S. (2013). Russian information warfare as domestic counterinsurgency. *American Foreign Policy Interests, 35*(1), 31–44. https://doi.org/10.1080/10803920.2013.757946; Hulcoop, A., Scott-Railton, J., Tanchak, P., Brooks, M., & Deibert, R. (2017). *Tainted leaks: Disinformation and phishing with*

a Russian nexus. Citizen Lab Research Report No. 92. Retrieved from https://citizenlab.ca/2017/05/tainted-leaks-disinformation-phish/

Organized criminal groups acting as proxies: Borogan, I., & Soldatov, A. (2012, April 25). The Kremlin and the hackers: Partners in crime? Retrieved from https://www.opendemocracy.net/en/odr/kremlin-and-hackers-partners-in-crime/; Galeotti, M. (2016). *Putin's hydra: Inside Russia's intelligence services*. European Council on Foreign Relations.

The St. Petersburg–based Internet Research Agency: For more on the IRA, see Chen, A. (2015, June 2). The agency. Retrieved from https://www.nytimes.com/2015/06/07/magazine/the-agency.html; See also Rid. *Active measures*.

IRA accounts purporting to belong to Black activists: Way, L. A., & Casey, A. (2018). Russia has been meddling in foreign elections for decades. Has it made a difference? Retrieved from https://www.washingtonpost.com/news/monkeycage/wp/2018/01/05/russia-has-been-meddling-in-foreign-elections-for-decades-has-it-made-adifference/; Rid. *Active measures*; Bail, C. A., Guay, B., Maloney, E., Combs, A., Hillygus, D. S., Merhout, F., . . . & Volfovsky, A. (2020). Assessing the Russian Internet Research Agency's impact on the political attitudes and behaviors of American Twitter users in late 2017. *Proceedings of the National Academy of Sciences, 117*(1), 243–250; Freelon, D., Bossetta, M., Wells, C., Lukito, J., Xia, Y., & Adams, K. (2020). Black trolls matter: Racial and ideological asymmetries in social media disinformation. *Social Science Computer Review*. https://doi.org/10.1177/0894439320914853

Take the Philippines, which is a good case study: Alba, D. (2019, March 19). Facebook removes hundreds of pages engaged in "inauthentic behavior" in the Philippines. Retrieved from https://www.buzzfeednews.com/article/daveyalba/facebook-removes-inauthentic-engagement-philippines-nic; Ong, J. C., & Cabanes, J. (2018). *Architects of networked disinformation: Behind the scenes of troll accounts and fake news production in the Philippines*. Newton Tech4Dev Network. https://doi.org/10.7275/2cq4-5396

The Philippines was "patient zero in the global information epidemic": Bengali, S., & Halper, E. (2019, November 19). Troll armies, a growth industry in the Philippines, may soon be coming to an election near you. Retrieved from https://www.latimes.com/politics/story/2019-11-19/troll-armies-routine-in-philippine-politics-coming-here-next

"Across the Philippines, it's a virtual free-for-all": Mahtani, S., & Cabato, R. (2019, July 26). Why crafty internet trolls in the Philippines may be coming to a website near you. Retrieved from https://www.washingtonpost.com/world/asia_pacific/why-crafty-internet-trolls-in-the-philippines-may-be-coming-to-a-website-near-you/2019/07/25/c5d42ee2-5c53-11e9-98d4-844088d135f2_story.html

In Indonesia, low-level military personnel coordinate disinformation campaigns: Allard, T., & Stubbs, J. (2020, January 7). Indonesian army wields internet 'news' as a weapon in Papua. Retrieved from https://www.reuters.com/article/us-indonesia-military-websites-insight/indonesian-army-wields-internet-news-as-a-weapon-in-papua-idUSKBN1Z7001

Taiwan is like a petri dish of disinformation: Zhong, R. (2020, January 16). Awash in disinformation before vote, Taiwan points finger at China. Retrieved from https://www.nytimes.com/2020/01/06/technology/taiwan-election-china-disinformation.html

Entire organizations, think tanks, and other front organizations: Lin. The existential threat.

"Manufactured doubt is everywhere": Michaels, D. (2020, January 28). Science for sale. Retrieved from https://bostonreview.net/science-nature/david-michaels-science-sale

Hard-wired cognitive biases and mental shortcuts are primed to push them along: Woolley, S., & Joseff, K. (2020). *Demand for deceit: How the way we think drives disinformation.* International Forum Working Paper. Retrieved from https://www.ned.org/demand-for-deceit-how-way-we-think-drives-disinformation-samuel-woolley-katie-joseff/

Attempts "to quash rumors through direct refutation may facilitate their diffusion": Berinsky, A. (2017). Rumors and health care reform: Experiments in political misinformation. *British Journal of Political Science, 47*(2), 241–262. https://doi.org/10.1017/S0007123415000186; Greenhill, K. M., & Oppenheim, B. (2017). Rumor has it: The adoption of unverified information in conflict zones. *International Studies Quarterly, 61*(3), 660–676. https://doi.org/10.1093/isq/sqx015

Efforts to correct falsehoods can ironically contribute to their further propagation: Phillips, W. (2018). *At a certain point you have to realize that you're promoting them: The ambivalence of journalistic amplification*. Data & Society Research Institute. Retrieved from https://datasociety.net/wp-content/uploads/2018/05/2-PART-2_Oxygen_of_Amplification_DS.pdf; Nyhan, B., & Reifler, J. (2010). When corrections fail: The persistence of political misperceptions. *Political Behavior, 32*(2), 303–330. https://doi.org/10.1007/s11109-010-9112-2

Citizens become fatigued trying to discern objective truth: Stevenson, A. (2018, October 9). Soldiers in Facebook's war on fake news are feeling overrun. Retrieved from https://www.nytimes.com/2018/10/09/business/facebook-philippines-rappler-fake-news.html

Questioning the integrity of all media can in turn lead to fatalism: MacFarquhar, N. (2016, August 29). A powerful Russian weapon: The spread of false stories. Retrieved from https://www.nytimes.com/2016/08/29/world/europe/russia-sweden-disinformation.html

"A plurality of unreality... encourages the listener to doubt everything": Zuckerman, E. (2019). QAnon and the emergence of the unreal. *Journal of Design and Science*, (6). https://doi.org/10.21428/7808da6b.6b8a82b9; Farrell, H., & Schneier, B. (2018). Common-knowledge attacks on democracy. Berkman Klein Center Research Publication 2018-7. http://dx.doi.org/10.2139/ssrn.3273111.

Social media remain polluted by misinformation and disinformation: Lewis, P. (2018). "Fiction is outperforming reality": How YouTube's algorithm distorts truth. Retrieved from https://www.theguardian.com/technology/2018/feb/02/how-youtubes-algorithm-distorts-truth; Vosoughi, S., Roy, D., & Aral, S. (2018). The spread of true and false news online. *Science, 359*(6380), 1146–1151. https://doi.org/10.1126/science.aap9559

Researchers posing as Russian trolls were still able to buy political ads: Warzel, C. (2018, September 4). This group posed as Russian trolls and bought political ads on Google. It was easy. Retrieved from https://www.buzzfeednews.com/article/charliewarzel/researchers-posed-as-trolls-bought-google-ads

Sheryl Sandberg made a startling admission: Vaidhyanathan, S. (2018, September 5). Why Facebook will never be free of fakes. Retrieved from https://www.nytimes.com/2018/09/05/opinion/facebook-sandberg-congress.html

Twitter was deleting on the order of a million accounts a day: Spangler, T. (2018, July 9). Twitter stock slides on report that it has been deleting over 1 million fake accounts daily. Retrieved from https://variety.com/2018/digital/news/twitter-stock-deleted-fake-accounts-1202868405/

Social media's inability to track inauthentic behaviour: Scott, M. (2018, October 7). Why we're losing the battle against fake news. Retrieved from https://www.politico.eu/article/fake-news-regulation-misinformation-europe-us-elections-midterms-bavaria/

Malicious actors are now using altered images and videos: Burgess, M. (2018, January 27). The law is nowhere near ready for the rise of AI-generated fake porn. Retrieved from https://www.wired.co.uk/article/deepfake-app-ai-porn-fake-reddit; Chesney, B., & Citron, D. (2019). Deep fakes: A looming challenge for privacy, democracy, and national security. *California Law Review, 107*, 1753. Retrieved from https://ssrn.com/abstract=3213954

In spite of the deletions, fact-checking, and monitoring systems they produce, social media will remain easy to exploit: Stewart, L. G., Arif, A., & Starbird, K. (2018, February). Examining trolls and polarization with a retweet network. In *Proceedings of WSDM workshop on Misinformation and Misbehavior Mining on the Web (MIS2)*. Retrieved from https://faculty.washington.edu/kstarbi/examining-trolls-polarization.pdf

"Continued corruption of the information ecosphere... has heightened the nuclear and climate threats": Bulletin of the Atomic Scientists. (2020, January 23). Closer than ever: It is 100 seconds to midnight. Retrieved from https://thebulletin.org/doomsday-clock/current-time/

H.G. Wells described an imaginary "World Encyclopedia": Wells, H. G. (1938). *World Brain*. Methuen.

An imagined state of affairs where truth and democracy reigned supreme; this never actually existed: Farkas, J., & Schou, J. (2019). *Post-truth, fake news and democracy: Mapping the politics of falsehood*. Routledge.

CHAPTER THREE: A GREAT LEAP FORWARD . . . FOR THE ABUSE OF POWER

The UN's special investigation into his execution: Callamard, A. (2019, June 19). Khashoggi killing: UN human rights expert says Saudi Arabia is responsible for "premeditated execution." Retrieved from https://www.ohchr.org/EN/NewsEvents/Pages/DisplayNews.aspx?NewsID=24713

One of the key figures . . . was Saud al-Qahtani: Hubbard, B. (2020, March 13). The rise and fall of M.B.S.'s digital henchman. Retrieved from https://www.nytimes.com/2020/03/13/sunday-review/mbs-hacking.html

Smaat used standard social media tactics to grow audiences and maximize its reach: DiResta, R., Grossman, S., K. H., & Miller, C. (2019). *Analysis of Twitter takedown of state-backed operation attributed to Saudi Arabian digital marketing firm Smaat*. Stanford Internet Observatory.

Twitter suspended eighty-eight thousand accounts connected to Smaat: Twitter Safety. (2019, December 20). New disclosures to our archive of state-backed information operations. Retrieved from https://blog.twitter.com/en_us/topics/company/2019/new-disclosures-to-our-archive-of-state-backed-information-operations.html

"The more victims he eats, the more he wants": dos Santos, N., & Kaplan, M. (2018, December 4). Jamal Khashoggi's private WhatsApp messages may offer new clues to killing. Retrieved from https://www.cnn.com/2018/12/02/middleeast/jamal-khashoggi-whatsapp-messages-intl/index.html

"God help us," Khashoggi replied to Omar: dos Santos & Kaplan. Khashoggi's private WhatsApp messages.

Power hierarchies are a thing of the past: See Tufekci, Z. (2017). *Twitter and tear gas: The power and fragility of networked protest*. Yale University Press.

What journalist Dana Priest called "Top Secret America": Priest, D. (2011). *Top secret America: The rise of the new American security state*. Little, Brown.

"Our upcoming March ISS 2013 World MEA in Dubai": Arnold, S. E. (2013, January 15). Telestrategies: An interview with Dr. Jerry Lucas. Retrieved from http://arnoldit.com/search-wizards-speak/telestrategies-2.html; See also Deibert, R. (2015). Authoritarianism goes global: Cyberspace under siege. *Journal of Democracy, 26*(3), 64–78; Anderson, C. (2014, July 31). Monitoring the lines: Sanctions and human rights policy considerations of TeleStrategies ISS world seminars. Retrieved from http://cda.io/notes/ monitoring-the-lines.

Marketed a mass surveillance system, called Evident: BBC News. (2017, June 15). How BAE sold cyber-surveillance tools to Arab states. Retrieved from https://www.bbc.com/news/world-middle-east-40276568

More than five hundred companies now "sell a wide range of systems used to identify, track, and monitor individuals": Privacy International. (2018, February 16). The global surveillance industry. Retrieved from https://privacyinternational.org/explainer/1632/global-surveillance-industry

"Zero days"—or "open doors that the vendor does not know it should lock": Lindsay, Restrained by design; Greenberg, A. (2012, March 23). Shopping for zero-days: A price list for hackers' secret software exploits. *Forbes*; Meakins, J. (2019). A zero-sum game: The zero-day market in 2018. *Journal of Cyber Policy, 4*(1), 60–71.

"We would read them, and we would wonder—how do they know?": Srivastava, M., & Wilson, T. (2019, October 30). Inside the WhatsApp hack: How an Israeli technology was used to surveil. Retrieved from https://www.ft.com/content/d9127eae-f99d-11e9-98fd-4d6c20050229

An extensive set of interviews with immigrant and refugee victims of spyware: Chisholm, B., Usiskin, C., & Whittaker-Howe, S. (n.d.). A grounded theory analysis of the psychological effects of covert digital surveillance on civil society actors [Unpublished manuscript].

For despots across time, says Montesquieu, "whatever inspires fear is the fittest spring of government": Montesquieu, C.-L. S., Nugent, T., & Alembert, J.-B. R. (1899). *The spirit of laws*. Colonial Press.

"In our online meetings we don't know if we can speak freely or not": Michaelsen, M. (2020, February). *Silencing across borders: Transnational repression and digital threats against exiled activists from Egypt, Syria, and Iran*. Retrieved from https://www.hivos.org/assets/2020/02/SILENCING-ACROSS-BORDERS-Marcus-Michaelsen-Hivos-Report.pdf

The backbone is the so-called Great Firewall: See Griffiths, J. (2019). *The great firewall of China: How to build and control an alternative version of the internet*. Zed Books; Roberts, M. E. (2018). *Censored: Distraction and diversion inside China's great firewall*. Princeton University Press; Marczak, B., Weaver, N., Dalek, J., Ensafi, R., Fifield, D., McKune, S., . . . & Paxson, V. (2015). *China's great cannon*. Citizen Lab Research Report No. 52. Retrieved from https://citizenlab.ca/2015/04/chinas-great-cannon/

Some of the Western media coverage of the social credit system has been sensationalistic: Ahmed, S. (2019, May 1). The messy truth about social credit. Retrieved from https://logicmag.io/china/the-messy-truth-about-social-credit/; Ahmed, S., & Weber, S. (2018). China's long game in techno-nationalism. *First Monday, 23*(5). Retrieved from https://firstmonday.org/ojs/index.php/fm/article/view/8085/7209

TikTok, the massively popular video streaming app: Ahmed. The messy truth.

In China, facial recognition systems have been deployed almost completely in the absence of any privacy protections: Qin, A. (2020, January 21). Chinese city uses facial recognition to shame pajama wearers. Retrieved from https://www.nytimes.com/2020/01/21/business/china-pajamas-facial-recognition.html

SenseTime's database had inadvertently exposed the . . . data of more than five hundred million people: Tao, L. (2019, April 12). SenseNets: The facial recognition company that supplies China's Skynet surveillance system. Retrieved from https://

www.scmp.com/tech/science-research/article/3005733/what-you-need-know-about-sensenets-facial-recognition-firm

Authorities also require locals to install QR barcodes on the doors of their homes: Wang, M. (2018). *"Eradicating ideological viruses": China's campaign of repression against Xinjiang's Muslims*. Retrieved from https://www.hrw.org/report/2018/09/09/eradicating-ideological-viruses/chinas-campaign-repression-against-xinjiangs

Xinjiang authorities have started systematically collecting biometric data: Wang. *"Eradicating ideological viruses"*; Leibold, J. (2020). Surveillance in China's Xinjiang region: Ethnic sorting, coercion, and inducement. *Journal of Contemporary China, 29*(121), 46–60.

Reports of arrests without due process are legion: Allen-Ebrahimian, B. (2019, November 24). Exposed: China's operating manuals for mass internment and arrest by algorithm. Retrieved from https://www.icij.org/investigations/china-cables/exposed-chinas-operating-manuals-for-mass-internment-and-arrest-by-algorithm/

"China is a major driver of AI surveillance worldwide": Feldstein, S. (2019, September). *The global expansion of AI surveillance*. Carnegie Endowment for International Peace. Retrieved from https://carnegieendowment.org/2019/09/17/global-expansion-of-ai-surveillance-pub-79847

An archetypal example is Brazil: Ionova, A. (2020, February 11). Brazil takes a page from China, taps facial recognition to solve crime. Retrieved from https://www.csmonitor.com/World/Americas/2020/0211/Brazil-takes-a-page-from-China-taps-facial-recognition-to-solve-crime

Argentina and Ecuador have purchased Chinese surveillance technology systems: Gershgorn, D. (2020, March 4). The U.S. fears live facial recognition. In Buenos Aires, it's a fact of life. Retrieved from https://onezero.medium.com/the-u-s-fears-live-facial-recognition-in-buenos-aires-its-a-fact-of-life-52019eff454d; Mozur, P., Kessel, J. M., & Chan, M. (2019, April 24). Made in China, exported to the world: The surveillance state. Retrieved from https://www.nytimes.com/2019/04/24/technology/ecuador-surveillance-cameras-police-government.html

An obscure facial recognition AI start-up called Clearview AI: Hill, K. (2020, January 18). The secretive company that might end privacy as we know it. Retrieved from https://www.nytimes.com/2020/01/18/technology/clearview-privacy-facial-recognition.html

People associated with 2,228 law enforcement agencies, companies, and institutions in twenty-seven countries had created accounts: Mac, R., Haskins, C., & McDonald, L. (2020, February 27). Clearview's facial recognition app has been used by the Justice Department, ICE, Macy's, Walmart, and the NBA. Retrieved from https://www.buzzfeednews.com/article/ryanmac/clearview-ai-fbi-ice-global-law-enforcement

Investors... even abused the app on dates and at parties: Hill, K. (2020, March 5). Before Clearview became a police tool, it was a secret plaything of the rich. Retrieved from https://www.nytimes.com/2020/03/05/technology/clearview-investors.html

Ton-That had close ties to several prominent alt-right extremists: O'Brien, L. (2020, April 7). The far-right helped create the world's most powerful facial recognition technology. Retrieved from https://www.huffingtonpost.ca/entry/clearview-ai-facial-recognition-alt-right_n_5e7d028bc5b6cb08a92a5c48

Nine law enforcement agencies... were in fact customers or employed individuals who were using the system: Allen, K., Gillis, W., & Boutilier, A. (2020, February 27). Facial recognition app Clearview AI has been used far more widely in Canada than previously known. Retrieved from https://www.thestar.com/news/canada/2020/02/27/facial-recognition-app-clearview-ai-has-been-used-far-more-widely-in-canada-than-previously-known.html

"The weaponization possiblities... are endless": Hill. The secretive company.

A "superpower that we haven't seen before in policing": Ferguson, A. G. (2017). *The rise of big data policing: Surveillance, race, and the future of law enforcement*. New York University Press; See also Eubanks, V. (2018). *Automating inequality: How high-tech tools profile, police, and punish the poor*. St. Martin's Press.

How fast, easy, and cheap it would be to identify specific individuals: Chinoy, S. (2019, April 16). We built an 'unbelievable' (but legal) facial recognition machine. Retrieved from https://www.nytimes.com/interactive/2019/04/16/opinion/facial-recognition-new-york-city.html

Equivalent to about eight hundred digital video cameras: Bloomberg. (2016, September 1). The surveillance firm recording crimes from Baltimore's skies [Video]. Retrieved from https://www.youtube.com/watch?reload=9&v=wRa-AucbN6k

"A department could potentially purchase a fleet of 500 drones in lieu of a single police chopper": Laperruque, J., & Janovsky, D. (2018, September 25). These police drones are watching you. Retrieved from https://www.pogo.org/analysis/2018/09/these-police-drones-are-watching-you/

One vendor of drones has bragged about a 518 percent growth in use by U.S. agencies: Dronefly. (n.d.). Police drone infographic. Retrieved June 16, 2020, from https://www.dronefly.com/police-drone-infographic

There are automatic licence plate readers: Howe, R. J. (October 2009). "Privacy impact assessment: Automatic license plate recognition (ALPR)." Royal Canadian Mounted Police (obtained through access to information request by Rob Wipond). Retrieved from https://robwipond.com/ref/RCMP%20ALPR%20PIA.pdf; Parsons, C. (2017, June 13). Who's watching where you're driving? Retrieved from https://www.priv.gc.ca/en/blog/20170613

Palantir technology "allows ICE agents to access a vast 'ecosystem' of data": Biddle, S., & Devereaux, R. (2019, May 2). Peter Thiel's Palantir was used to bust relatives of migrant children, new documents show. Retrieved from https://theintercept.com/2019/05/02/peter-thiels-palantir-was-used-to-bust-hundreds-of-relatives-of-migrant-children-new-documents-show/

The trends towards data fusion have helped blur military and civilian applications: Schneier, B. (2016). *Data and Goliath: The hidden battles to collect your data and control your world.* W. W. Norton.

National security regulations … shield many of these agencies: Richardson, R., Schultz, J., & Crawford, K. (2019). *Dirty data, bad*

predictions: How civil rights violations impact police data, predictive policing systems, and justice. Social Science Research Network Scholarly Paper No. ID 3333423.

The U.S. government began checking social media feeds for immigration vetting in 2014: Brennan Centre. (2019, June 25). Timeline of social media monitoring for vetting by the Department of Homeland Security and the State Department. Retrieved from https://www.brennancenter.org/our-work/research-reports/timeline-social-media-monitoring-vetting-department-homeland-security-and

Huge defence contractors... began lobbying for legislation that would bolster border security: Lipton, E. (2013, June 6). U.S. military firms eye border security contracts. Retrieved from https://www.nytimes.com/2013/06/07/us/us-military-firms-eye-border-security-contracts.html

"Immigration and Customs Enforcement... ordered $2 million worth of... phone and laptop hacking technology": Brewster, T. (2017, April 13). US Immigration splurged $2.2 million on phone hacking tech just after Trump's travel ban. Retrieved from https://www.forbes.com/sites/thomasbrewster/2017/04/13/post-trump-order-us-immigration-goes-on-mobile-hacking-spending-spree

The company's advertising describes... cloud-based private data from "over 50 of the most popular social media": mySociety. (2020, January 29). This is what the Cellebrite software promises police. If that concerns you, why not join @privacyint's campaign to discover whether your local force are using this surveillance software? [Tweet]. Retrieved from https://twitter.com/mySociety/status/1222488330732032001

The acquisition of masses of big data has pushed the agencies to find contractors who specialize in social media analytics: Brewster, T. (2017, September 27). Trump's immigration cops just spent $3 million on these ex-DARPA social media data miners. Retrieved from https://www.forbes.com/sites/thomasbrewster/2017/09/27/trump-immigration-social-media-surveillance-giant-oak-penlink-palantir/

Amazon had pitched its facial recognition technology to ICE: Laperruque, J., & Peterson, A. (2018, October 23). Amazon pushes ICE to buy its face recognition surveillance tech. Retrieved from https://www.thedailybeast.com/amazon-pushes-ice-to-buy-its-face-recognition-surveillance-tech; Lutz, E. (2019, August 14). Amazon's creepy surveillance tech can now detect fear. Retrieved from https://www.vanityfair.com/news/2019/08/amazon-creepy-surveillance-tech-rekognition-can-now-detect-fear

Ring and Neighbors…have reflexively undertaken racial profiling: Haskins, C. (2019, February 7). Amazon's home security company is turning everyone into cops. Retrieved from https://www.vice.com/en_us/article/qvyvzd/amazons-home-security-company-is-turning-everyone-into-cops

A Fresno police department used a social media monitoring firm: Cagle, M. (2015, December 15). This surveillance software is probably spying on #BlackLivesMatter. Retrieved from https://www.aclunc.org/blog/surveillance-software-probably-spying-blacklivesmatter; *Economist*. (2019, February 21). America's cops take an interest in social media. Retrieved from https://www.economist.com/united-states/2019/02/21/americas-cops-take-an-interest-in-social-media

Banjo, a small AI startup: Koebler, J., Maiberg, E., & Cox, J. (2020, March 4). This small company is turning Utah into a surveillance panopticon. Retrieved from https://www.vice.com/en_us/article/k7exem/banjo-ai-company-utah-surveillance-panopticon

At least seventy-five companies receive "anonymous, precise location data from apps": Valentino-DeVries, J., Singer, V., Keller, M. H., & Krolik, A. (2018, December 10). Your apps know where you were last night, and they're not keeping it secret. Retrieved from https://www.nytimes.com/interactive/2018/12/10/business/location-data-privacy-apps.html

Cox was able to locate a phone by paying $300 to a bounty hunter: Cox, J. (2019, January 8). I gave a bounty hunter $300. Then he located our phone. Retrieved from https://www.vice.com/en_us/article/nepxbz/i-gave-a-bounty-hunter-300-dollars-located-phone-microbilt-zumigo-tmobile

The portal for one location tracking service, called LocationSmart, was improperly secured: Goodin, D. (2018, May 17). Website leaked real-time location of most US cell phones to almost anyone. Retrieved from https://arstechnica.com/information-technology/2018/05/service-leaked-locations-of-us-cell-phones-for-free-no-password-required/

A spokesperson for Securus said the company "is neither a judge nor a district attorney": Valentino-DeVries, J. (2018, May 10). Service meant to monitor inmates' calls could track you, too. Retrieved from https://www.nytimes.com/2018/05/10/technology/cellphone-tracking-law-enforcement.html

Cell phone tracking laws vary widely in the U.S.: American Civil Liberties Union. (n.d.). Cell phone location tracking laws by state. Retrieved June 16, 2020, from https://www.aclu.org/issues/privacy-technology/location-tracking/cell-phone-location-tracking-laws-state?redirect=map/cell-phone-location-tracking-laws-state

Canada's RCMP use a social media monitoring system: Carney, B. (2019, March 25). "Project Wide Awake": How the RCMP watches you on social media. Retrieved from https://thetyee.ca/News/2019/03/25/Project-Wide-Awake/; Craig, S. (2016, November 13). RCMP tracked 89 indigenous activists considered 'threats' for participating in protests. *National Post*.

A Toronto Star *investigation, which analyzed RCMP logs*: Allen, K. (2019, April 8). What you should know about the 'Stingray' surveillance device used by police. Retrieved from https://www.thestar.com/news/gta/2019/04/08/cellphone-surveillance-technology-what-you-need-to-know.html; Israel, T., & Parsons, C. (2016). *Gone opaque? An analysis of hypothetical IMSI catcher overuse in canada*. Telecon Transparency Project, Citizen Lab. Retrieved from https://citizenlab.ca/wp-content/uploads/2016/09/20160818-Report-Gone_Opaque.pdf

Seventy-five federal, state, and municipal agencies in the U.S. that used cell site simulators: American Civil Liberties Union. (2018, November). Stingray tracking devices: Who's got them? Retrieved from https://www.aclu.org/issues/privacy-technology/surveillance-technologies/stingray-tracking-devices-whos-got-them

Local police in Maryland had been using cell site simulators for over a decade before publicly disclosing them: Mabeus, C. (2016, May 3). Battlefield technology gets spotlight in Maryland courts: Secrecy and defense concerns surround cell phone trackers. Retrieved from https://cnsmaryland.org/interactives/spring-2016/maryland-police-cell-phone-trackers/index.html

Some of the measures many countries adopted or proposed were deeply unsettling: Capatides, C. (2020, April 2). "Shoot them dead": Philippine president Rodrigo Duterte orders police and military to kill citizens who defy coronavirus lockdown. Retrieved from https://www.cbsnews.com/news/rodrigo-duterte-philippines-president-coronavirus-lockdown-shoot-people-dead/?ftag=CNM-00-10aab7e&linkId=85694802; Gebrekidan, S. (2020, March 30). For autocrats, and others, coronavirus is a chance to grab even more power. Retrieved from https://www.nytimes.com/2020/03/30/world/europe/coronavirus-governments-power.html; Gershgorn, D. (2020, April 9). We mapped how the coronavirus is driving new surveillance programs around the world. Retrieved from https://onezero.medium.com/the-pandemic-is-a-trojan-horse-for-surveillance-programs-around-the-world-887fa6f12ec9

Drones were being offered up and used as part of COVID mitigation efforts: Gaulkin, T. (2020, April 1). Drone pandemic: Will coronavirus invite the world to meet Big Brother? Retrieved from https://thebulletin.org/2020/04/drone-pandemic-will-coronavirus-invite-the-world-to-meet-big-brother/

How easy it is to unmask real identities contained in large personal data sets: Narayanan, A., & Shmatikov, V. (2008). Robust de-anonymization of large sparse datasets. IEEE *Symposium on Security and Privacy*, 111–125. http://doi.org/10.1109/SP.2008.33

"At least eight surveillance and cyber-intelligence companies attempting to sell repurposed spy and law enforcement tools": Schectman, J., Bing, C., & Stubbs, J. (2020, April 28). Cyber-intel firms pitch governments on spy tools to trace coronavirus. Retrieved from https://www.reuters.com/article/us-health-coronavirus-spy-specialreport/

special-report-cyber-intel-firms-pitch-governments-on-spy-tools-to-trace-coronavirus-idUSKCN22A2G1

"The world's business has slid into a world of personal devices": Scott-Railton, J. (2020, March 23). Another critical COVID-19 shortage: Digital security. Retrieved from https://medium.com/@_jsr/another-critical-covid-19-shortage-digital-security-374b1617fea7

Zoom had been plagued by security issues for a number of years: Wells, D. (2018, December 3). Remotely hijacking Zoom clients. Retrieved from https://medium.com/tenable-techblog/remotely-exploiting-zoom-meetings-5a811342ba1d; Cox, J. (2020, March 26). Zoom iOS app sends data to Facebook even if you don't have a Facebook account. Retrieved from https://www.vice.com/en_us/article/k7e599/zoom-ios-app-sends-data-to-facebook-even-if-you-dont-have-a-facebook-account

Highly disturbing instances of "Zoom-bombing": Setera, K. (2020, March 30). FBI warns of teleconferencing and online classroom hijacking during COVID-19 pandemic. Retrieved from https://www.fbi.gov/contact-us/field-offices/boston/news/press-releases/fbi-warns-of-teleconferencing-and-online-classroom-hijacking-during-covid-19-pandemic

Our Citizen Lab team reverse-engineered Zoom: Marczak, B., & Scott-Railton, J. (2020, April 3). Move fast and roll your own crypto: A quick look at the confidentiality of Zoom meetings. Retrieved from https://citizenlab.ca/2020/04/move-fast-roll-your-own-crypto-a-quick-look-at-the-confidentiality-of-zoom-meetings

What I have elsewhere referred to as "event-based" information controls: Deibert, R., & Rohozinski, R. (2008). Good for liberty, bad for security? Internet securitization and global civil society. In R. Deibert, J. Palfrey, R. Rohozinski, & J. Zittrain (Eds.). *Access denied: The practice and policy of internet filtering* (123–165). MIT Press; Bennett, C., & Haggerty, K. (Eds.). (2011). *Security games: Surveillance and control at mega-events.* Routledge.

"Crises are a time-tested means of subverting democracy": Levitsky, S., & Ziblatt, D. (2019, January 12). Why autocrats love emergencies. Retrieved from https://www.nytimes.com/2019/01/12/opinion/

sunday/trump-national-emergency-wall.html; Shammas, M. (2019, December 12). *What's behind rising authoritarianism: Answers from political psychology & the Third Reich.* Retrieved from https://papers.ssrn.com/sol3/papers.cfm?abstract_id=3503164

"If you've got nothing to hide, you've got nothing to fear": For a detailed examination of the flaws concerning the arguments around "nothing to hide," see Solove, D. J. (2011). *Nothing to hide: The false tradeoff between privacy and security.* Yale University Press.

Abuse-of-power episodes within ostensibly liberal democratic societies: Weiner, T. (2012). *Enemies: A history of the FBI.* Random House; Ross, C. A. (2007). Ethics of CIA and military contracting by psychiatrists and psychologists. *Ethical Human Psychology and Psychiatry, 9*(1), 25–34; Hewitt, S. (2018). Cold war counter-terrorism: The evolution of international counter-terrorism in the RCMP Security Service, 1972–1984. *Intelligence and National Security, 33*(1), 67–83; In Canadian criminal law, there are numerous examples of recognized violations of constitutionally protected rights of individuals by law enforcement agencies (see, e.g., *R v. Grant,* 2009 SCC 32; *R v. Le,* 2019 SCC 34; *R v. Evans,* 1996 1 SCR 8; *R v. Nasogaluak,* 2010 SCC 6; *R v. Cole,* 2012 SCC 53); Savage, C., & Risen, J. (2010, March 31). Federal judge finds NSA wiretaps were illegal. *New York Times;* Greenwald, G. (2014). *No place to hide: Edward Snowden, the NSA, and the US surveillance state.* Picador.

A large and influential class of kleptocrats: Cooley, A., Heathershaw, J., & Sharman, J. (2018). The rise of kleptocracy: Laundering cash, whitewashing reputations. *Journal of Democracy, 29*(1), 39–53. https://doi.org/10.1353/jod.2018.0003

"The 13th consecutive year of decline in global freedom": Freedom House. (2019). *Freedom in the world 2019: Democracy in retreat.* Retrieved from https://freedomhouse.org/report/freedom-world/2019/democracy-retreat

"The political uses of the internet in autocracies and democracies are becoming harder to distinguish" Gunitsky, S. (2020, February 19). The great online convergence: Digital authoritarianism comes to democracies. Retrieved from https://warontherocks.com/2020/02/the-great-online-convergence-digital-authoritarianism-comes-to-democracies/

CHAPTER FOUR: BURNING DATA

Jio, launched in 2016 by India's richest man: Pham, S. (2020, May 7). India's Jio Platforms lands $1.5 billion from Vista Equity, marking 3 big investments in 3 weeks. Retrieved from https://www.cnn.com/2020/05/07/tech/reliance-jio-vista-india-intl-hnk/index.html

Under the reign of prime minister Narendra Modi ... the country has rapidly descended into authoritarianism: Filkins, D. (December 2, 2019). Blood and soil in Narendra Modi's India. Retrieved from https://www.newyorker.com/magazine/2019/12/09/blood-and-soil-in-narendra-modis-india

Our very first report on cyber-espionage: Citizen Lab. (2009, March 28). *Tracking GhostNet: Investigating a cyber espionage network*. Retrieved from https://citizenlab.ca/2009/03/tracking-ghostnet-investigating-a-cyber-espionage-network/

Delhi has "turned into a gas chamber": Arvind Kejriwal. (2019, November 1). Delhi has turned into a gas chamber due to smoke from crop burning in neighbouring states. It is very imp that we protect ourselves from this toxic air. Through pvt & govt schools, we have started distributing 50 lakh masks today. I urge all Delhiites to use them whenever needed. [Tweet]. Retrieved from https://twitter.com/ArvindKejriwal/status/1190124368241795073

Coal-fired power plants accounted for 44 percent of new energy production in India in 2019: Saurabh. (2020, January 20). Coal makes a comeback in India, new capacity up 73% in 2019. Retrieved from https://cleantechnica.com/2020/01/20/coal-makes-a-comeback-in-india-new-capacity-up-73-in-2019/

Only one of them is complying with a law requiring the installation of equipment to cut emissions of sulphur oxides: Varadhan, S. (2020, February 5). India's pollution regulator threatens to shut 14 coal-fired power plants. Retrieved from https://www.reuters.com/article/us-india-pollution-coal/indias-pollution-regulator-threatens-to-shut-14-coal-fired-power-plants-idUSKBN1ZZ2A3

Warns Apple, "Unauthorized modification of iOS can cause security vulnerabilities": Apple. (n.d.). Unauthorized modification of iOS can cause security vulnerabilities, instability, shortened battery life, and other issues. Retrieved December 2019 from https://support.apple.com/en-us/HT201954

Extraordinary steps to discourage users from getting too curious about what goes on "beneath the hood": Gordon, W. (2019, April 17). The most common ways manufacturers prevent you from repairing your devices. Retrieved from https://www.ifixit.com/News/15617/the-most-common-ways-manufacturers-prevent-you-from-repairing-your-devices

The production of each and every device involves hundreds of kilograms of fossil fuels: UN News. (2004, March 8). Computer manufacturing soaks up fossil fuels, UN University study says. Retrieved from https://news.un.org/en/story/2004/03/96452-computer-manufacturing-soaks-fossil-fuels-un-university-study-says

Data centres... consume hundreds of thousands of gallons of fresh water a day: Ensmenger, N. (2018). The environmental history of computing. *Technology and Culture, 59*(4), S7–S33. https://doi.org/10.1353/tech.2018.0148

Non-renewable resources, manufacturing, shipping, energy, labour, and non-recyclable waste: Gies, E. (2017, November 29). The real cost of energy. Retrieved from https://www.nature.com/articles/d41586-017-07510-3

Around seventy of the eighty-three stable and non-radioactive elements in the entire periodic table: Nield, D. (2015, August 4). Our smartphone addiction is costing the Earth. Retrieved from https://www.techradar.com/news/phone-and-communications/mobile-phones/our-smartphone-addiction-is-costing-the-earth-1299378

China holds the world's largest reserves of rare earth elements: Hearty, G. (2019, August 20). Rare earths: Next element in the trade war? Retrieved from https://www.csis.org/analysis/rare-earths-next-element-trade-war

China did just that, shutting off exports of the elements to Japan for two months: Funabashi, Y. (2019, August 9). The Mideast has oil, China has rare earths. Retrieved from https://www.japantimes.

co.jp/opinion/2019/08/09/commentary/japan-commentary/mideast-oil-china-rare-earths/

The mining and refining activities consume vast amounts of water while generating a large quantity of CO2 emissions: Crawford & Joler. Anatomy of an AI system.

Rare earth elements are mined either by stripping away layers of topsoil or by drilling holes into the ground: Standaert, M. (2019, July 2). China wrestles with the toxic aftermath of rare earth mining. Retrieved from https://e360.yale.edu/features/china-wrestles-with-the-toxic-aftermath-of-rare-earth-mining

"Only 0.2 percent of the mined clay contains the valuable rare earth elements": Abraham, D. S. (2015). *The elements of power: Gadgets, guns, and the struggle for a sustainable future in the rare metal age*. Yale University Press.

The element cerium (which is used to polish the glass on our device screens): Maughan, T. (2015, April 2). The dystopian lake filled by the world's tech lust. Retrieved from https://www.bbc.com/future/article/20150402-the-worst-place-on-earth

For every one tonne of rare earth elements mined and processed: Crawford & Joler. Anatomy of an AI system.

High levels of contaminants in the region's ground and surface water: Standaert. China wrestles with the toxic aftermath.

Grotesque deformities in local livestock: Kaiman, J. (2014, March 20). Rare earth mining in China: The bleak social and environmental costs. Retrieved from https://www.theguardian.com/sustainable-business/rare-earth-mining-china-social-environmental-costs

"Damaged crops, homes and belongings covered in soot, polluted drinking water": Whoriskey, P. (2020, October 2). China pollution caused by graphite mining for smartphone battery. Retrieved from https://www.washingtonpost.com/graphics/business/batteries/graphite-mining-pollution-in-china/

Bayan Obo is the closest thing to "hell on earth": Maughan. The dystopian lake; Liu, H. (2016, June). *Rare earths: Shades of grey; Can China*

continue to fuel our global clean & smart future? Retrieved from http://www.chinawaterrisk.org/wp-content/uploads/2016/07/CWR-Rare-Earths-Shades-Of-Grey-2016-ENG.pdf

The mine "has put a death-curse on nearby villages," and the giant waste pond... is "a time bomb": Liu. *Rare earths.*

Satellite images show dozens of them spread throughout the region's hills and mountains: Standaert. China wrestles with the toxic aftermath.

There is also a black market for rare earth element mining: Liu. *Rare earths.*

About forty thousand tonnes of rare earth metals were smuggled out of China each year: Stanway, D. (2015, July 7). Fate of global rare earth miners rests on China smuggling crackdown. Retrieved from https://www.reuters.com/article/us-china-rareearth/fate-of-global-rare-earth-miners-rests-on-china-smuggling-crackdown-idUSKCN0PH2DO20150707

Lynas Corporation exports its rare earth metal processing: Liu. *Rare earths.*

The company built the largest refining facility in the world in Malaysia: Bradsher, K. (2011, June 30). Engineers fear rare earth refinery in Malaysia is dangerous. Retrieved from https://www.nytimes.com/2011/06/30/business/global/30rare.html

Around 580,000 tonnes of low-level radioactive waste: Lipson, D., & Hemingway, P. (2019, August 21). Australian mining company Lynas gets permission to dispose of radioactive waste in Malaysia, dividing locals. Retrieved from https://www.abc.net.au/news/2019-08-22/malaysians-divided-on-radioactive-waste-from-aussie-miner-lynas/11434122

Take lithium, also known as "grey gold": Crawford & Joler. Anatomy of an AI system.

Lithium production is booming: Shankleman, J., Biesheuvel, T., Ryan, J., & Merrill, D. (2017, September 7). We're going to need more lithium. Retrieved from https://www.bloomberg.com/graphics/2017-lithium-battery-future/

A single Tesla car requires about seven kilograms of lithium for each of its battery packs: Crawford & Joler. Anatomy of an AI system.

"What links the battery in your smartphone with a dead yak floating down a Tibetan river": Katwala, A. (2018, August 5). The spiralling environmental cost of our lithium battery addiction. Retrieved from https://www.wired.co.uk/article/lithium-batteries-environment-impact

Lithium is found in the brine of salt flats: Zacune, J. (n.d.). Lithium. Retrieved June 16, 2020, from https://www.foeeurope.org/sites/default/files/publications/13_factsheet-lithium-gb.pdf

The lithium carbonate is then extracted through a chemical process that… can harm nearby communities: Karlis, N. (2019, June 17). Electric cars are still better for the environment. But lithium mining has some problems. Retrieved from https://www.salon.com/2019/06/17/lithium-mining-for-green-electric-cars-is-leaving-a-stain-on-the-planet/

In Chile's Atacama and Argentina's Salar de Hombre Muerto regions: Zacune. Lithium.

More than half of the world's cobalt supply is sourced from the Democratic Republic of Congo: U.S. Department of the Interior. (n.d.). Cobalt statistics and information. Retrieved June 16, 2020, from https://www.usgs.gov/centers/nmic/cobalt-statistics-and-information; Eichstaedt, P. (2011). *Consuming the Congo: War and conflict minerals in the world's deadliest place.* Chicago Review Press.

Cobalt mining operations in the DRC routinely use child labour: Amnesty International. (2016). *"This is what we die for": Human rights abuses in the Democratic Republic of the Congo power the global trade in cobalt.* Retrieved from https://www.amnesty.org/en/documents/afr62/3183/2016/en/

Health officials have linked breathing problems and birth defects: Frankel, T. C. (2016, September 30). Cobalt mining for lithium ion batteries has a high human cost. Retrieved from https://www.washingtonpost.com/graphics/business/batteries/congo-cobalt-mining-for-lithium-ion-battery/

"Urinary concentrations of cobalt that were 43 times as high as that of a control group": Frankel. Cobalt mining.

Around four thousand children worked at mining sites in the southern DRC city of Kolwezi alone: Frankel. Cobalt mining.

"A child working in a mine in the Congo would need more than 700,000 years of non-stop work": Crawford & Joler. Anatomy of an AI system.

Indonesia's tin mining operations are "an orgy of unregulated mining": Ensmenger. The environmental history of computing.

Most of the tin is sourced by... PT Timah: Crawford & Joler. Anatomy of an AI system.

"If you own a mobile, it's probably held together by tin from the Indonesian island of Bangka": Hodal, K. (2012, November 23). Death metal: Tin mining in Indonesia. Retrieved from https://www.theguardian.com/environment/2012/nov/23/tin-mining-indonesia-bangka

"A complex structure of supply chains within supply chains": Crawford & Joler. Anatomy of an AI system.

The company undertook site visits to eighty-five smelters and refiners in twenty-one countries: Intel. (2014, May). Intel's efforts to achieve a "conflict free" supply chain. Retrieved from https://www.intel.com/content/dam/doc/policy/policy-conflict-minerals.pdf

One container ship can produce the same amount of pollution as about fifty million cars: Piesing, M. (2018, January 4). Cargo ships are the world's worst polluters, so how can they be made to go green? Retrieved from https://inews.co.uk/news/long-reads/cargo-container-shipping-carbon-pollution-515489

Foxconn and another manufacturer, Unimicron, were dumping heavy metals: Myslewski, R. (2013, August 5). Chinese Apple suppliers face toxic heavy metal water pollution charges. Retrieved from https://www.theregister.co.uk/2013/08/05/chinese_apple_suppliers_investigated_for_water_pollution/

Working conditions at the Catcher Technology Company's factory in China: Bloomberg News. (2018, January 16). Apple supplier workers describe noxious hazards at China factory. Retrieved from https://www.bloomberg.com/news/articles/2018-01-16/workers-at-apple-supplier-catcher-describe-harsh-conditions

Factory employees reported they were "exposed to toxic chemicals every day": China Labor Watch. (2019, September 8). iPhone 11 illegally produced in China: Apple allows supplier factory Foxconn to violate labor laws. Retrieved from http://www.chinalaborwatch.org/report/144

Foxconn's Longhua factory is notorious for its suicide nets: Merchant, B. (2017, June 18). Life and death in Apple's forbidden city. Retrieved from https://www.theguardian.com/technology/2017/jun/18/foxconn-life-death-forbidden-city-longhua-suicide-apple-iphone-brian-merchant-one-device-extract; See also Merchant, B. (2017). *The one device: The secret history of the iPhone*. Little, Brown.

In response to reports of worker suicides, Steve Jobs promised to take action: Fullerton, J. (2018, January 7). Suicide at Chinese iPhone factory reignites concern over working conditions. Retrieved from https://www.telegraph.co.uk/news/2018/01/07/suicide-chinese-iphone-factory-reignites-concern-working-conditions/

Eight years later... working conditions had not improved: China Labor Watch. iPhone 11 illegally produced in China.

Foxconn and Apple disputed the majority of these allegations: Toh, M. (2019, September 9). Apple says a supplier's factory in China violated labor rules. Retrieved from https://www.cnn.com/2019/09/09/tech/apple-foxconn-china-labor-watch-trnd/index.html

A ten-by-forty-mile strip of land around Santa Clara County, California: Ensmenger. The environmental history of computing; United States Environmental Protection Agency. (n.d.). What is Superfund? Retrieved from https://www.epa.gov/superfund/what-superfund

Fluorinated greenhouse gases... have "extremely high global warming potentials": United States Environmental Protection Agency. (2018, April). Center for Corporate Climate Leadership sector spotlight: Electronics. Retrieved from https://www.epa.gov/climateleadership/center-corporate-climate-leadership-sector-spotlight-electronics

Together with mining, manufacturing processes account for about 95 percent of waste: Lepawsky, J. (2018, January 19). 'Wasted': Why recycling isn't enough when it comes to e-waste. Retrieved from https://www.cbc.ca/radio/day6/episode-373-trump-s-year-in-tweets-impeach-o-meter-diplomacy-on-ice-e-waste-and-more-1.4489635/wasted-why-recycling-isn-t-enough-when-it-comes-to-e-waste-1.4489672

"No amount of post-consumer recycling can recoup the waste": Lepawsky, J. (2018, May 17). Almost everything we know about e-waste is wrong. Retrieved from https://thenarwhal.ca/almost-everything-we-know-about-e-waste-is-wrong/

The internet appeared to be holding up, in spite of usage surging: Beech, M. (2020, March 25). COVID-19 pushes up internet use 70% and streaming more than 12%, first figures reveal. Retrieved from https://www.forbes.com/sites/markbeech/2020/03/25/covid-19-pushes-up-internet-use-70-streaming-more-than-12-first-figures-reveal/#63dcee3a3104

Air traffic, automobile, and other forms of fossil-fuelled transportation plummeted: Henriques, M. (2020, March 27). Will Covid-19 have a lasting impact on the environment? Retrieved from https://www.bbc.com/future/article/20200326-covid-19-the-impact-of-coronavirus-on-the-environment

Americans waste up to $19 billion annually in electricity costs: University of Utah. (2016, October 25). A complete waste of energy: Engineers develop process for electronic devices that stops wasteful power leakage. Retrieved from https://www.sciencedaily.com/releases/2016/10/161025114525.htm

The world's communication ecosystem currently consumes approximately 7 percent of global electricity: Jones, N. (2018, September 12). How to stop data centres from gobbling up the world's electricity. Retrieved from https://www.nature.com/articles/d41586-018-06610-y

A smartphone streaming an hour of video on a weekly basis uses more power annually than a new refrigerator: Burrington, I. (2016, December 16). The environmental toll of a Netflix binge. Retrieved from https://www.theatlantic.com/technology/archive/2015/12/there-are-no-clean-clouds/420744/

Sending sixty-five emails is roughly equivalent to driving one kilometre in a car: Villazon, L. (2020, January 3). The thought experiment: What is the carbon footprint of an email? Retrieved from https://www.sciencefocus.com/planet-earth/the-thought-experiment-what-is-the-carbon-footprint-of-an-email/

A major study by a team of researchers at Canada's McMaster University: Belkhir, L., & Elmeligi, A. (2018). Assessing ICT global emissions footprint: Trends to 2040 & recommendations. *Journal of Cleaner Production, 177*, 448–463. https://doi.org/10.1016/j.jclepro.2017.12.239

"From Bitcoin 'mines' to server 'farms' to data 'warehouses'": Ensmenger. The environmental history of computing.

Central Asian countries... advertise for Bitcoin mining operations to be hosted in their jurisdictions: Redman, J. (2020, February 12). 3 cents per kWh — Central Asia's cheap electricity entices Chinese bitcoin miners. Retrieved from https://news.bitcoin.com/central-asias-cheap-electricity-chinese-bitcoin-miners/

Estimates put electric energy consumption associated with Bitcoin mining at around 83.67 terawatt-hours per year: Digiconomist. (n.d.). Bitcoin energy consumption index. Retrieved May 27, 2020, from https://digiconomist.net/bitcoin-energy-consumption

The electricity consumed by the Bitcoin network in one year could power all the teakettles used to boil water in the entire United Kingdom for nineteen years: Cambridge Centre for Alternative Finance. (n.d.). Cambridge Bitcoin electricity consumption index. Retrieved from https://cbeci.org/cbeci/comparisons

A life-cycle assessment for training several common large AI models: Hao, K. (2019, June 6). Training a single AI model can emit as much carbon as five cars in their lifetimes. Retrieved from https://www.technologyreview.com/2019/06/06/239031/training-a-single-ai-model-can-emit-as-much-carbon-as-five-cars-in-their-lifetimes/; Strubell, E., Ganesh, A., & McCallum, A. (2019). Energy and policy considerations for deep learning in NLP. Retrieved from https://arxiv.org/abs/1906.02243

Data centres are "hidden monuments" to our excessive data consumption: Hogan, M. (2015). Facebook data storage centers as the archive's underbelly. *Television & New Media, 16*(1), 3–18. https://doi.org/10.1177/1527476413509415

What one author appropriately called "energy hogs": Pearce, F. (2018, April 3). Energy hogs: Can world's huge data centers be made more efficient? Retrieved https://e360.yale.edu/features/energy-hogs-can-huge-data-centers-be-made-more-efficient

Energy consumption by data centres will treble in the next decade: Bawden, T. (2016, January 23). Global warming: Data centres to consume three times as much energy in next decade, experts warn. Retrieved from https://www.independent.co.uk/environment/global-warming-data-centres-to-consume-three-times-as-much-energy-in-next-decade-experts-warn-a6830086.html

As much as 70 percent of the entire world's internet traffic passes through data centres housed in a single county in Virginia: Upstack. (n.d.). Why is Ashburn known as Data Center Alley? Retrieved May 29, 2020, from https://upstack.com/data-center/why-ashburn-is-data-center-alley

The electricity demand of data centre alley is estimated to be about 4.5 gigawatts: Craighill, C. (2019, February 13). Greenpeace finds Amazon breaking commitment to power cloud with 100% renewable energy. Retrieved from https://www.greenpeace.org/usa/news/greenpeace-finds-amazon-breaking-commitment-to-power-cloud-with-100-renewable-energy/

As much as 360,000 gallons of clean, chilled water a day: Ensmenger. The environmental history of computing.

Roughly as much water as about one hundred acres of almond trees: FitzGerald, D. (2015, June 24). Data centers and hidden water use. Retrieved from https://www.wsj.com/articles/SB10007111583511843695404581067903126039290

U.S. server farms will have used 174 billion gallons of water by 2020: Shehabi, A., Smith, S., Sartor, D., Brown, R., Herrlin, M., Koomey, J.... & Lintner, W. (2016). *United States Data Center energy usage report.* Lawrence Berkeley National Lab. Retrieved from https://eta.lbl.gov/publications/united-states-data-center-energy

Mesa, Arizona, made a deal with Google to permit construction of a massive server farm: Mesa Council, Board, and Committee Research Center. (2019, July 1). Resolution 19-0809. Retrieved from http://mesa.legistar.com/LegislationDetail.aspx?ID=3998203&GUID=FC6B9CE4-208A-4AC1-AB2A-40255C1E9F74

Google... considers its water use a proprietary trade secret: Sattiraju, N. (2020, April 1). Google data centers' secret cost: Billions of gallons of water. Retrieved from https://www.bloomberg.com/news/features/2020-04-01/how-much-water-do-google-data-centers-use-billions-of-gallons

An extensive ranking of social media platforms: Cook, G. (2017). *Clicking clean: Who is winning the race to build a green internet?* Retrieved from http://www.clickclean.org/international/en/

Among the worst is Amazon: Hern, A. (2019, April 9). Amazon accused of abandoning 100% renewable energy goal. Retrieved from https://www.theguardian.com/technology/2019/apr/09/amazon-accused-of-abandoning-100-per-cent-renewable-energy-goal

AWS alone brings in more revenue than McDonald's: Merchant, B. (2019, April 8). Amazon is aggressively pursuing big oil as it stalls out on clean energy. Retrieved from https://gizmodo.com/amazon-is-aggressively-pursuing-big-oil-as-it-stalls-ou-1833875828

Amazon also runs one of the largest warehouse, transportation, distribution, and logistical operations in the world: Ensmenger. The environmental history of computing; McCarthy, L. (2020, January 30). Amazon: accelerating decline in shipping costs are driving future valuation. Retrieved from https://seekingalpha.com/article/4320147-amazon-accelerating-decline-in-shipping-costs-are-driving-future-valuation

Amazon owns 850 facilities in twenty-two countries: Bearth, D. (2019, April 8). Is Amazon a logistics company? All signs point to that. Retrieved from https://www.ttnews.com/articles/amazon-logistics-company-all-signs-point

It is also almost completely non-transparent about its energy footprint: Crawford & Joler. Anatomy of an AI system.

"The world's largest cloud computing company is... still powering its corner of the internet with dirty energy": Craighill, C. (2019, February 13). Greenpeace finds Amazon breaking commitment to power cloud with 100% renewable energy. Retrieved from https://www.greenpeace.org/usa/news/greenpeace-finds-amazon-breaking-commitment-to-power-cloud-with-100-renewable-energy/

It's a good bet that both Alibaba and Tencent: Pearce. Energy hogs.

Many cloud computing companies are actually seeking out revenues from fossil fuel industries: Merchant, B. (2019, February 21). How Google, Microsoft, and big tech are automating the climate crisis. Retrieved from https://gizmodo.com/how-google-microsoft-and-big-tech-are-automating-the-1832790799

Chevron, ExxonMobile, Total, and Equinor have signed billion-dollar contracts with Google, Microsoft, and others: Matthews, C. M. (2018, July 24). Silicon Valley to big oil: We can manage your data better than you. Retrieved from https://www.wsj.com/articles/silicon-valley-courts-a-wary-oil-patch-1532424600

Amazon... has reportedly "aggressively courted" the fossil fuel sector: Merchant. Amazon is aggressively pursuing big oil.

India is currently the world's second-largest smartphone market: Bhattacharya, A. (2017, December 21). There's an e-waste crisis lurking behind India's cheap-phone boom. Retrieved from https://qz.com/india/1161447/theres-an-e-waste-crisis-lurking-behind-indias-boom-in-cheap-phones/

Indian authorities have introduced laws and measures to try to standardize the industry: Lahiry, S. (2019, April 17). Recycling of e-waste in India and its potential. Retrieved from https://www.downtoearth.org.in/blog/waste/recycling-of-e-waste-in-india-and-its-potential-64034

Most of India's recycling and processing... is still managed by the informal sector: Kumar, R., & Shah, D. J. (2014). Review: Current status of recycling of waste printed circuit boards in India. *Journal of Environmental Protection, 5*(1), 9–16. http://doi.org/10.4236/jep.2014.51002

An estimated one million people... depend for their livelihood on these manual recycling operations: Bhattacharya. There's an e-waste crisis lurking.

A sizable proportion of e-waste trade is actually highly regionalized: Lepawsky, J. (2015), The changing geography of global trade in electronic discards. *Geographical Journal, 181*(2), 147–159. https://doi.org/10.1111/geoj.12077; Lepawsky, J., & McNabb, C. (2010). Mapping international flows of electronic waste. *Canadian Geographer / Le Géographe canadien, 54*(2), 177–195. https://doi.org/10.1111/j.1541-0064.2009.00279.x

"There is definitely a topography to the e-waste trade": Lepawsky, J. (2016, March 10). Trading on distortion. Retrieved from https://resource-recycling.com/e-scrap/2016/03/10/trading-on-distortion/

While India's reuse economy is truly remarkable, that doesn't mean that there are no waste or other issues: Corwin, J. E. (2018). "Nothing is useless in nature": Delhi's repair economies and value-creation in an electronics "waste" sector. *Environment and Planning A: Economy and Space, 50*(1), 14–30. https://doi.org/10.1177/0308518X17739006; See also Toxics Link. (2019). Informal e-waste recycling in Delhi. Retrieved from http://www.toxicslink.org/docs/Informal%20E-waste.pdf

Raw sewage combined with acid wash... flows directly into the Yamuna River: Bhaduri, A. (2017, November 30). Why does the world's e-waste reach India? Retrieved from https://yourstory.com/2017/11/e-waste

Apple churns out a bewildering variety of new components and accessories: Leber, R. (2020, March 3). Your plastic addiction is bankrolling big oil. Retrieved from https://www.motherjones.com/environment/2020/03/your-plastic-addiction-is-bankrolling-big-oil/

Take AirPods: Haskins, C. (2019, May 6). AirPods are a tragedy. Retrieved from https://www.vice.com/en_ca/article/neaz3d/airpods-are-a-tragedy

Even highly efficient recycling is an energy-intensive industrial process: Pickering, D. (Producer). (2018, February 7). *Restart* [Audio podcast]. Episode 9. Tracing global flows of electronic 'discards' with Josh Lepawsky. Retrieved from https://therestartproject.org/podcast/discards/

Adding extra life to computers saves between five and twenty times more energy than recycling them outright: Ives, M. (2014, February 6). In developing world, a push to bring e-waste out of shadows. Retrieved from https://e360.yale.edu/features/in_developing_world_a_push_to_bring_e-waste_out_of_shadows

Rising sea levels risk flooding critical infrastructure located in coastal areas: Borunda, A. (2018, July 16). The internet is drowning. Retrieved from https://www.nationalgeographic.com/science/2018/07/news-internet-underwater-sea-level-rise/

The risk of high temperatures overheating data centres: Bogle, A. (2015, January 14). Will climate change burn up the internet? Retrieved from https://grist.org/climate-energy/will-climate-change-burn-up-the-internet/

"For the most part, we experience only the positive benefits of information technology": Ensmenger. The environmental history of computing.

CHAPTER FIVE: RETREAT, REFORM, RESTRAINT

"We were both playing Columbo to each other": Contenta, S. (2019, December 13). How these Toronto sleuths are exposing the world's digital spies while risking their own lives. Retrieved from https://www.thestar.com/news/canada/2019/12/13/from-a-tower-in-toronto-they-watch-the-watchers-how-citizen-lab-sleuths-are-exposing-the-worlds-digital-spies-while-risking-their-own-lives.html

The ensuing AP story was a bombshell: Satter, R. (2019, February 11). Undercover spy exposed in NYC was 1 of many. Retrieved from https://apnews.com/9bdbbfe0c8a2407aac14a1e995659de4

"Our very tools and techniques threaten to wipe us out": Vaidhyanathan. *Antisocial media.*

Companies trumpet their powerful machine learning and artificial intelligence systems: Klein, N. (2020, May 13). How big tech plans to profit from the pandemic. Retrieved from https://www.theguardian.com/news/2020/may/13/naomi-klein-how-big-tech-plans-to-profit-from-coronavirus-pandemic

The luxurious Grand Velas Riviera Nayarit: Grand Velas Riviera Maya. (2019, January 4). Velas Resorts introduces the 'detox concierge' as part of 2019 digital detox program. Retrieved from https://rivieramaya.grandvelas.com/newsroom/hotel/velas-resorts-detox-concierge

Guidelines for a thirty-day "digital declutter" process: Newport, C. (2019). *Digital minimalism: Choosing a focused life in a noisy world.* Portfolio; See also Allcott, H., Braghieri, L., Eichmeyer, S., & Gentzkow, M. (2020). The welfare effects of social media. *American Economic Review, 110*(3), 629–76; Hill, K. (2019). I cut the 'Big Five' tech giants from my life. It was hell. Retrieved from https://gizmodo.com/i-cut-the-big-five-tech-giants-from-my-life-it-was-hel-1831304194

These don't go far enough for virtual reality pioneer Jaron Lanier: Lanier, J. (2018). *Ten arguments for deleting your social media accounts right now.* Henry Holt.

Bill McKibben's The Age of Missing Information*... or Lewis Mumford's* The Pentagon of Power: McKibben, B. (2006). *The age of missing information.* Random House; Mumford, L. (1970). *The pentagon of power: The myth of the machine.* Vol. 2. Harcourt Brace Jovanovich.

We now live in a "global village" (to borrow McLuhan's phrasing): McLuhan, M. (1962). *The Gutenberg galaxy: The making of typographic man.* University of Toronto Press.

A single habitat that... Buckminster Fuller once aptly called "Spaceship Earth": Fuller, R. B. (1969). *Operating manual for spaceship Earth.* Southern Illinois University Press.

Facebook refers cases to the board, whose decisions are binding but not enforced by law: Douek, E. (2020, May 11). "What kind of oversight board have you given us?" Retrieved from https://lawreviewblog.uchicago.edu/2020/05/11/fb-oversight-board-edouek/

There are as many as 188 fact-checking entities in more than sixty countries: Woolley & Joseff. *Demand for deceit.*

Advocates of fact-checking also assume that everyone reasons the same way: Woolley & Joseff. *Demand for deceit.*

Fact-checking can actually reinforce the spread of false information: Pennycook, G., & Rand, D. (2020, March 24). The right way to fight fake news. Retrieved from https://www.nytimes.com/2020/03/24/opinion/fake-news-social-media.html; Pennycook, G., Bear, A., Collins, E. T., & Rand, D. G. (2020). The implied truth effect: Attaching warnings to a subset of fake news headlines increases perceived accuracy of headlines without warnings. *Management Science* [Forthcoming]. http://dx.doi.org/10.2139/ssrn.3035384

General warnings about the veracity of news can actually reduce confidence in all news sources: Clayton, K., Blair, S., Busam, J. A., Forstner, S., Glance, J., Green, G., ... & Sandhu, M. (2019). Real solutions for fake news? Measuring the effectiveness of general warnings and fact-check tags in reducing belief in false stories on social media. *Political Behavior,* 1–23. https://doi.org/10.1007/s11109-019-09533-0

Media literacy is incomplete: See Boyd, D. (2017). "Did media literacy backfire?" *Journal of Applied Youth Studies, 1*(4), 83–89. Retrieved from https://search.informit.com.au/documentSummary;dn=607936397466888;res=IELNZC; Bulger, M., & Davison, P. (2018). *The promises, challenges, and futures of media literacy.* Data & Society Research Institute. Retrieved from https://datasociety.net/output/the-promises-challenges-and-futures-of-media-literacy/

Oops! It was a "bug," said Guy Rosen: Associated Press. (2020, March 17). Facebook bug wrongly deleted authentic coronavirus news. Retrieved from https://www.ctvnews.ca/health/coronavirus/facebook-bug-wrongly-deleted-authentic-coronavirus-news-1.4857517; Human social media content moderators have extremely stressful jobs, given the volume of potentially offensive and harmful posts: Roberts, S. T. (2019). *Behind the screen: Content moderation in the shadows of social media*. Yale University Press; Kaye, D. A. (2019). *Speech police: The global struggle to govern the internet*. Columbia Global Reports.

There is no shortage of proposals to reform and regulate social media: Owen, T. (2019, November). *The case for platform governance*. Centre for International Governance Innovation.

Some advocate for giving users a legal right "not to be tracked": United States of America. (2019). Do Not Track Act, S.1578, 116th Cong. Retrieved from https://www.congress.gov/bill/116th-congress/senate-bill/1578

Calls for more scrutiny of the machine-based algorithms companies use to sort their users: United States of America. (2019). Algorithmic Accountability Act of 2019, H.R.2231, 116th Cong. Retrieved from https://www.congress.gov/bill/116th-congress/house-bill/2231/all-info; Raji, I. D., Gebru, T., Mitchell, M., Buolamwini, J., Lee, J., & Denton, E. (2020). Saving face: Investigating the ethical concerns of facial recognition auditing. *Proceedings of the 2020 AAAI/ACM Conference on AI, Ethics, and Society (AIES '20)*. https://doi.org/10.1145/3375627.3375820; Pasquale, F. (2015). *The black box society*. Harvard University Press.

Proposals have been made to legislate greater transparency in the social media advertising space: Friedersdorf, C. (2019, November 1). Doubt anyone who's confident that Facebook should ban political ads. Retrieved from https://www.theatlantic.com/ideas/archive/2019/11/twitter-facebook-political-ads/601174/

Many advocate for social media platforms to be forced (or otherwise encouraged) to incorporate human rights due diligence: Amnesty International. (2019). *Surveillance giants: How the business model of Google and Facebook threatens human rights*; Kaye. *Speech police*.

The development of "civic media" as a "social" or "public" (instead of commercial) "good": Owen. *The case for platform governance*.

Everyone's efforts are weaving something larger than their own separate struggles: Deudney, D., & Mendenhall, E. (2016). Green Earth: The emergence of planetary civilization. In S. Nicholson & S. Jinnah (Eds.),

New Earth politics: Essays from the Anthropocene (43–72). MIT Press. https://doi.org/10.2307/j.ctt1b349c4.8

The social media equivalent of Rachel Carson's Silent Spring, *Barry Commoner's* The Closing Circle, *and Paul Ehrlich's* The Population Bomb: Carson, R. (1962). *Silent spring.* Houghton Mifflin; Commoner, B. (1971). *The closing circle: Nature, man, and technology.* Alfred A. Knopf; Ehrlich, P. R. (1971). *The population bomb.* Ballantine.

Republican political theory enjoys a "ghostly afterlife": Deudney, D. (2007). *Bounding power: Republican security theory from the polis to the global village.* Princeton University Press. https://doi.org/10.2307/j.ctt7sj7t

Republican polities tend to be rare and relatively fragile: Deudney, D. (2000). Geopolitics as theory: Historical security materialism. *European Journal of International Relations, 6*(1), 77–107. https://doi.org/10.1177/1354066100006001004

"Republicanism is an institutionalized system of decentralized power constraint": Deudney, D. (1995). The Philadelphian system: Sovereignty, arms control, and balance of power in the American states-union, circa 1787–1861. *International Organization, 49*(2), 191–228. Retrieved from https://jstor.org/stable/2706970

"Every man invested with power is apt to abuse it": Montesquieu. *The spirit of laws.*

"You must first enable the government to control the governed; and next oblige it to control itself": Madison, J. (1788). *Federalist no. 51: The structure of the government must furnish the proper checks and balances between the different departments.* The New-York Packet.

These devices are a form of "friction" introduced into political processes: Stein, J. G. (2002). *The Cult of Efficiency.* House of Anansi Press.

Some oversight bodies have simply been eliminated altogether: Brookings Institution. (2020, May 22). Tracking deregulation in the Trump era. Retrieved from https://www.brookings.edu/interactives/tracking-deregulation-in-the-trump-era/

What Levitsky and Ziblatt call "the soft guardrails of democracy": Levitsky, S., & Ziblatt, D. (2018). *How democracies die: What history reveals about our future*. Crown.

Numerous proposals worldwide to employ cell location data to assist in the effort to combat the spread of COVID-19: Glanz, J., Carey, B., Holder, J., Watkins, D., Valentino-DeVries, J., Rojas, R., & Leatherby, L. (2020, April 2). Where America didn't stay home even as the virus spread. Retrieved from https://www.nytimes.com/interactive/2020/04/02/us/coronavirus-social-distancing.html; Landau, S. (2020, March 25). Location surveillance to counter COVID-19: Efficacy is what matters. Retrieved from https://www.lawfareblog.com/location-surveillance-counter-covid-19-efficacy-what-matters; Anderson, R. (2020, May 12). Contact tracing in the real world. Retrieved from https://www.lightbluetouchpaper.org/2020/04/12/contact-tracing-in-the-real-world/

Such apps will be wide open to malfeasance that could distort the utility of the data: Anderson. Contact tracing in the real world.

The safeguards around them must be exceptionally strong: Geist, M. (2020, March 24). How Canada should ensure cellphone tracking to counter the spread of coronavirus does not become the new normal. Retrieved from https://www.michaelgeist.ca/2020/03/how-canada-should-ensure-cellphone-tracking-to-counter-the-spread-of-coronavirus-does-not-become-the-new-normal/; The turn to apps to solve contact tracing challenges during the COVID pandemic is a good example of what Evgeny Morozov calls "technological solutionism." See Morozov, E. (2013). *To save everything, click here: The folly of technological solutionism*. PublicAffairs.

"It is insufficient to say that a comprehensive system for control and use of targeted surveillance technologies is broken": United Nations Office of the High Commissioner for Human Rights. (2019, May 28). *Surveillance and human rights: Report of the Special Rapporteur on the Promotion and Protection of the Right to Freedom of Opinion and Expression*. Retrieved from https://digitallibrary.un.org/record/3814512

States purchasing spyware are at liberty to abuse it: Anstis, S., Deibert, R. J., & Scott-Railton, J. (2019, July 19). A proposed response to the commercial surveillance emergency. Retrieved from https://www.lawfareblog.com/proposed-response-commercial-surveillance-emergency

Government military, intelligence, and law enforcement agencies have... stockpiled knowledge of software bugs: Deibert, R. (2014, November 25). The cyber security syndrome. Retrieved from https://www.opencanada.org/features/the-cyber-security-syndrome/; Deibert, R. (2013). Divide and rule: Republican security theory as civil society cyber strategy. *Georgetown Journal of International Affairs*, 39–50.

These could include mandated transparency and reporting, greater accountability to legislators, and independent oversight bodies: Parsons, C. (2019). "Once more, preventing the breach: The rationale, and implications of, adopting human security practices for vulnerabilities equities process policies" [Working paper]; Herpig, S., & Schwartz, A. (2019, January 4). The future of vulnerabilities equities processes around the world. Retrieved from https://www.lawfareblog.com/future-vulnerabilities-equities-processes-around-world

Abuses and built-in discrimination around the use of some of these technologies today: O'Neil, C. (2016). *Weapons of math destruction*. Crown Random House; Tanovich, D. (2006). *The colour of justice*. Irwin Law; Ontario Human Rights Commission. (2017, April). *Under suspicion: Research and consultation report on racial profiling in Ontario*. Retrieved from http://www.ohrc.on.ca/en/under-suspicion-research-and-consultation-report-racial-profiling-ontario; Ontario Human Rights Commission. (2018, November). *A collective impact: Interim report on the inquiry into racial profiling and racial discrimination of Black persons by the Toronto Police Service*. Retrieved from http://www.ohrc.on.ca/en/public-interest-inquiry-racial-profiling-and-discrimination-toronto-police-service/collective-impact-interim-report-inquiry-racial-profiling-and-racial-discrimination-black; Howe, M., & Monaghan, J. (2018). Strategic incapacitation of Indigenous dissent: Crowd theories, risk management, and settler colonial policing. *Canadian Journal of Sociology*, 43(4), 325–348. Retrieved from https://journals.library.ualberta.ca/cjs/index.php/CJS/article/view/29397/21432?fbclid=IwARogOWPQ6ZE6Om8Tq4uovO1rF2ndSSfvbtjLOeM4U_B2F_YzYeqRNuipHQw; Facial recognition software trained predominantly on the faces of white and lighter-skinned people may be less capable of accurately identifying individuals with darker skin tones. See Molnar & Gill. *Bots at the gate*; Garvie, C., Bedoya, A., & Frankle, J. (2016). *The perpetual line-up*. Georgetown Law: Center on Privacy and Technology; Klare, B. F., Burge, M. J., Klontz, J. C., Bruegge, R. W. V., & Jain, A. K. (2012). Face recognition performance: Role of demographic information. *IEEE Transactions on Information Forensics and Security, 7*(6), 1789–1801.

A recurring theme in science fiction but one that seems increasingly less far-fetched: Deudney, D. (2020). *Dark skies: Space expansionism, planetary geopolitics, and the ends of humanity*. Oxford University Press; Kerr, I. R., Calo, R., & Froomkin, M. (Eds.). (2016) *Robot law*. Edward Elgar.

A wholesale ban on the use of AI and facial recognition until proper accountability mechanisms are in place: Fight for the Future. (n.d.). Ban facial recognition. Retrieved June 16, 2020, from https://www.banfacialrecognition.com/; Schneier, B. (2020, January 20). We're banning facial recognition. We're missing the point. Retrieved from https://www.nytimes.com/2020/01/20/opinion/facial-recognition-ban-privacy.html

Restraints . . . can begin in one or several jurisdictions and then develop more broadly: Lu, D. (2020, January 23). It's too late to ban face recognition — Here's what we need instead. Retrieved from https://www.newscientist.com/article/2231066-its-too-late-to-ban-face-recognition-heres-what-we-need-instead/; Access Now. (May 16, 2018). Toronto declaration: Protecting the rights to equality and non-discrimination in machine learning systems. Retrieved from https://www.accessnow.org/the-toronto-declaration-protecting-the-rights-to-equality-and-non-discrimination-in-machine-learning-systems/; Université de Montréal. Montreal declaration for responsible AI. Retrieved from https://www.montrealdeclaration-responsibleai.com/; Fairness, Accountability, and Transparency in Machine Learning. (n.d.). Principles for accountable algorithms and a social impact statement for algorithms. Retrieved June 16, 2020, from www.fatml.org/resources/principles-for-accountable-algorithms

Erik Learned-Miller...feels that the negative aspects of these technologies are growing and simply too dangerous to leave unregulated: Gershgorn, D. (2019, July 26). An A.I. pioneer wants an FDA for facial recognition. Retrieved from https://onezero.medium.com/an-a-i-pioneer-wants-an-fda-for-facial-recognition-cdde309cf553

Since 9/11...the most secretive and martial wings of the state have ballooned in size: Deibert. The cyber security syndrome; It is also very important to note that the mere recognition by citizens that their governments are undertaking mass surveillance can have a chilling effect on free expression. See Penney, J. W. (2017). Internet surveillance, regulation, and chilling effects online: A comparative case study. *Internet Policy Review, 6*(2), 22. https://doi.org/10.14763/2017.2.692

The platforms' legal appropriation of users' data: Cohen. *Between truth and power.*

"There is a theoretical point—call it the Skinnerlarity": Wu, T. (2020, April 9). Bigger Brother. Retrieved from https://www.nybooks.com/articles/2020/04/09/bigger-brother-surveillance-capitalism/

The EU's General Data Protection Regime...and California's Consumer Privacy Act are by far the most well known: On GDPR, see Bennett, C. J. (2018). The European General Data Protection Regulation: An instrument for the globalization of privacy standards? *Information Polity, 23*(2), 239–246; Hartzog, W., & Richards, N. M. (2020). Privacy's constitutional moment and the limits of data protection. *Boston College Law Review, 61*(5), 1687. http://dx.doi.org/10.2139/ssrn.3441502

A true "codified antisurveillance regime": Wu. Bigger Brother; Balkin, J. M., & Zittrain, J. (2016, October 3). A grand bargain to make tech companies trustworthy. Retrieved from https://www.theatlantic.com/technology/archive/2016/10/information-fiduciary/502346/; Hartzog, W. (2018). *Privacy's blueprint: The battle to control the design of new technologies*. Harvard University Press.

A "protective counter movement": Cohen. *Between truth and power.*

Laws pertaining specifically to the freewheeling data broker industry: Pasquale, F. (2014, October 17). The dark market for personal data. *New York Times*; Schneier. *Data and Goliath.*

Hasty decisions are usually bad: Rosen, J. (2018, October). America is living James Madison's nightmare. Retrieved from https://www.theatlantic.com/magazine/archive/2018/10/james-madison-mob-rule/568351/

A technical tweak a group of Brazilian researchers explicitly described as introducing friction into the application: Romm, T. (2020, March 2). Fake cures and other coronavirus conspiracy theories are flooding WhatsApp, leaving governments and users with a 'sense of panic.' Retrieved from https://www.washingtonpost.com/technology/2020/03/02/whatsapp-coronavirus-misinformation/; de Freitas Melo, P., Vieira, C. C., Garimella, K., de Melo, P. O. V., & Benevenuto, F. (2019, December). Can WhatsApp counter misinformation by limiting message forwarding? Retrieved from https://arxiv.org/abs/1909.08740

They even issued a rare joint statement: Statt, N. (2020, March 16). Major tech platforms say they're 'jointly combating fraud and misinformation' about COVID-19. Retrieved from https://www.theverge.com/2020/3/16/21182726/coronavirus-covid-19-facebook-google-twitter-youtube-joint-effort-misinformation-fraud

"Platforms should be forced to earn the kudos they are getting": Douek, E. (2020, March 25). COVID-19 and social media content moderation. Retrieved from https://www.lawfareblog.com/covid-19-and-social-media-content-moderation

Mandatory or poorly constructed measures could be perverted as an instrument of authoritarian control: Lim, G., & Donovan, J. (2020, April 3). Republicans want Twitter to ban Chinese Communist Party accounts. That's a dangerous idea. Retrieved from https://slate.com/technology/2020/04/republicans-want-twitter-to-ban-chinese-communist-party-accounts-thats-dangerous.html; Lim, G. (2020). *Securitize/counter-securitize: The life and death of Malaysia's anti-fake news act.* Retrieved from https://datasociety.net/library/securitize-counter-securitize/

Some commentators have called for additional exceptions to Section 230's immunity clauses: Sylvain, O. (2018, April 1). Discriminatory designs on user data. Retrieved from https://knightcolumbia.org/

content/discriminatory-designs-user-data; Citron, D. K., & Penney, J. (2019, January 2). When law frees us to speak. *Fordham Law Review, 87*(6). Retrieved from https://ssrn.com/abstract=3309227; Citron, D.K., & Wittes, B. (2018). The problem isn't just backpage: Revising Section 230 immunity. *Georgetown Law Tech Review*, 453. Retrieved from https://georgetownlawtechreview.org/wp-content/uploads/2018/07/2.2-Citron-Wittes-453-73.pdf; The most accessible and comprehensive account of Section 230 of the CDA is Kosseff, J. (2019). *The twenty-six words that created the internet*. Cornell University Press.

The key will be to make sure that social media platforms manage content in ways that are transparent: Kaye. *Speech police*.

"Shaped by geometry rather than natural morphology": Deudney. The Philadelphian system.

Brandeis "believed that great economic power results in immense political power": Wu, T. (2018, November 10). Be afraid of economic 'bigness.' Be very afraid. Retrieved from https://www.nytimes.com/2018/11/10/opinion/sunday/fascism-economy-monopoly.html

Amazon... "the titan of twenty-first century commerce": Khan, L. M. (2017). Amazon's antitrust paradox. *Yale Law Journal, 126*(3), 710.

Bezos was named... the "richest man in modern history": Au-Yeung, A. (2018, October 3). How Jeff Bezos became the richest person in America and the world. Retrieved from https://www.forbes.com/sites/angelauyeung/2018/10/03/how-jeff-bezos-became-the-richest-person-in-the-world-2018-forbes-400/

Amazon, Facebook, and Google spent nearly half a billion dollars on lobbying efforts in Washington: Romm, T. (2020, January 22). Amazon, Facebook spent record sums on lobbying in 2019 as tech industry ramped up Washington presence. Retrieved from https://www.washingtonpost.com/technology/2020/01/22/amazon-facebook-google-lobbying-2019/

Justice Brandeis lamented the "curse of bigness": *United States v. Columbia Steel Co.*, 74 F. Su671 (D. Del. 1947).

"Antitrust law... was meant fundamentally as a kind of constitutional safeguard": Wu. Be afraid; See also Hughes, C. (May 9, 2019). It's time to break up Facebook. Retrieved from https://www.nytimes.com/2019/05/09/opinion/sunday/chris-hughes-facebook-zuckerberg.html; Srinivasan, D. (2019). The antitrust case against Facebook: A monopolist's journey towards pervasive surveillance in spite of consumers' preference for privacy. *Berkeley Business Law Journal, 16*(1), 39–101.

That the large tech platforms be designated as public utilities: Economist. (2020, April 4). Winners from the pandemic — Big tech's covid-19 opportunity. Retrieved from https://www.economist.com/leaders/2020/04/04/big-techs-covid-19-opportunity?fsrc=scn/tw/te/bl/ed/winnersfromthepandemicbigtechscovid19opportunityleaders

"These firms have done things that, say, a litany of mini-Googles could not have done": Scott, M. (2020, March 25). Coronavirus crisis shows Big Tech for what it is — a 21st century public utility. Retrieved from https://www.politico.eu/article/coronavirus-big-tech-utility-google-facebook/

"A well-regulated Militia, being necessary to the security of a free State": United States of America. U.S. Const. amend. II.

Another recessed power might be "data portability" and "interoperability" requirements: Gasser, U. (2015, July 6). Interoperability in the digital ecosystem. http://dx.doi.org/10.2139/ssrn.2639210; Doctorow, C. (July 11, 2019). Interoperability: Fix the internet, not the tech companies. Retrieved from https://www.eff.org/deeplinks/2019/07/interoperability-fix-internet-not-tech-companies

The COVID emergency may have helped kick the right-to-repair movement into high gear: Motherboard staff. (2020, March 20). The world after this. Retrieved from https://www.vice.com/en_us/article/wxekvw/the-world-after-coronavirus-healthcare-labor-climate-internet

Technicians scrambled to circumvent the software and other controls: Doctorow, C. (2020, March 19). Right to repair in times of pandemic. Retrieved from https://www.eff.org/deeplinks/2020/03/right-repair-times-pandemic

Active forms of resistance...may be appropriate: For an argument for the value of "conscience-driven" lawbreaking, see Schneier. *Data and Goliath*; See also Deibert, R. J. (2003). Black code: Censorship, surveillance, and the militarisation of cyberspace. *Millennium, 32*(3), 501–530; Menn, J. (2019). *Cult of the dead cow: How the original hacking supergroup might just save the world*. PublicAffairs.

What most observers saw as a "war on whistleblowing": Risen, J. (2014). *Pay any price: Greed, power, and endless war*. Houghton Mifflin Harcourt.

Well-intentioned moderation could very easily slide into heavy-handed suppression: For more on how strong content moderation requirements for social media platforms could backfire, see Donahoe, E. (2017, August 21). Protecting democracy from online disinformation requires better algorithms, not censorship. Retrieved from https://www.cfr.org/blog/protecting-democracy-online-disinformation-requires-better-algorithms-not-censorship; MacKinnon, R. (2012). *Consent of the networked: The worldwide struggle for internet freedom*. Basic Books.

According to Deudney: Deudney, The Philadelphian system.

To turn this around would require a major rethink: On the importance of public education and civics as a way to create a healthy online public sphere, see Greenspon, E., & Owen, T. (2018). *Democracy divided: Countering disinformation and hate in the digital public sphere*. Public Policy Forum. Retrieved from https://www.ppforum.ca/publications/socialmarketing-hate-speech-disinformation-democracy/; Lucas, E., & Pomerantsev, P. (2016). *Winning the information war: Techniques and counter-strategies to Russian propaganda in Central and Eastern Europe*. Center for European Policy Analysis; Bjola, C., & Papadakis, K. (2020). Digital propaganda, counterpublics and the disruption of the public sphere: The Finnish approach to building digital resilience. *Cambridge Review of International Affairs*, 1–29; Cederberg, G. (2018). *Catching Swedish phish: How Sweden is protecting its 2018 elections*. Belfer Center for Science and International Affairs; Bulger & Davison. *The promises, challenges, and futures of media literacy*.

Environmentalism's ideals — getting "back to nature": Davis, W. (2009). *The Wayfinders*. House of Anansi Press.

"It is this human right... with which the University has a duty above all to be concerned": Office of the Governing Council. (n.d.). University of Toronto Statement of Institutional Purpose. Retrieved June 1, 2020, from https://governingcouncil.utoronto.ca/university-toronto-statement-institutional-purpose

"Researchers who test online platforms for discriminatory and rights-violating data practices": American Civil Liberties Union. (2020, March 28). Federal court rules 'big data' discrimination studies do not violate federal anti-hacking law. Retrieved from https://www.aclu.org/press-releases/federal-court-rules-big-data-discrimination-studies-do-not-violate-federal-anti

An alternative "human-centric" approach to cybersecurity: Deibert, R. (2018). Toward a human-centric approach to cybersecurity. *Ethics & International Affairs, 32*(4), 411–424. https://doi.org/10.1017/S0892679418000618

I witnessed first-hand well-intentioned and hard-working government bureaucrats: Freedom Online Coalition. (2016, October). Freedom Online coalition statement on a human rights based approach to cybersecurity policy making. Retrieved from https://freedomonlinecoalition.com/wp-content/uploads/2019/11/FOC-Statement-on-a-Human-Rights-Based-Approach-to-Cybersecurity.pdf; See also DeNardis, L. (2014). *The global war for internet governance.* Yale University Press.

ACKNOWLEDGEMENTS

THE INVITATION TO DELIVER the Massey Lectures is a professional dream come true. I have been influenced by many of the books and lectures in the series since my undergraduate days. To contribute one myself is phenomenal (and a little surreal). Thanks to Greg Kelly and Philip Coulter at CBC, Janie Yoon, Sarah MacLachlan, Peter Norman, Gillian Watts, Alysia Shewchuk, and Maria Golikova at House of Anansi Press, and Michael Levine at Westwood Creative Artists. Special thanks to Massey College's John Fraser, Hugh Segal, and Nathalie Des Rosiers. I am especially grateful to colleagues at the University of Toronto, and especially the chairs, deans, principals, and executive directors at the Department of Political Science and Munk School of Global Affairs and Public Policy, for supporting my research at the Citizen Lab for close to twenty years. Special thanks to Janice Stein, Rob Vipond, David Cameron, Louis Pauly, Antoinette Handley, Stephen Toope, Randall Hansen, Michael Sabia,

Margaret McKone, Ariana Bradford, and president Meric Gertler. We appreciate your having our backs!

Although I have been researching and writing on the topics covered in *Reset* for decades, the genesis of this particular book was at the Ninth Global Assembly of the World Movement for Democracy, held from May 6 to 9, 2018, in Dakar, Senegal. During a panel at the assembly, I made remarks about the "painful truths of social media." Carl Gershman, Larry Diamond, Christopher Walker, and Marc Plattner encouraged me to write them up in an essay for the *Journal of Democracy*, which appeared as "The Road to Digital Unfreedom: Three Painful Truths about Social Media" in the January 2019 issue. *Reset* builds upon and updates this essay.

Numerous people have generously provided feedback, comments, and suggestions as I researched and wrote this book. I am especially grateful to Daniel Deudney, with whom I have been having a conversation about these and other topics for more than twenty-five years. Dan's suggestions and insights about republicanism were invaluable. Thanks to Stephanie Tran, Ethan Deibert, and Gabby Lim for research assistance and comments on earlier drafts, and to Alexei Abraham, Neal Roese, Cynthia Khoo, Christopher Parsons, Siena Anstis, Michael Deibert, Jane Gowan, and Jon Penney for detailed reviews and comments. All errors and omissions that remain are solely my fault.

The themes that I cover in *Reset* are inseparably linked to the work of the Citizen Lab — the extraordinary research group I have had the great fortune to help direct and participate in for twenty years. Each and every Citizen Lab researcher from the first day to the present has inspired, informed, and influenced me in countless ways. Thanks to Nart Villeneuve, Graeme Bunton, Michelle Levesque — the original crew. Special thanks to Masashi Crete-Nishihata, Adam Senft, John Scott-Railton, Jakub Dalek, Ivy Lo, Irene Poetranto, Christopher Parsons, Siena Anstis, Bill Marczak, Bahr Abdul Razzak, Noura Al-Jizawi, Miles Kenyon, Matthew Braga, Lotus Ruan, Sharly Chan, William Chan, Stephanie Tran, Sarah McKune, Mari Zhou, Joshua Gold, Simon Humbert, Pellaeon Lin, Matthew Brooks, Lex Gill, Alexei Abraham, Ruohan Xiong, Kate Robertson, Etienne Maynier, Ned Moran, Adam Hulcoop, Cynthia Khoo, Gabby Lim, Jon Penney, Bill Robinson, Moses Karanja, Lennart Maschmeyer, Jennie Phillips, Ksenia Ermoshina, Jeffrey Knockel, Phillipa Gill, Stefania Milan, Chris Davis, Claudio Guarnieri, Seth Hardy, Katie Kleemola, Joshua Oliver, Helmi Noman, Greg Wiseman, Byron Sonne, Jason Ng, Andrew Hilts, Brandon Dixon, Alberto Fittarelli, Adam Molnar, James Tay, Igor Valentovich, and Peter Tanchak. To be part of the Citizen Lab is like waking up each day and going on a great adventure with a group of smart, dedicated, principled, and supportive people. I am grateful for every minute we work together.

Thanks also to my many students in political science and the Munk School's Master of Global Affairs program.

Many of the themes in this book were the subject of discussions in our seminars, and I learned a great deal from our time together.

I am also very grateful to colleagues in the digital security and human rights space with whom we often collaborate, and whose own research and writing have been influential to me: Rebecca MacKinnon, Gus Hosein, Edin Omanovic, Ashkan Soltani, Anriette Esterhuysen, Jillian York, Danny O'Brien, Eva Galperin, Cory Doctorow, Annie Game, Joseph Nye, Martha Finnemore, Duncan Hollis, Eileen Donahoe, Christopher Bronk, Myriam Dunn Cavelty, Florian Egloff, Phil Howard, Thomas Rid, Camille François, Lokman Tsui, Herb Lin, Petra Molnar, Brendan de Caires, Michael Geist, Christopher Gore, Tamir Israel, Susan Morgan, Dinah PoKempner, Bruce Schneier, Malte Spitz, Amie Stepanovich, Meredith Whittaker, Collin Anderson, Dennis Broeders, Mikkel Flyverbom, Dirk Matten, Anita Gohdes, Tina Freyburg, Christopher Soghoian, Sunil Abraham, Robert Guerra, Brett Solomon, Peter Micek, Gustaf Björksten, Rex Hughes, Didier Bigo, James Der Derian, Misha Glenny, Ellery Biddle, Mallory Knodel, Moez Chakchouk, Kilnam Chon, James Lewis, Donny B. U., Mark Raymond, Laura DeNardis, Tim Maurer, Paul Meyer, Harvey Rishikof, Steve Weber, Sean Brooks, Marietje Schaake, Stéphane Duguin, David Kaye, Cynthia Wong, Jon Lindsay, Thomas Biersteker, Christopher Prince, Brenda McPhail, Holly Porteus, Seva Gunitsky, John Ruggie, Jonathan Zittrain, Arturo Filastò, Maria Xynou, Danna Ingleton, and Edward Snowden.

Thanks especially to our partners in the Cyber Stewards Network and other organizations worldwide, including Walid Al-Saqaf, Hisham Al-Miraat, Ramsey George, Reem al Masri, Kelly Kim, K. S. Park, Leandro Ucciferri, Valeria Milanes, Anja Kovacs, Gbenga Sesan, Pirongrong Ramasoota, Sinta Dewi Rosadi, Lhadon Tethong, Lobsang Gyatso Sither, Nathan Freitas, Sonny Zulhuda, Luis Fernando García, Ashnah Kalemera, Lillian Nalwoga, Wairagala Wakabi, Olga Paz, Ariel Barbosa, Maria Paz Canales, Vladimir Garay, Nica Dumlao, Yerry Borang, Clara Gutteridge, Brock Chisholm, Renata Ávila, Sonny Zulhuda, and Kemly Camacho.

Special thanks to Omar Abdulaziz and Ahmed Mansoor, as well as all the other victims and targets who have been the subject of our research. Your bravery in the face of despotism and corruption is inspiring.

Thanks to the many dedicated journalists with whom we have collaborated, and in particular Colin Freeze, Mark Harrison, Joseph Menn, Barton Gellman, Ellen Nakashima, Irina Borogan, Andrei Soldatov, Andy Greenberg, Robert Steiner, Lorenzo Franceschi-Bicchierai, Jeremy Wagstaff, Dave Seglins, Noah Shachtman, Shane Harris, Ryan Tate, Trevor Timm, David Walmsley, Avi Asher-Schapiro, Joseph Cox, Chris Bing, Nathan VanderKlippe, Glenn Greenwald, Robert McMillan, John Markoff, Mark MacKinnon, Nahlah Ayed, Josh Rogin, Ronen Bergman, Suzanne Smalley, Michael Isikoff, Raphael Satter, Nicole Perlroth, Eva Dou, Thomas Brewster, Kim Zetter, Sandro Contenta,

Mehul Srivastava, Zack Whittaker, Kate Allen, Amy Goodman, and Stephanie Kirchgaessner.

Special thanks to Eric Sears and John Palfrey at the MacArthur Foundation, Vera Franz and Hannah Draper at OSF, Jenny Toomey, Lori McGlinchey, Alberto Cerda Silva, Matt Mitchell, and Michael Brennan at the Ford Foundation, Eli Sugarman and Patrick Collins at the Hewlett Foundation, Laurent Elder, Ruhiya Seward, Matthew Smith, and Phet Sayo at IDRC, Adam Lynn and Libby Liu at OTF, Michael Madnick at Mountain, and the Oak Foundation and Sigrid Rausing Trust.

Last, I would like to thank my family: my wife, Jane Gowan, and my children, Emily, Rosalind, Ethan, and Michael. I am deeply grateful for the support and love you give to me, to each other, and to everyone around you. You make the world a better place, and I love you all dearly.

INDEX

ABOUT THE AUTHOR

Ronald J. Deibert is professor of Political Science and director of the Citizen Lab at the Munk School of Global Affairs and Public Policy, University of Toronto. The Citizen Lab undertakes interdisciplinary research at the intersection of global security, information and communications technologies, and human rights. The research outputs of the Citizen Lab are routinely covered in global media, including more than two dozen reports that received exclusive front-page coverage in the *New York Times*, the *Washington Post*, and other global media over the past decade. Deibert is the author of *Black Code: Surveillance, Privacy, and the Dark Side of the Internet*, as well as numerous books, chapters, articles, and reports on internet censorship, surveillance, and cybersecurity. In 2013, he was appointed to the Order of Ontario and awarded the Queen Elizabeth II Diamond Jubilee medal, for being "among the first to recognize and take measures to mitigate growing threats to communications rights, openness, and security worldwide."